Test Your
I.Q. & REASONING

Test Your I.Q. & REASONING

Vijaya Khandurie

Ocean Books Pvt. Ltd.
ISO 9001:2008 Publishers

Published by
Ocean Books (P) Ltd.
4/19 Asaf Ali Road,
New Delhi-110 002 (INDIA)

ISBN 978-81-8430-235-6
Test Your IQ & Reasoning
by Vijaya Khandurie

Edition
2018

Price
₹ 250.00 (Rupees Two Hundred Fifty Only)

Printed at
Narula Printers, Delhi

Preface

I. Q. stands for "Intelligence Quotient", originally coined by a German psychologist William Stern. An I.Q. test is a method employed by psychologists to assess 'intelligence'. First introduced in 1904 by Alfred Binet, a French psychologist it later became *Stanford–Binet test*. I.Q. score is a statistically derived number, obtained by dividing the 'Mental Age' by 'Chronological Age' which when further multiplied by 100 determines the level of intelligence. Thus, if a child aged ten has the mental ability of a 13-year old his I.Q. score will be 130, which is pretty high and will come in the category of 'gifted'. The I.Q. spectrum ranges from 'idiot' (10) to 165 (genius). The highest IQ ever recorded was by an American magazine columnist Marilyn vos Savant (228). Physicist Steven Hawking (200), Former World Chess Champion Bobby Fisher (187), and Albert Einstein (160) all fall in the 'genius' category.

In order to judge the I.Q. of a person, a series of verbal and non-verbal tests are conducted which give an idea of his/her intelligence in relation to the other people of the same age. There are several factors of intelligence that I.Q. test measures like general intelligence, language, visual-spatial concept, mathematical skills, logical reasoning and general knowledge. Normally I.Q. tests asses your intellectual potential.

In modern times I.Q. or Mentally Ability Test has become an important instrument to select a candidate in competitive examinations whether it is the National Talent Search Examination or I. A. S. There is hardly any competition where such tests are not conducted. Every child aspires for a better future, and endeavours hard to make it a reality.

This book on I.Q. and Reasoning Tests contains forty tests each consisting of twenty five exercises comprising different types. They are not arranged according to gradation; therefore the reader can begin from anywhere. Even if these exercises do not gauge your I.Q. they will definitely enhance it. However there is one suggestion: start when you are completely free of stress and finish one task at a time and in one sitting. Take note of the time spent completing one set of test. This will reflect your mental ability, agility and also give an idea of your potential. The answers with explanations are given at the end of the book.

Have fun and enjoy!

New Delhi **—Vijaya Khandurie**

Acknowledgement

While working in the Directorate of Education, NCT Delhi, in various capacities, I had the opportunity to interact with countless students studying in schools. One such occasion was to deal with National Talent Search Examination (NTSE), one of the most prestigious competitions sponsored by the National Council of Educational Research and Training (NCERT). During the period of my service in the Science Branch of the Directorate of Education, I conducted Mental Ability Tests to help students attain this scholarship. I am grateful to the Directorate of Education, NCT of Delhi and NCERT that allowed me to access the question papers of the two stages of the NTSE, some of the questions might per chance have found a place in this book.

I am also grateful to my wife Manju Khandurie who rendered her full support in this endeavour.

—Vijaya Khandurie

Contents

TEST-1

1. Put the key word inside the box to make a two-word phrase from the list of words that follow? For example: FOLK TALE/MUSIC/DANCE

   [   ] BAR/TOOTH/SHAKE

2. Which three-letter word should be inserted within the parenthesis to form two new words?

   M (__ __ __) H
   F (__ __ __) E

3. Choose the missing number ("?") from the given alternatives.

   97, 89, 83, 79, ?

   (a) 73 (b) 71
   (c) 67 (d) 61

4. What number replaces the question mark?

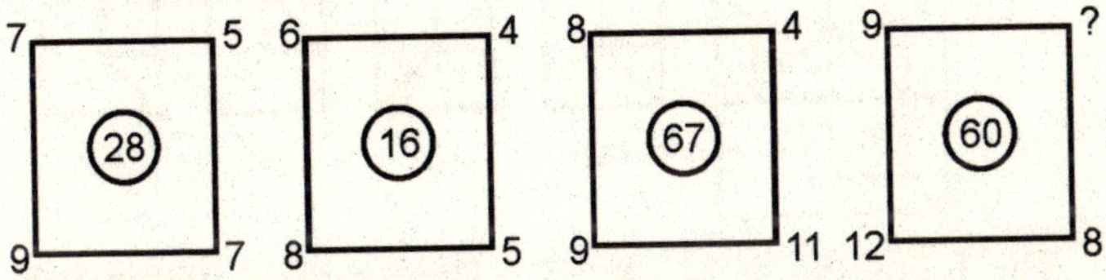

5. The first two letters of the following five-letter word are missing. Find out the missing letters to form a word?

   __ __ CID

6. Find the missing letter ("?").

   J, F, M, A, M, J, ?

   (a) J (b) A
   (c) S (d) O

7. Which among the four options should occupy the position indicated by a question mark to continue the sequence?

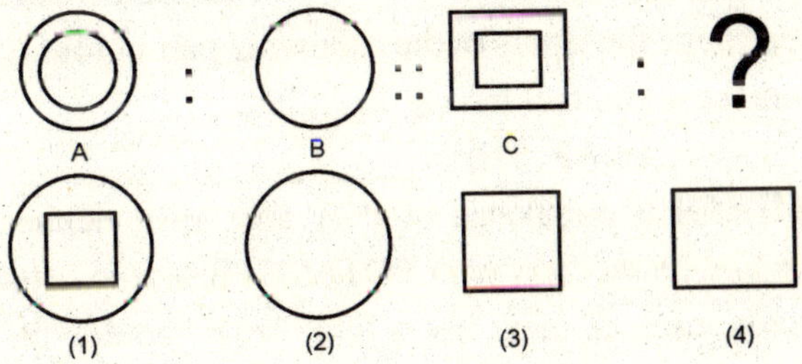

8. Find a single word that defines both the words. For example: Quick bird would be SWIFT.
   Unyielding company ____________

9. Find the group which is different from others.
   (a) ECA (b) JHF
   (c) YWT (d) QOM

10. Which among the following units is different from others?
    CALORIE
    LAMBERT
    GILBERT
    OERSTED

11. Select the correct figure among the four options to complete the first figure to make it symmetrical?

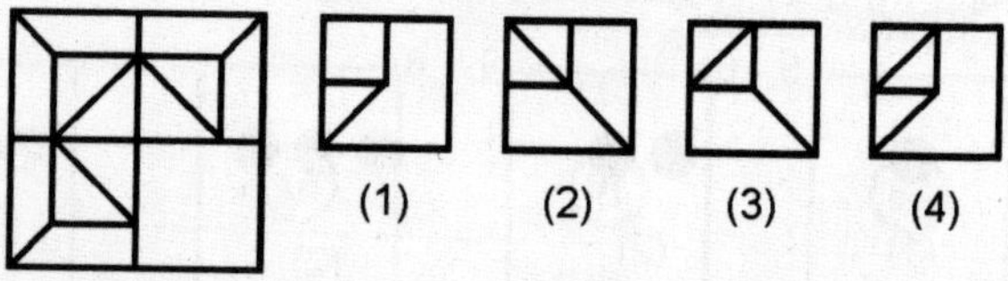

12. The following word carries a shorter word within it in the normal sequence which conveys the same meaning as the longer word. Find the shorter synonym?
    FALSITIES

13. Barkha is as old as Astha but half as young as Ekta. Champa is half the age of Astha but is twice older than Deeksha. Which two ladies form the pair of the oldest and the youngest?
    (a) Ekta and Deeksha (b) Ekta and Astha
    (c) Ekta and Barkha (d) Astha and Deeksha

14. Rearrange the letters of the following pair of four-letter words to make an animal having eight letters?
    LEAP THEN _ _ _ _ _ _ _ _

15. POTASH is composed of POT and ASH, neither of which has any connection with POTASH. Below is listed a pair of words, each of them has a three-letter word as its meaning.

The two three-letter words combine to form a six-letter word which is defined. Find the 6-letter word. For example: Male child + Trap = SONNET

Central + Obtain = ___________ (Dwarf)

16. Find a single word that defines both the words. For example: Quick bird would be Swift.

Hit branch = ________

17. Which of the four alternatives is exactly the mirror image of the object placed in front of two plane mirrors inclined at 90º?

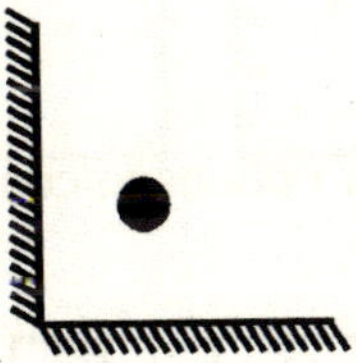

(1) (2) (3) (4)

18. Find the group which is different from others.

(a) trsq (b) jhik

(c) kijl (d) ywxz

19. Which among the following figures is different from others?

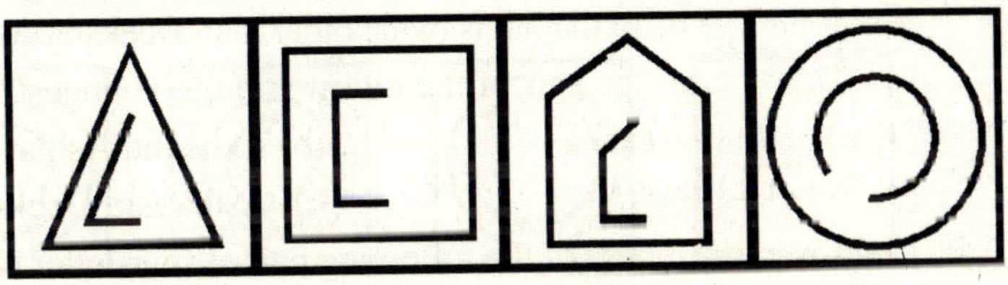

A B C D

20. If 5 × 4 = 14 and 7 × 4 = 18 then what is the value of 9 x 4?

(a) 12 (b) 22

(c) 32 (d) 42

21. A square sheet of paper is folded as shown by arrows and then a hole is punched in it. Which option suggests its look when it is unfolded?

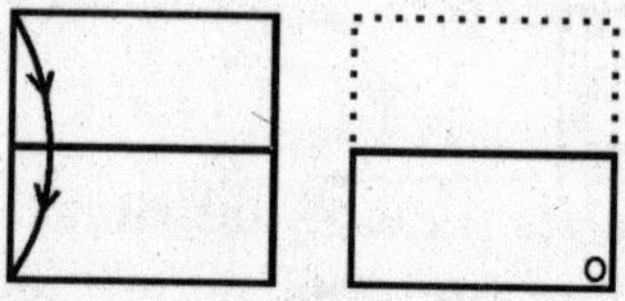

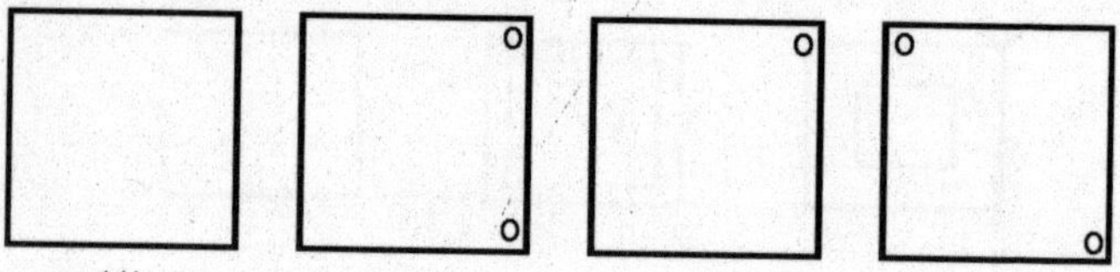

(1) (2) (3) (4)

22. Insert a 3-letter word in the blank spaces which completes the first word and starts the second.

FEAT (__ __ __) RING

23. Which among the four options should occupy the position indicated by a question mark to continue the sequence?

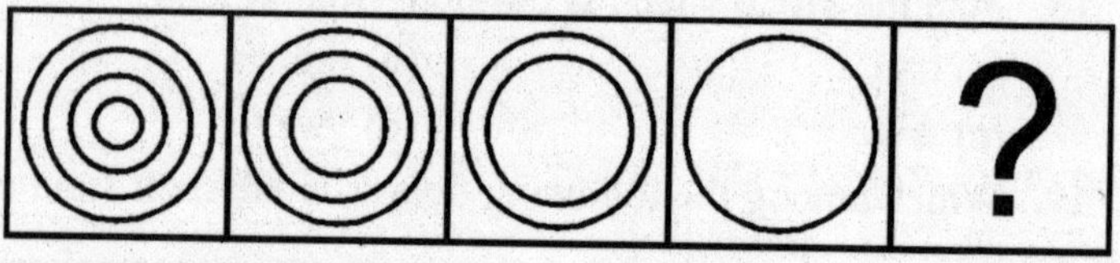

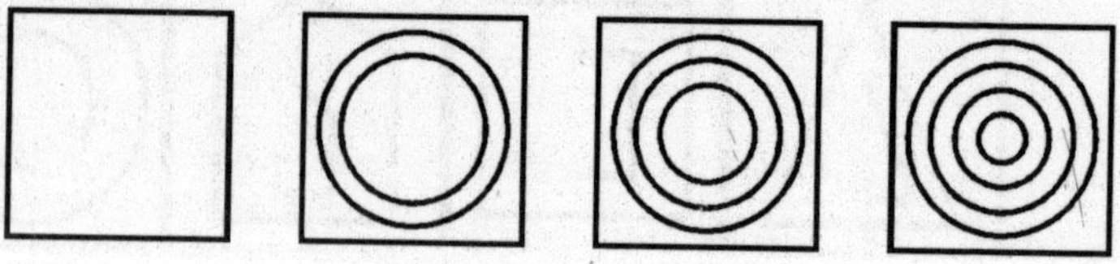

(1) (2) (3) (4)

24. Make a six-letter word to match the definition by putting letters in the blank spaces. Clue is given.

__ __ __ KER = Dealer

25. Which figure in the lower row should replace the question mark so that C and the chosen figure maintain the same relationship as A and B?

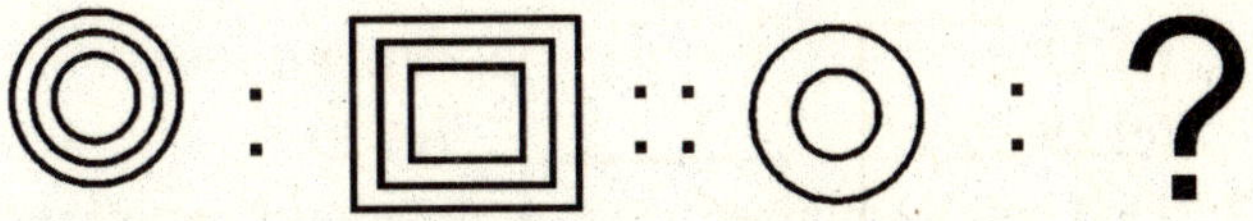

A B C

(1) (2) (3) (4)

TEST-2

1. Choose the missing number ("?") from the given alternatives?

   3, 4, 6, 8, 12, 14, ?

   (a) 17 (b) 18
   (c) 19 (d) 20

2. Find out the number which is different from others?

   (a) 91 (b) 117
   (c) 153 (d) 169

3. If α stands for "+", β stands for "–", γ stands for "÷" and δ stands for "x", find the value of 50 γ 5 δ 5 β 27 α 4

   (a) 9 (b) 18
   (c) 27 (d) 36

4. What number replaces the question mark?

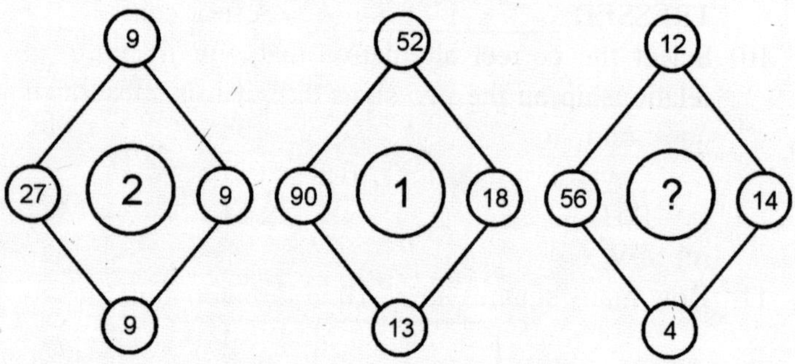

5. Which three-letter word should be inserted within the parenthesis to form two new words?

   H (___ ___ ___) Y
   L (___ ___ ___) R

6. Make a seven-letter word to match the definition by putting letters in the blank spaces. Clue is given.

   ___ ___ ___ ___ AGE (Domestic refuge)

7. Insert a three-letter word in the blank spaces which completes the first word and starts the second?

   MIMI(___ ___ ___)STAL

8. Which of the four alternatives is exactly the mirror image of the object placed in front of a plane mirror AB?

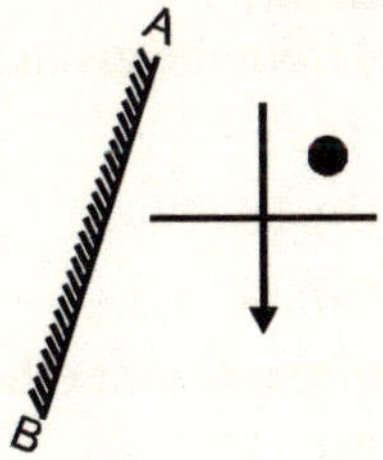

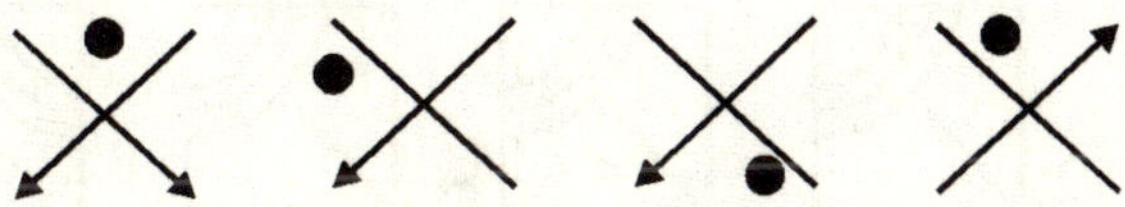

(1) (2) (3) (4)

9. Unscramble the letters of the following word to make a new one to match it with the clue?

TRESSED ____________ = A fruit course

10. Select the correct alternative that will maintain the same relationship on the two signs "::", if it is substituted for the question mark "?".

QDU: PCT::?: TGX

(a) UMJ (b) SFJ

(c) SFW (d) UHJ

11. How many squares are there in the following figure?

12. Rearrange the letters on the left side to make a word that matches the clue?

AAAILMR ____________ (a disease)

13. Select the correct figure among the four options to complete the first figure to make it symmetrical?

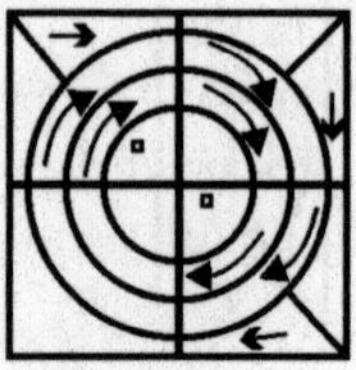

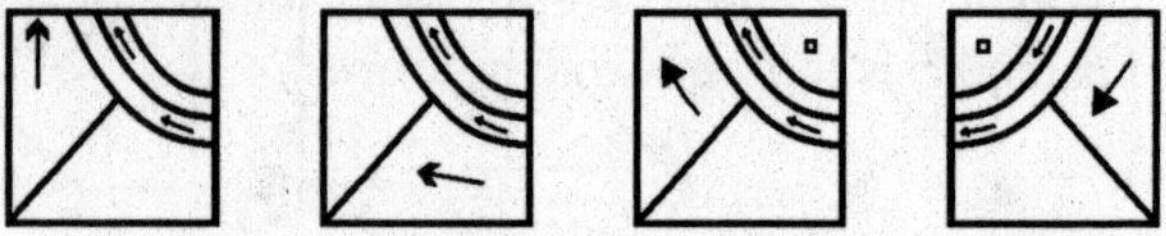

(1) (2) (3) (4)

14. The first two letters of the following five-letter word are missing. Find out the missing letters to form a word?

___ ___ CTI

15. Which among the four options should occupy the position indicated by a question mark to continue the sequence?

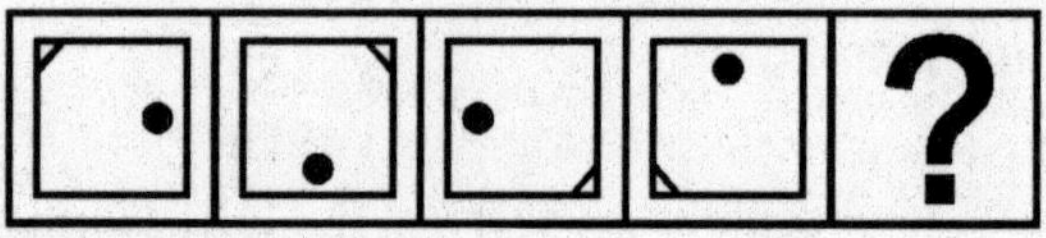

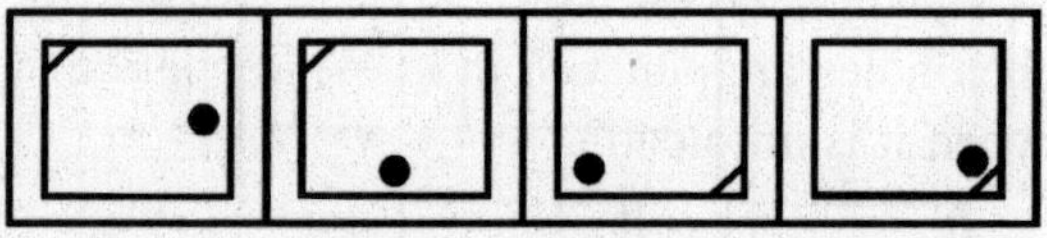

(1) (2) (3) (4)

16. Select the alternative whose alphabet when placed at the missing spaces complete the following series?

p __ pp __ p __ ppq __ qppq

(a) qqqp (b) qqpq

(c) qqpp (d) qppq

17. Five boys are sitting in a row. Prakash is on the right of Mohan. Naresh is on the left of Mohan, but is on the right of

Kailash. Prakash is on the left of Akash. Who is on the extreme left?

(a) Prakash (b) Kailash

(c) Akash (d) Mohan

18. Put the key word inside the box to make a two-word phrase from the list of words that follow. For example:

BEAUTY	SPOT/SALOON/QUEEN
	COPY/NOTICE/BOOKING

19. Which three-letter word should be inserted within the parenthesis to form two new words?

S (___ ___ ___) R

S (___ ___ ___) K

20. Which among the following figures is different from others?

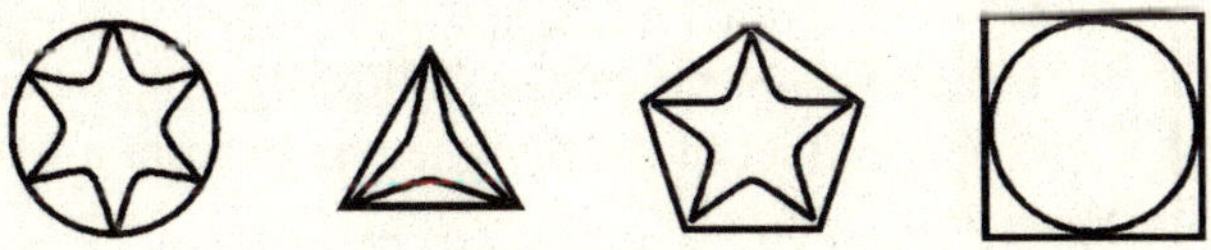

(1) (2) (3) (4)

21. Which among the following words is different from others?

GARAGE

ORATOR

EDITED

CHURCH

22. A square sheet of paper is folded as shown by arrows and then holes are punched in it. Which option suggests its look when it is unfolded?

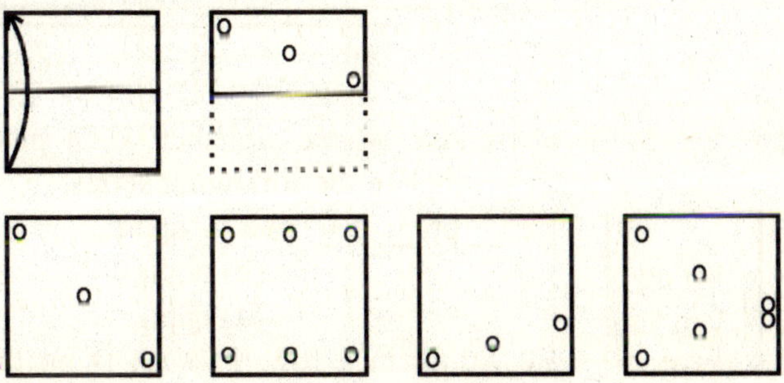

(1) (2) (3) (4)

23. Which among the following words is different from others?

A C C E S S
B E L L O W
B O N N E T
C H I N T Z
E F F L U X

24. Make word to match the definition by putting letters in the blank spaces?

___ ___ ___ TION = Part

25. Which figure in the lower row should replace the question mark so that C and the chosen figure maintain the same relationship as A and B?

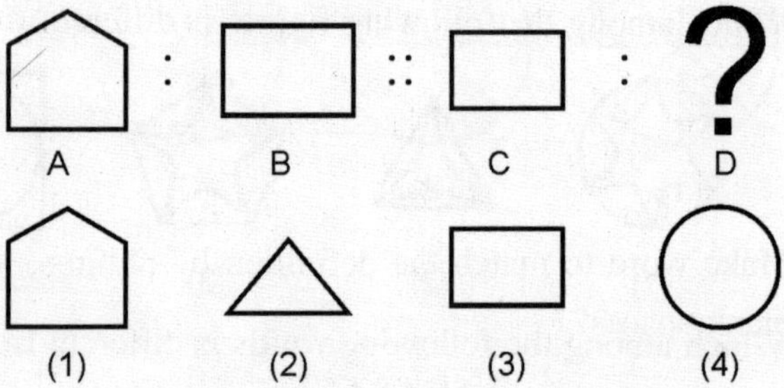

TEST-3

1. Select the correct alternative that will maintain the same relationship on the two signs "::", if it is substituted for the question mark "?".

ZXUV: TROP:: PNKL:?

(a) IFDE (b) JHFE

(c) JGEF (d) JHEF

2. Which among the following figures is different from others?

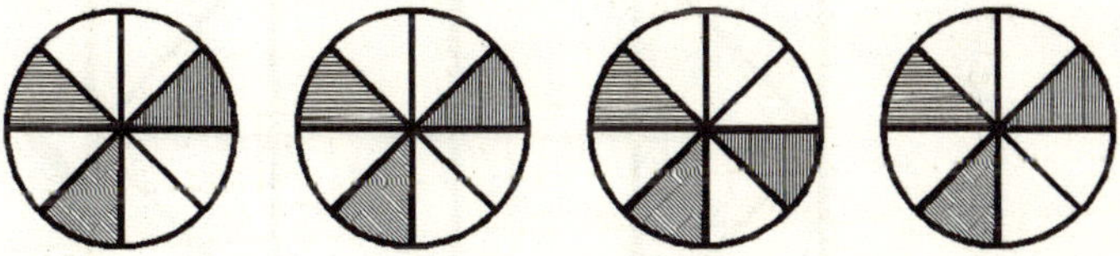

(1) (2) (3) (4)

3. Make word to match the definition by putting letters in the blank spaces?

___ ___ ___ ___ ANT = Refined

4. Insert a four-letter word in the blank spaces which completes the first word and starts the second?

GANG(_ _ _ _)LING

5. Which among the four options should occupy the position indicated by a question mark to continue the sequence?

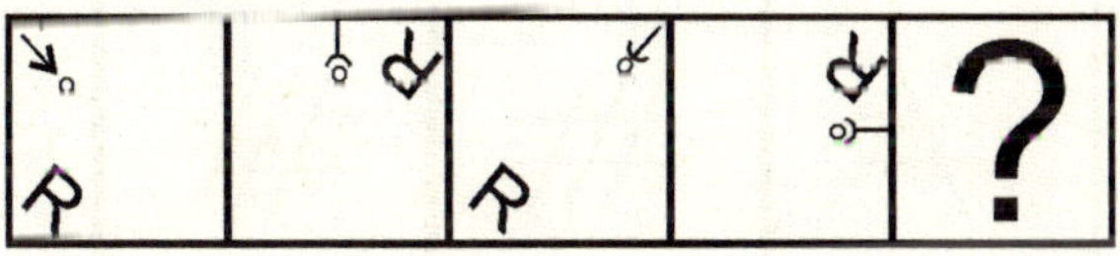

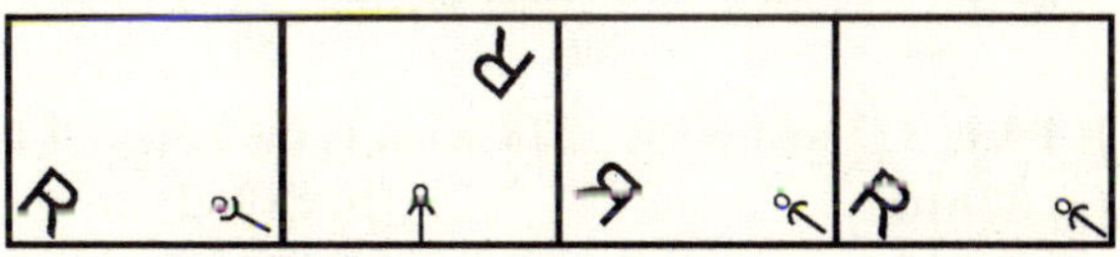

(1) (2) (3) (4)

6. Choose the missing number ("?") from the given alternatives?
3, 7, 14, 23, 36, ?
(a) 45 (b) 47
(c) 49 (d) 51

7. How many right-angled triangle are there in the following figure?

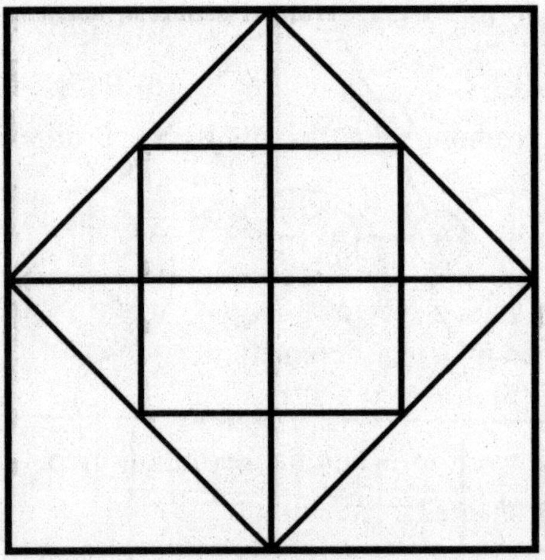

8. Apply your intelligence to fill in the blank spaces so that the three words have the same five letters?

E___ R ___ ___
___ ___ ___ A ___
L ___ Y ___ ___

9. Which among the following figures is different from others?

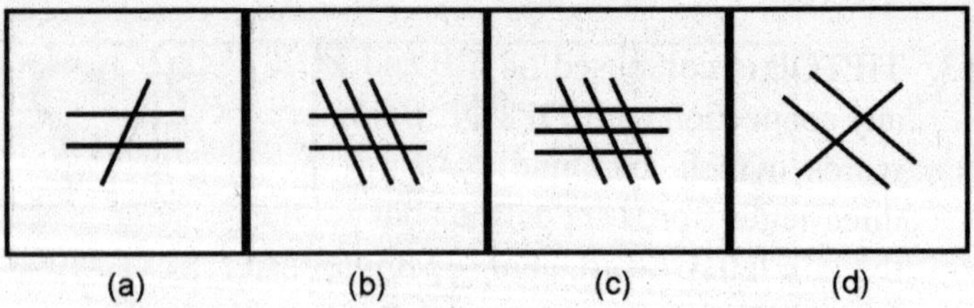

10. If PA is 322 and NI is 2818 what is the value of DECA?
(a) 82610 (b) 81062
(c) 81602 (d) 86102

11. Which number should replace the question mark?

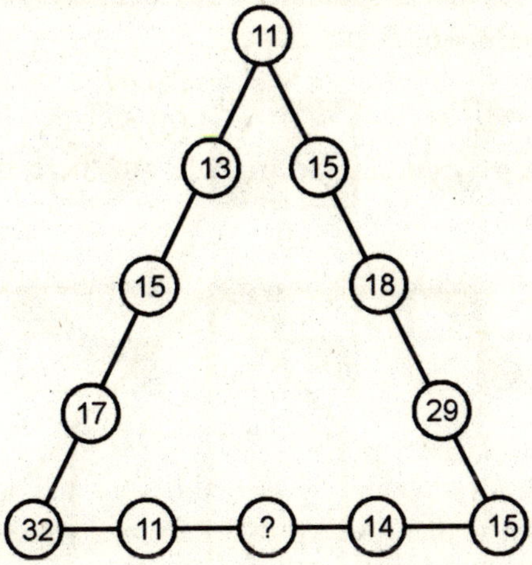

12. Which among the four options should occupy the position indicated by a question mark to continue the sequence?

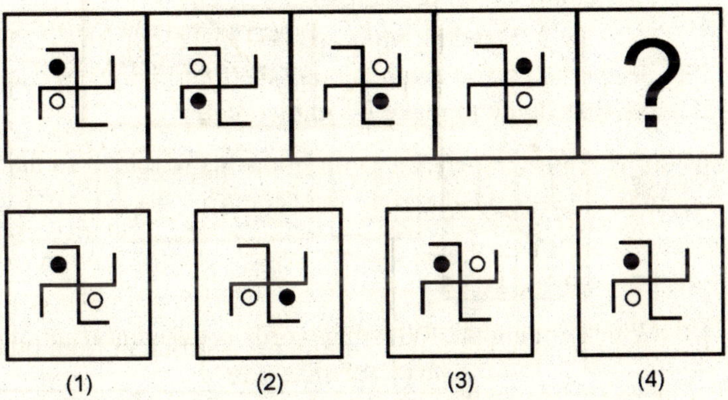

13. TIPTOP is composed of TIP and TOP, neither of which has any connection with TIPTOP. Below are given two three-letter words which combine to form a six-letter word. The three-letter words are defined but not the six-letter word. Find the six-letter word. For example Male child + Trap = SONNET

Devil + Skill = ____________ (Pass on)

14. Which figure in the lower row should replace the question

mark so that C and the chosen figure maintain the same relationship as A and B?

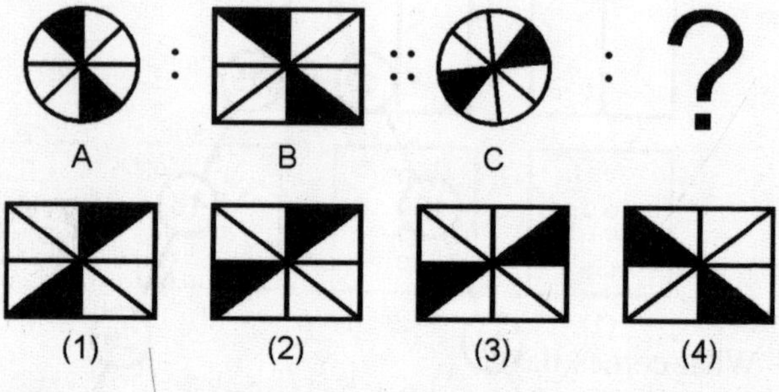

15. Which letter should be placed before and after the following alphabet so that four words are formed which spell the same—forward and backword?

__ U __

16. Find a single word that defines both the words. For example: Quick bird would be Swift.

Standing supporter = ________

17. Select the correct figure among the four options to complete the first figure to make it symmetrical?

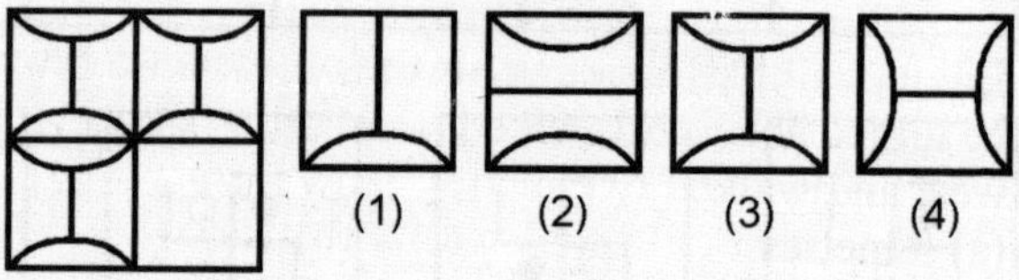

18. Which among the following words is different from others?

MOTHER-IN-LAW
SWITCHBOARD
INFORMALITY
LUTHERANISM
BOXING MATCH

19. Discover the name of a World Cup cricketer hidden in the following sentence?

After renewal, shall we shift?

20. A square sheet of paper is folded as shown by arrows and

then holes are punched in it. Which option suggests its look when it is unfolded?

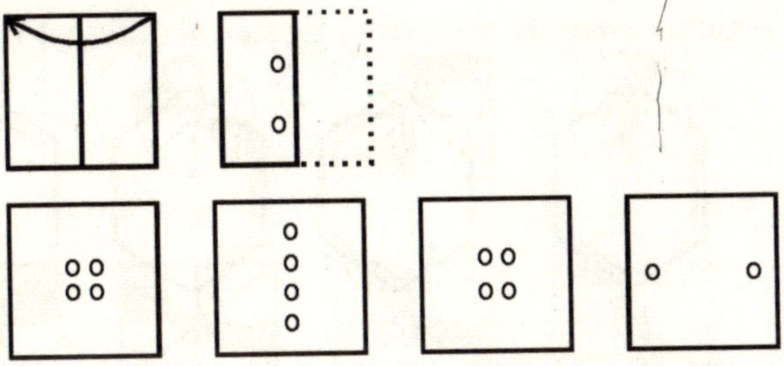

(1) (2) (3) (4)

21. What comes next?

8 5 4 9 1 7 6 10 3 2 ?

22. Which among the following figures is different from others?

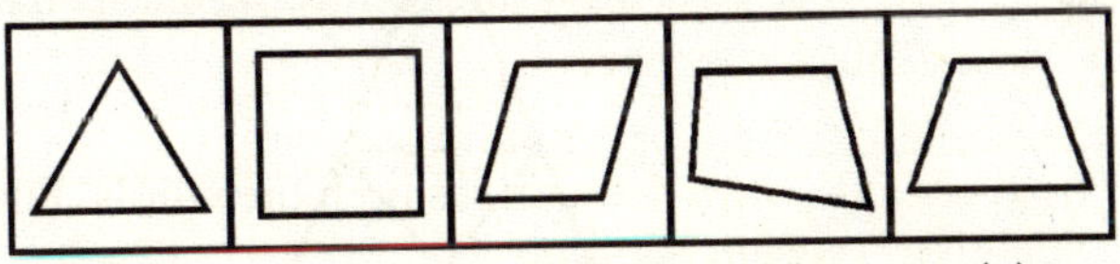

(a) (b) (c) (d) (e)

23. The following word carries a shorter word within it in the normal sequence which conveys the same meaning as the longer word. Find the shorter synonym?

A R M A M E N T S

24. David walks five metres towards the east of his house. Then he turned north and walked ten metres straight, then he turned west and walked five metres. How far is he from his house?

(a) 5 metres (b) 10 metres

(c) 15 metres (d) 20 metres

25. Which among the four options is the correct image of the object in front of the plane mirror?

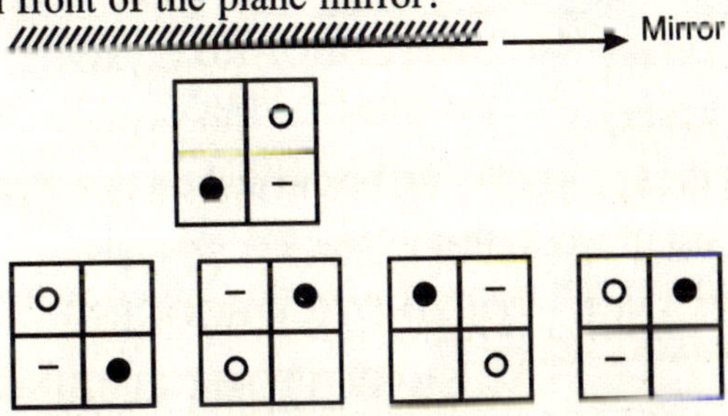

(a) (b) (c) (d)

❑

TEST-4

1. Which among the following figures is different from others?

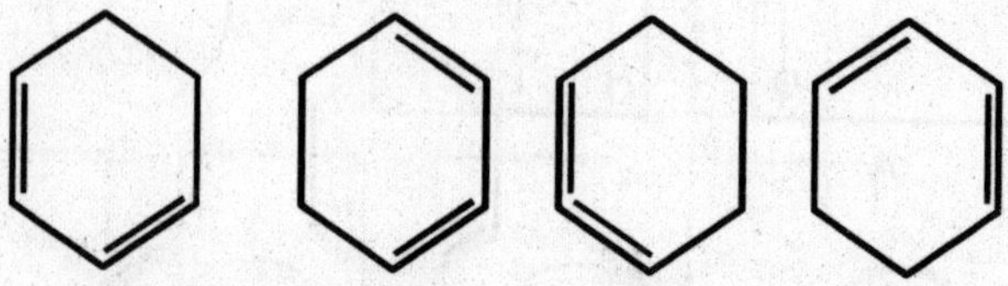

(1) (2) (3) (4)

2. How many triangles are there in the following figure?

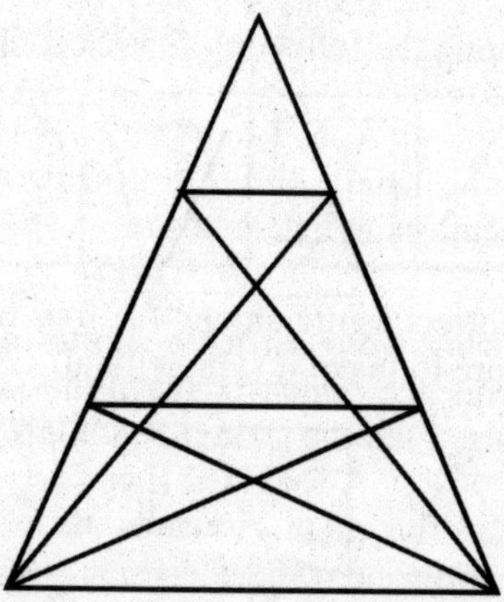

3. Select the alternative whose alphabet when placed at the missing spaces complete the following series?

x __ z ____ xy __ __ z __ xxy __ yz

(a) xyyzxy (b) yxyxyz

(c) yxyzxy (d) yxyzyx

4. Put the key word in the box to make a two-word phrase from the list of words that follow. For example:

ADVANCE	COPY/NOTICE/BOOKING
	MUSIC/BOTTOM/CLIMBING

5. Which figure in the lower row should replace the question

mark so that C and the chosen figure maintain the same relationship as A and B?

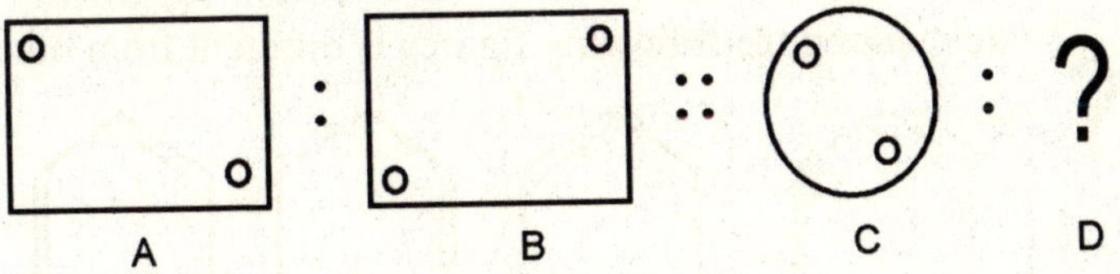

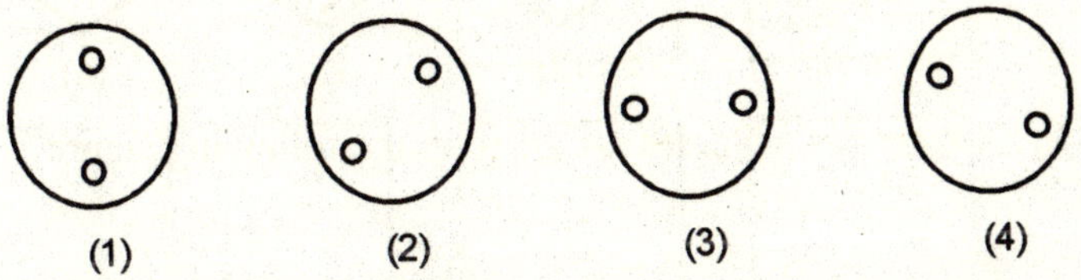

6. What comes next?

A, E, F, H, I, K, ?

7. The first three letters of the following word are missing. Discover the missing letters to form a word?

___ ___ ___ PHY

8. Select the correct figure among the four options to complete the first figure to make it symmetrical?

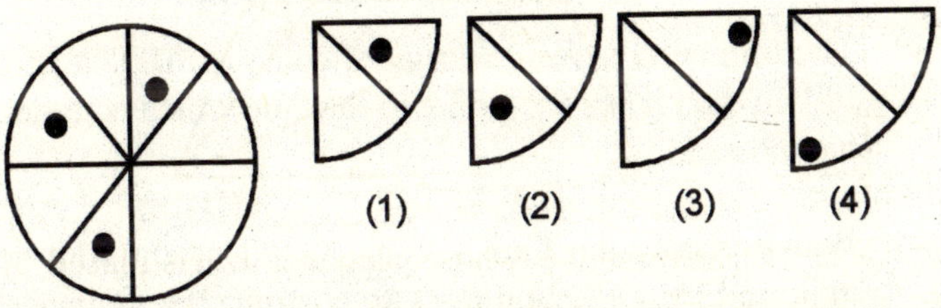

9. Which three-letter word should be inserted within the parenthesis to form two new words?

G (___ ___ ___) E
G (___ ___ ___) H

10. Which number should replace the question mark?

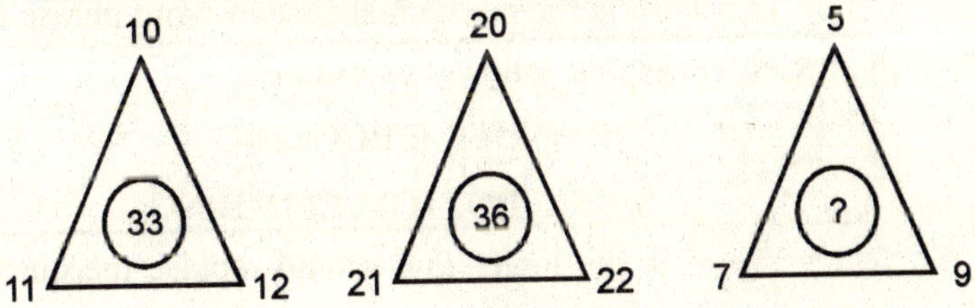

11. A square sheet of paper is folded as shown by arrows and then a hole is punched in it. Which option suggests its look when it is unfolded?

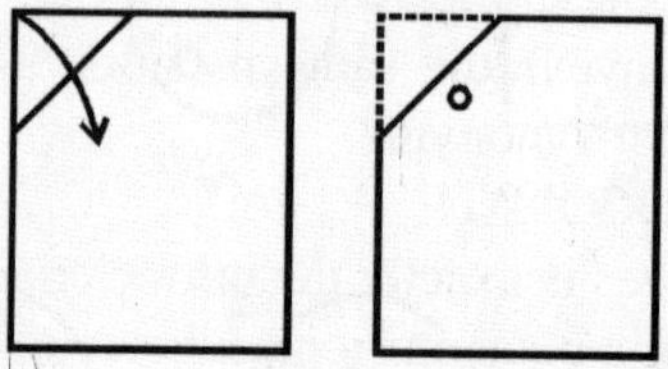

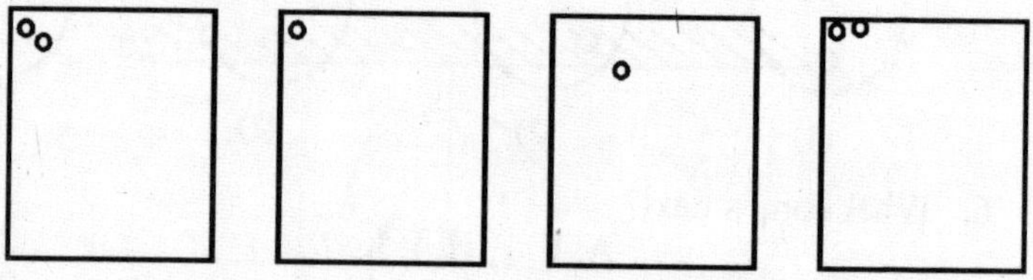

(1) (2) (3) (4)

12. Anushka is 16 years old. In four years time she will be twice as old as Mona was a year ago. How old is Mona?

(a) 10 (b) 11

(c) 12 (d) 13

13. The following seven-letter word contains ART at its centre. Fill up the blanks according to the clue which is given in the parenthesis?

___ ___ A R T ___ ___ (Dark)

14. Which among the four options should occupy the position indicated by a question mark to continue the sequence?

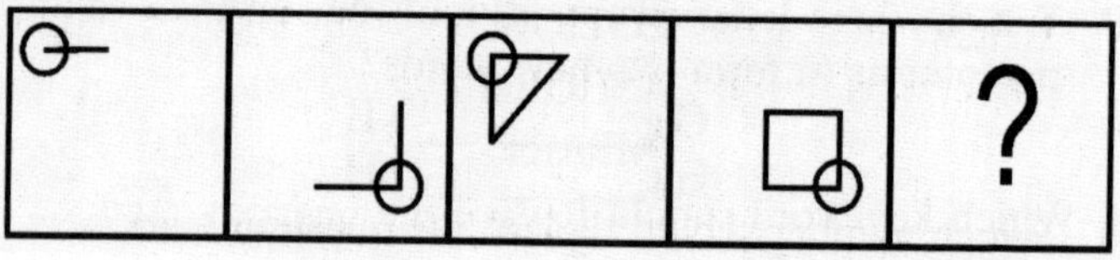

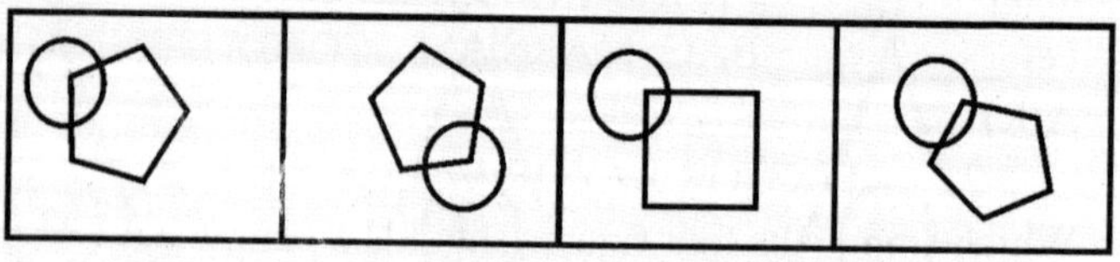

(1) (2) (3) (4)

15. Insert a three-letter word in the blank spaces which complete the first word and starts the second?

RIB(__ __ __)NET

16. The following word carries a shorter word within it in the normal sequence which conveys the same meaning as the longer word. Find the shorter synonym?

CHOCOLATE

17. Which of the four alternatives is exactly the mirror image of the object placed in front of a plane mirror AB?

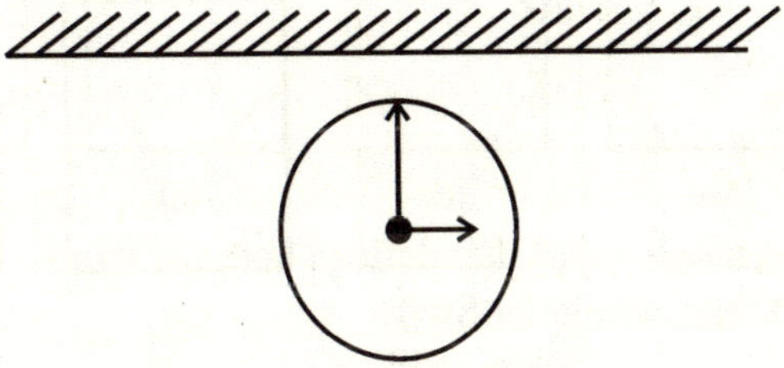

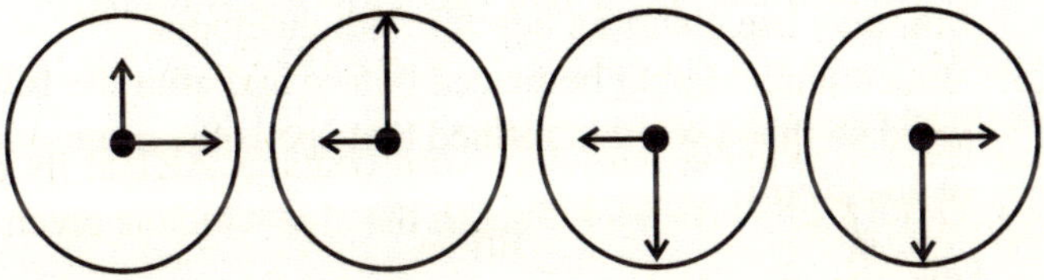

(a) (b) (c) (d)

18. Which among the following words is different from others?

POISON
LOTION
ASHORE
IMPART

19. Which key word should replace the question mark so as to make a two-word phrase from the list of words that follows, i.e. ____?____: BAG, MARSHAL, CONDITIONING (? is AIR)

____?___ FACTOR/RAZOR/VALVE

20. Which among the four figures should be placed at the question mark so as to complete the pattern?

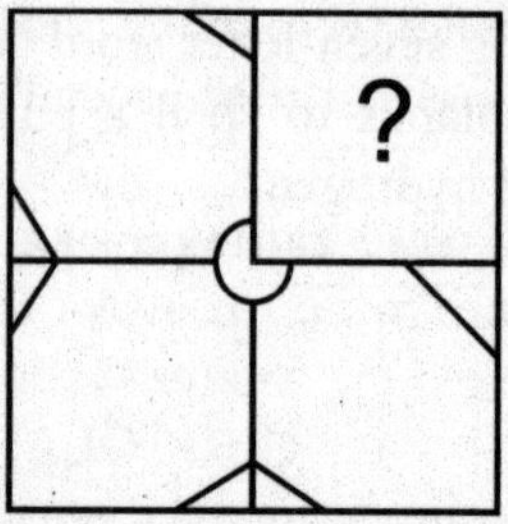

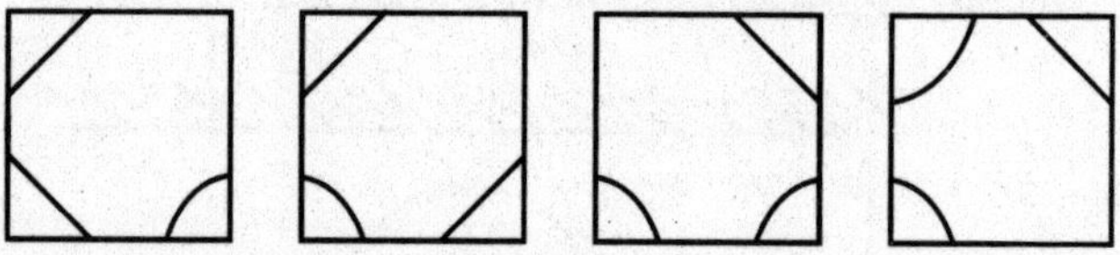

(a) (b) (c) (d)

21. Find a single word that defines both the words. For example: Quick bird would be Swift.

Weary drill = ________

22. Which animal is hidden in the following sentence?
You may use common key for both the doors.

23. Which letter should be placed before and after the following word so that a word is formed that spells the same—forward or backward?

__ EIFIE __

24. Which figure in the lower row should replace the question mark so that C and the chosen figure maintain the same relationship as A and B?

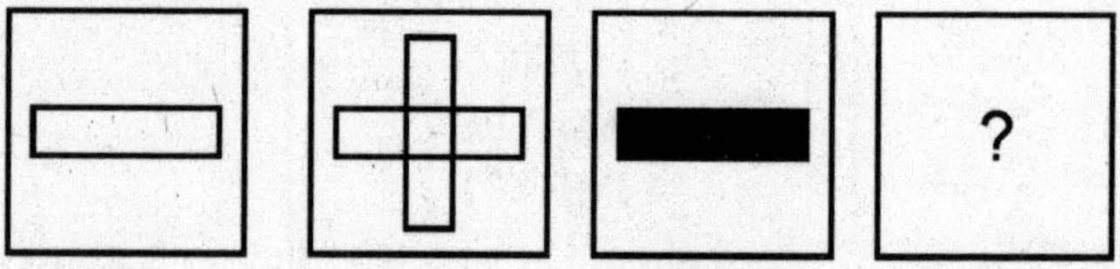

(a) (b) (c) (d)

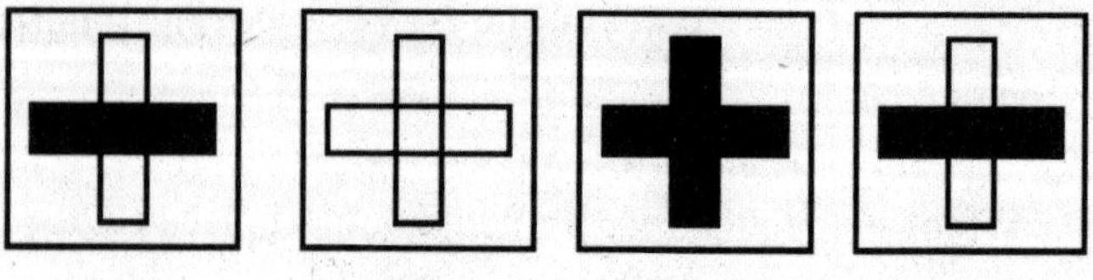

(1) (2) (3) (4)

25. The following seven-letter word contains MON at its centre. Fill up the blanks to spell a pungent gas compounded of nitrogen and hydrogen.

___ ___ M O N ___ ___

❑

TEST-5

1. Insert a three-letter word in the blank spaces which completes the first word and starts the second?

   FOOT(__ __ __)LESS

2. Which among the following words is different from others?

   IMPUGNABLE
   BLASTODERM
   DECALOGIST
   DIAGNOSTIC
   PLEONASTIC
   UNTOWARDLY

3. Which key word should replace the question mark so as to make a two-word phrase from the list of words that follows, i.e. ____?____: BAG, MARSHAL, CONDITIONING (? is AIR)

   ____?___ AGE/EAGLE/HANDSHAKE

4. Choose the missing number ("?") from the given alternatives?

   2, 6, 14, 30, 62, ?, 254

   (a) 124 (b) 126
   (c) 132 (d) 142

5. Select the correct figure among the four options to complete the first figure to make it symmetrical?

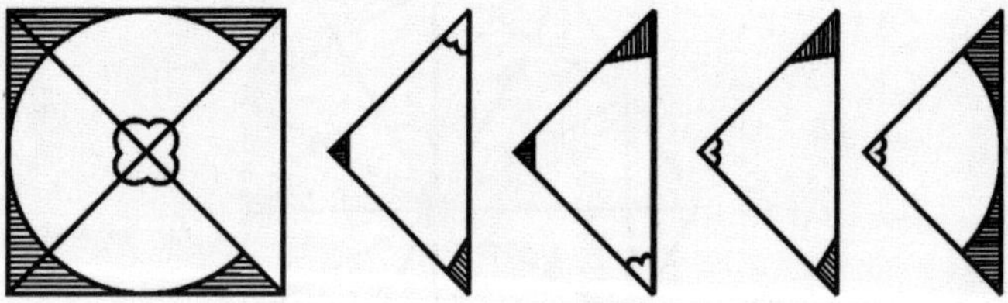

(1) (2) (3) (4)

6. Find a single word that defines both the words. For example: Quick bird would be Swift.

   Dull apartment ____________

7. Which number should replace the question mark?

1	4	2	6	5
9	9	?	9	9
3	6	8	1	0

8. Which among the following figures is different from others?

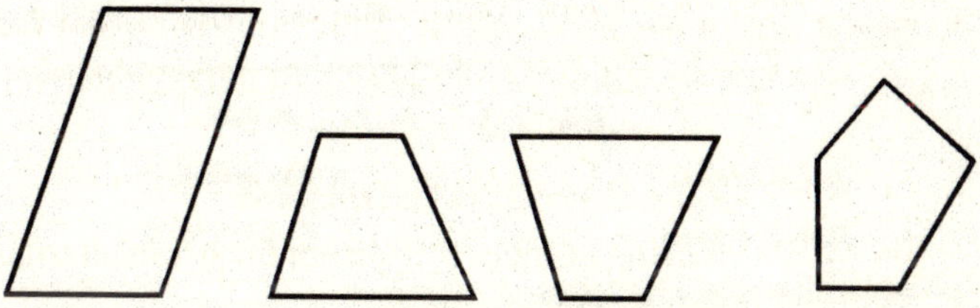

(1) (2) (3) (4)

9. If TRY is 792 then what is the value of IQ?

(a) 917 (b) 179

(c) 1018 (d) 1810

10. How many triangles are there in the following figure?

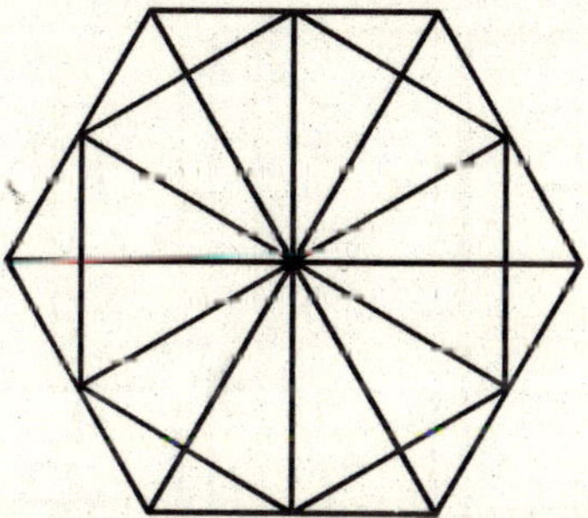

11. Make a six-letter word to match the definition by putting letters in the blank spaces. Clue is given.

___ ___ ___ LET = Cluster of cottages

12. A square sheet of paper is folded as shown by arrows and then holes are punched in it. Which option suggests its look when it is unfolded?

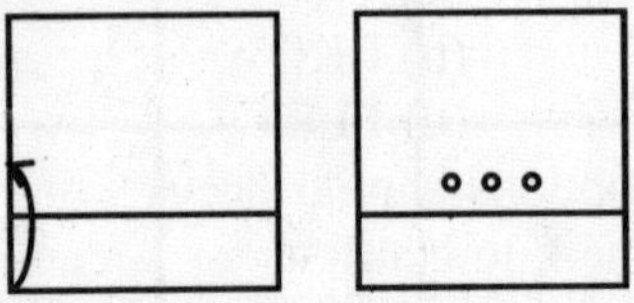

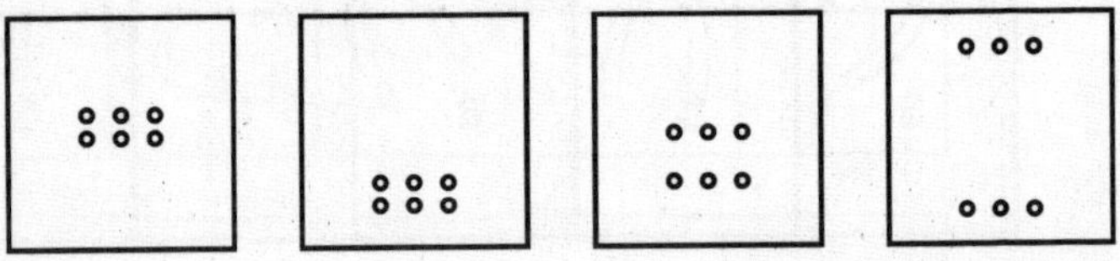

(1) (2) (3) (4)

13. Select the alternative whose figures when placed at the missing spaces complete the following sequence?

—♦♣—♣—♣——♣♣♦—

(a) ♣♦♦♣♣♦ (b) ♦♦♠♣♣♦

(c) ♣♣♦♦♣♣ (d) ♣♦♠♠♣♦

14. Find the missing letter ("?").

z, v, r, n, j, ?

(a) d (b) e (c) f (d) g

15. Which figure in the lower row should replace the question mark so that C and the chosen figure maintain the same relationship as A and B?

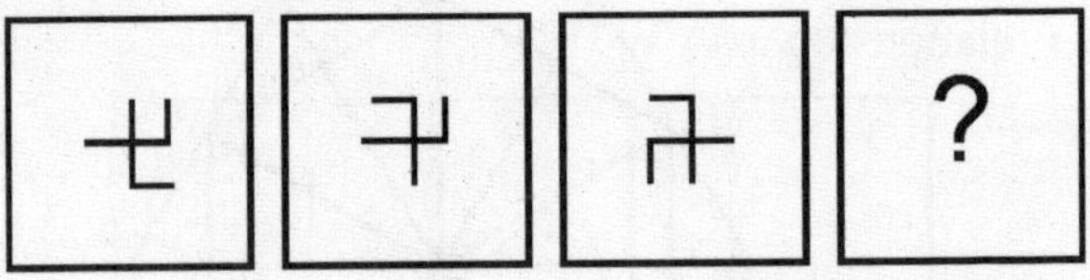

A B C D

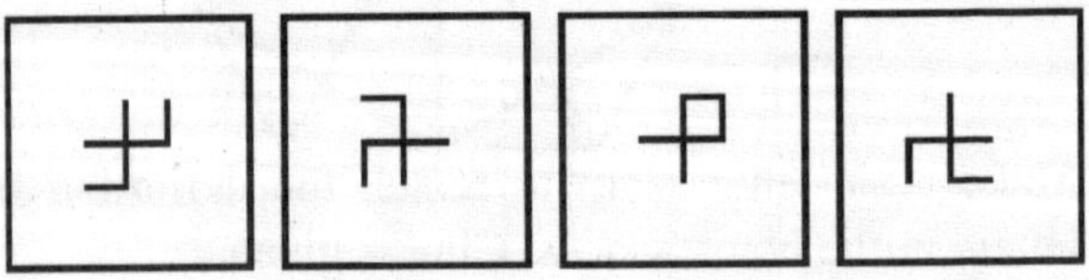

(1) (2) (3) (4)

16. Select the correct alternative that will maintain the same relationship on the two signs "::", if it is substituted for the question mark "?".

AGMS: DJPV:: BHNT: ?

(a) EKQV (b) EKQW
(c) KQVC (d) FLRY

17. Which among the four options should occupy the position indicated by a question mark to continue the sequence?

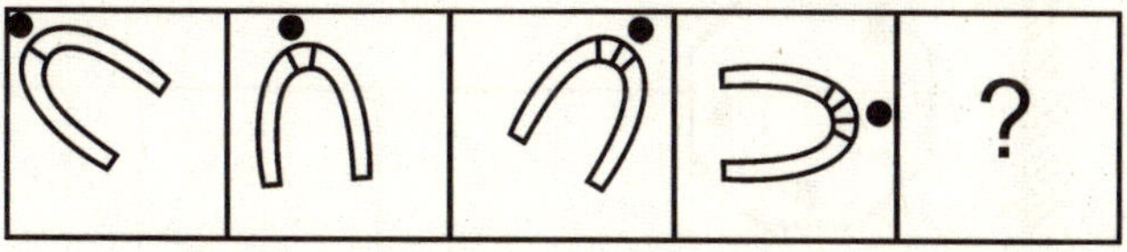

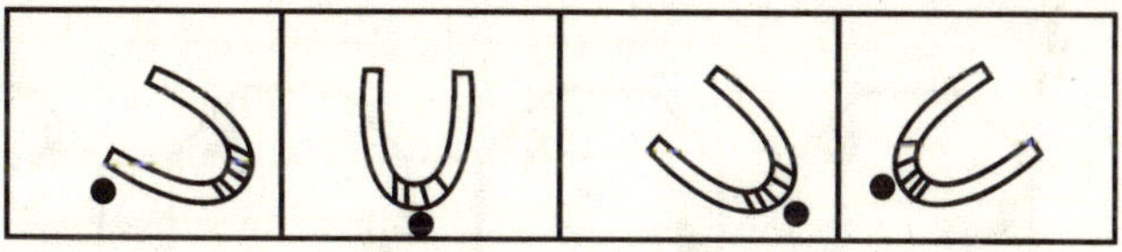

(1) (2) (3) (4)

18. Make three meaningful seven-letter words from the following set of letters?

ACILOPT ________ ________ ________

19. Which three-letter word should be inserted within the parenthesis to form two new words?

D (__ __ __) N
C (__ __ __) L

20. Which figure in the lower row should replace the question mark so that C and the chosen figure maintain the same relationship as A and B?

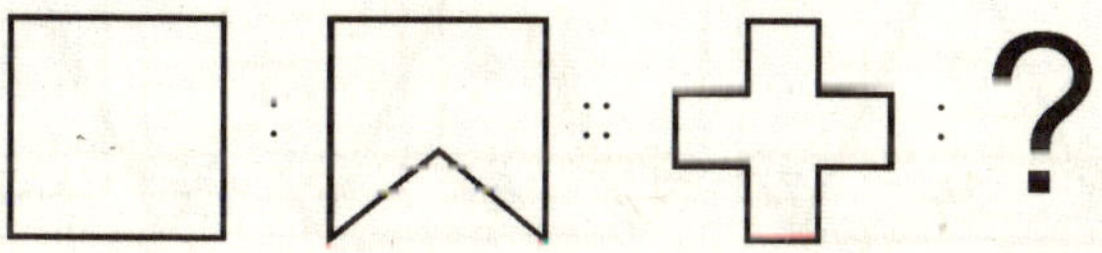

A B C D

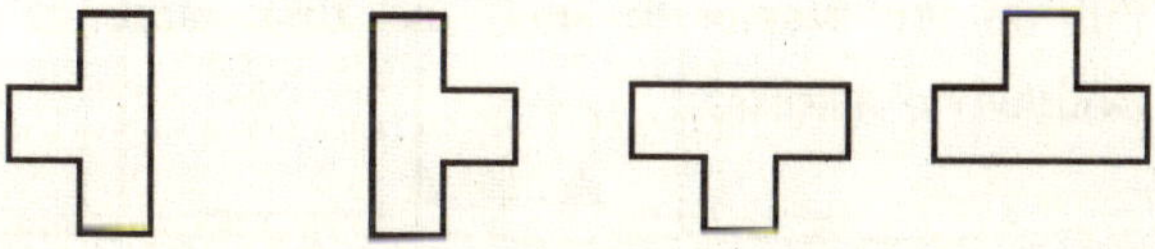

(1) (2) (3) (4)

21. Which of the four alternatives is exactly the mirror image of the object placed in front of a plane mirror AB?

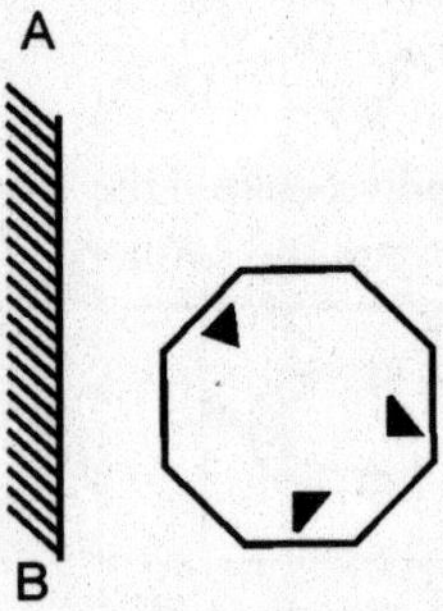

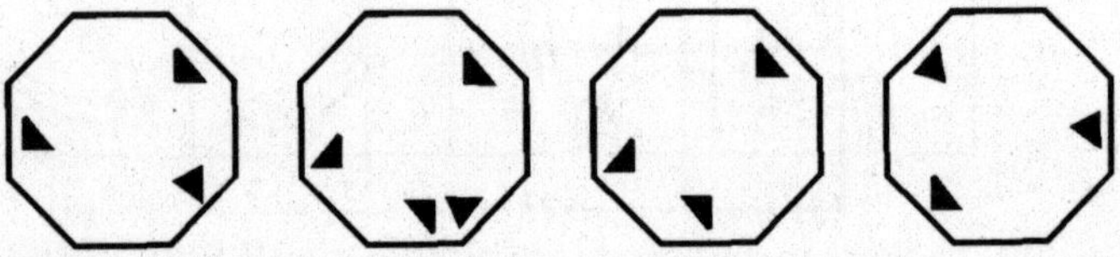

(1) (2) (3) (4)

22. The first two letters of the following five-letter word are missing. Find out the missing letters to form a word.

___ ___ URB

23. What number should replace the question mark?

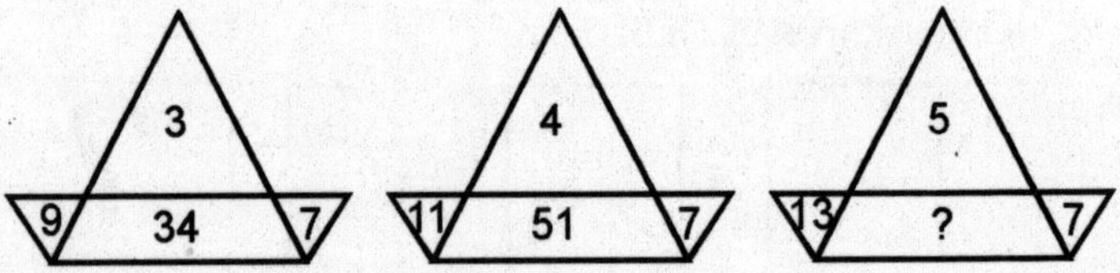

24. The following seven-letter word contains ABA at its centre. Fill up the blanks to spell the first name of a famous Bollywood actress?

___ ___ A B A ___ ___

25. Which letters should be placed in the empty spaces so that

you read the same words across and down in the following word game?

S	C	O	L	D
C				E
O				L
L				A
D	E	L	A	Y

❑

TEST-6

1. Select the correct alternative that will maintain the same relationship on the two signs "::", if it is substituted for the question mark "?".

   AHNR: GNTX:: HOUY: ?

   (a) HOUZ (b) IPVZ
   (c) IPVY (d) IFDE

2. A square sheet of paper is folded as shown by the dotted lines and then a cut on the corner is made. Which option suggests its look when it is unfolded?

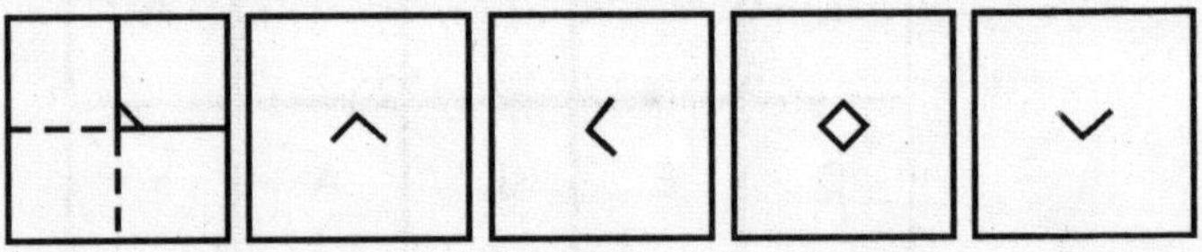

(1) (2) (3) (4)

3. Find the missing letter ("?")?

   c, x, f, u, i, r, ??

   (a) l, o (b) o, l
   (c) m, n (d) n, o

4. Select the correct figure among the four options to complete the first figure to make it symmetrical? [C 6] 4/6

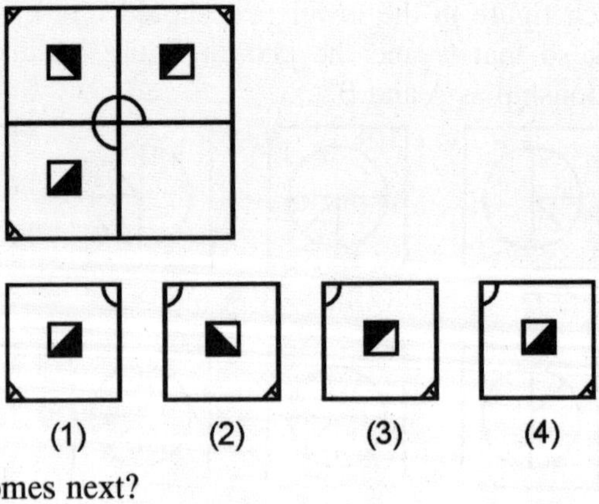

(1) (2) (3) (4)

5. What comes next?

   O, T, T, F, F, S, S, E, ?

6. Find out the number which is different from others?
   (a) 1232 (b) 2343
   (c) 3454 (d) 4525
7. How many squares are there in the following figure?

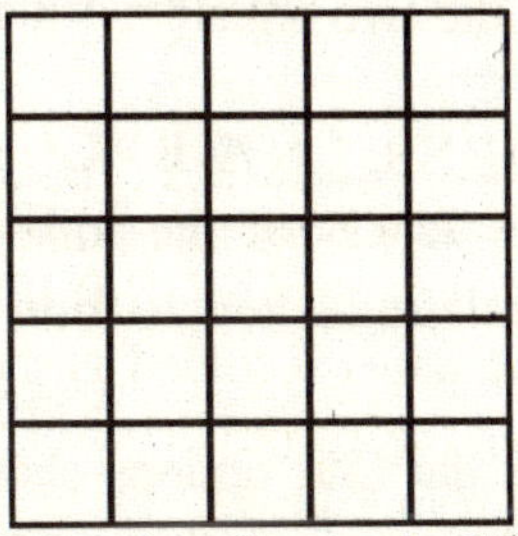

8. Which among the following figures is different from others?

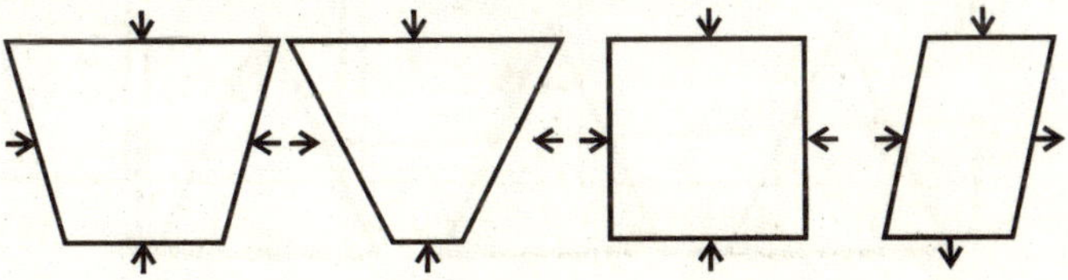

(1) (2) (3) (4)

9. If BAD is 214, what is GOOD?
   (a) 20121223 (b) 2012124
   (c) 712124 (d) 715154
10. Find the group which is different from others?
   (a) FI (b) JN
   (c) MP (d) UX
11. Which figure in the lower row should replace the question mark so that C and the chosen figure maintain the same relationship as A and B?

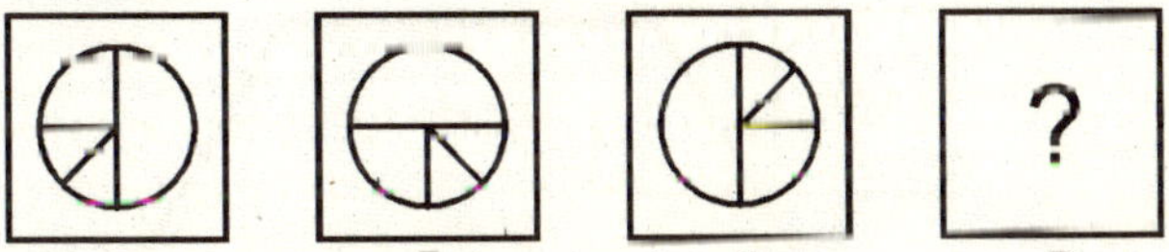

A B C D

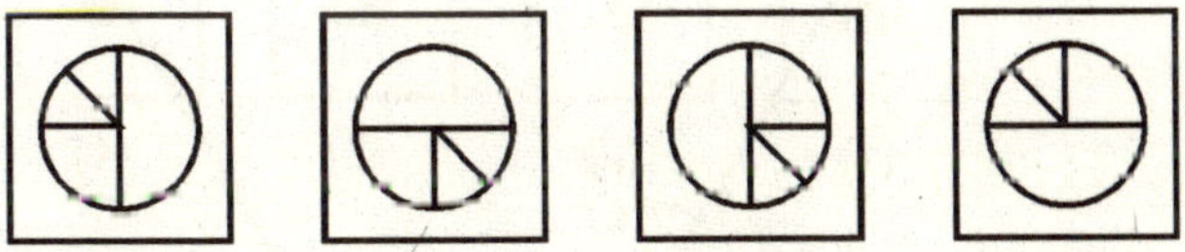

(1) (2) (3) (4)

12. What does the following word equation suggest?

6 D in a PC

13. The following seven-letter word contains ARK at its centre. Fill up the blanks to spell the surname of a former Indian Test player?

___ ___ A R K ___ ___

14. The first three letters of the following word are missing. Discover the missing letters to form a word?

___ ___ ___ UMA

15. Which among the four options should occupy the position indicated by a question mark to continue the sequence?

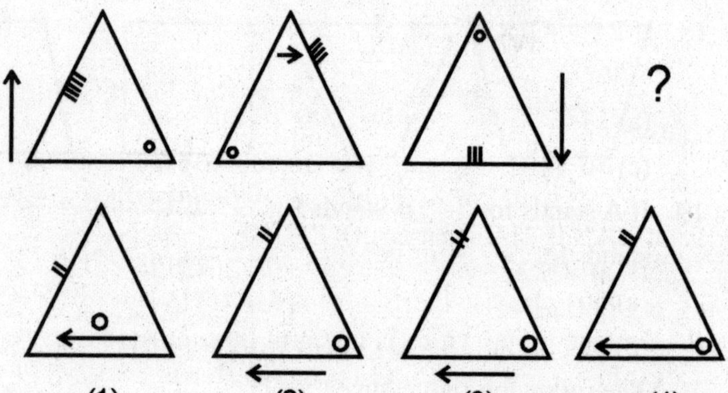

(1) (2) (3) (4)

16. What angle should replace the question mark in the following hexagon?

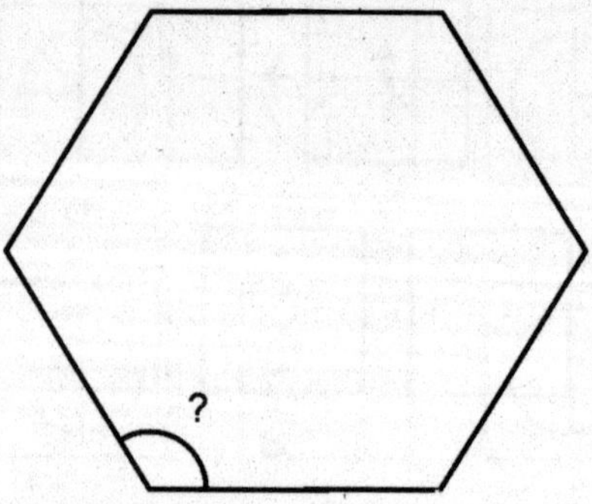

17. In which options the following figure is embedded?

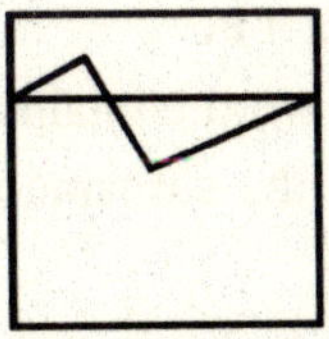

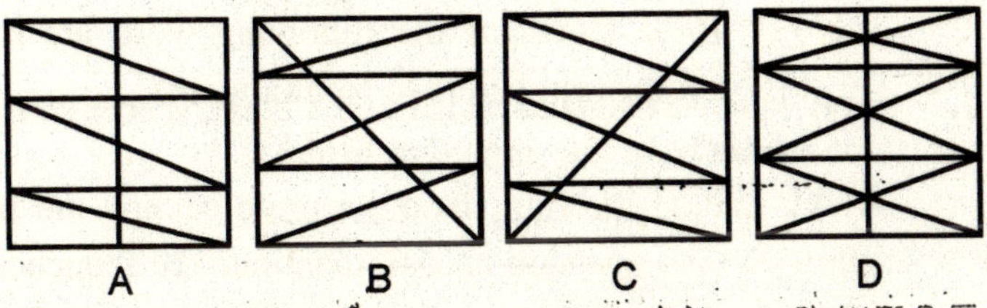

18. If 24 + 42 = 24 and 31 + 13 = 16 then find the value of 63 + 36?

(a) 14 (b) 16

(c) 36 (d) 20

19. If A stands for "–", B stands for "+", C stands for "×" and D stands for "÷" then find the value of 21 D 3 A 1 B 8 C 5?

(a) 36 (b) 46

(c) 56 (d) 66

20. The following figure appears when a square sheet of paper is folded twice and a punch is made shown by a dot. Which option justifies the formation of the given figure?

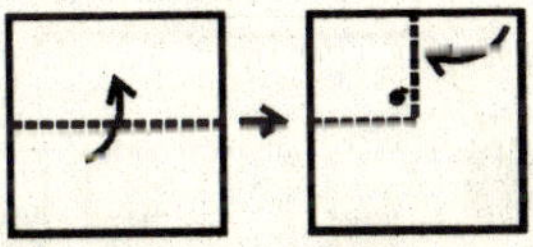

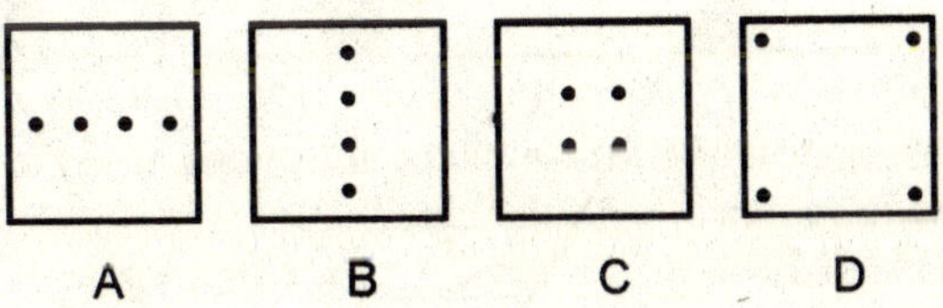

21. Which among the following number is odd one out?

12	18	15
54	72	87
79	78	24

22. Apply your intelligence to fill in the blank spaces so that the three words have the same five letters?

__ __ R __ __

__ __ N __ E

__ __ I __ S

23. Which among the four options should occupy the position indicated by a question mark to continue the sequence?

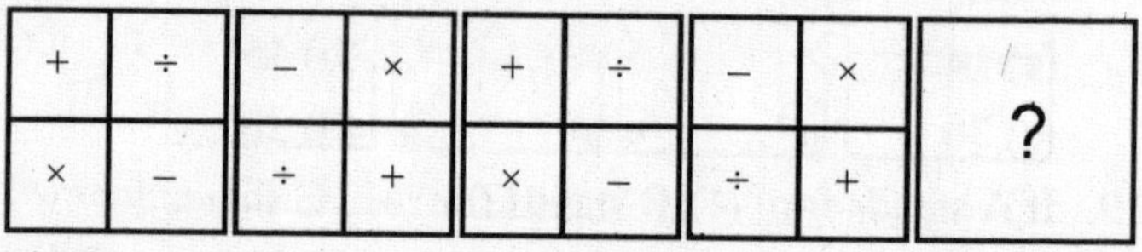

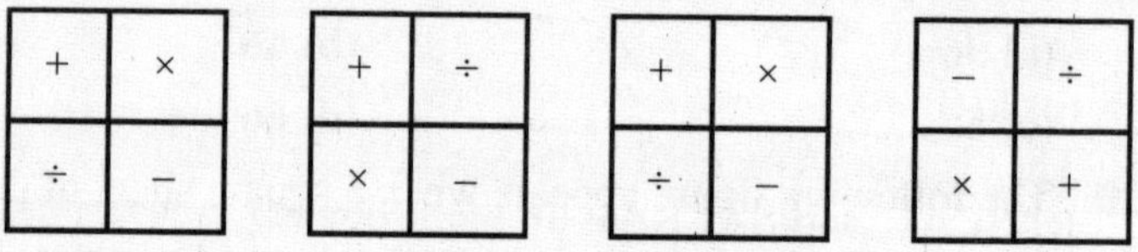

(1) (2) (3) (4)

24. Which of the four alternatives is exactly the mirror image of the object placed in front of a plane mirror AB?

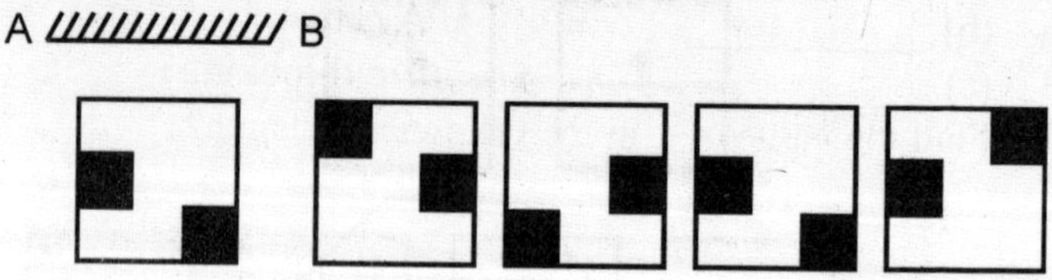

(1) (2) (3) (4)

25. Unscramble the letters of the following word to make a new one to match it with the clue?

BEAMLESS ____________ = Congregate

❑

TEST-7

1. Find the missing number ("?")?

13, 25, 38, 51, 66, ?

(a) 78 (b) 79
(c) 80 (d) 81

2. Find the missing letter ("?")?

AD, ZW, EH, TQ, ?, ?

(a) LN, NL (b) MN, NM
(c) NK, KN (d) KN, NK

3. A square sheet of paper is folded as shown by the dotted lines and then a hole is punched and a cut at the corner is made. Which option suggests its look when it is unfolded?

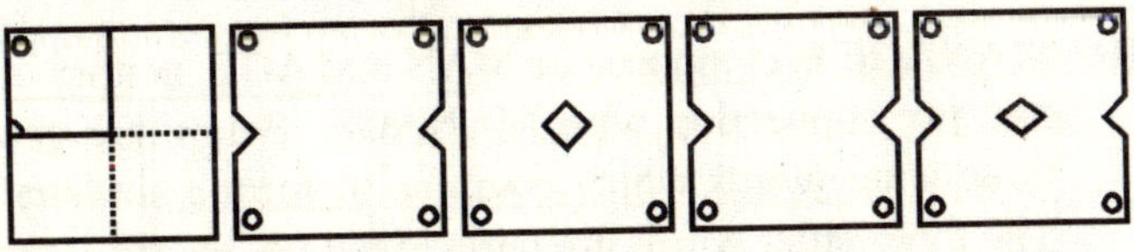

(1) (2) (3) (4)

4. Find the group which is different from others?

(a) GJN (b) EIM
(c) LPT (d) NRV

5. The letters AACLRS when rearranged form LASCAR, RASCAL, and SACRAL. In the following groups rearrange the letters to form anagrams. Clues are given.

ABELRY

(a) ____________ Only just
(b) ____________ A cereal
(c) ____________ Tired-looking

6. Find the value of x in the following octagon?

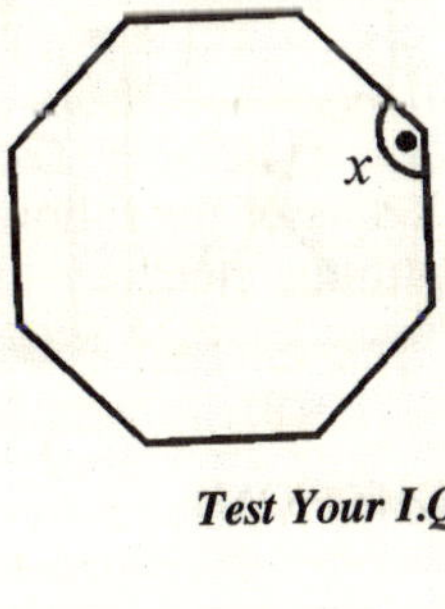

7. Which three-letter word should be inserted within the parenthesis to form two new words?

B (___ ___ ___) Z
E (___ ___ ___) E

8. Which among the following figures is different from others?

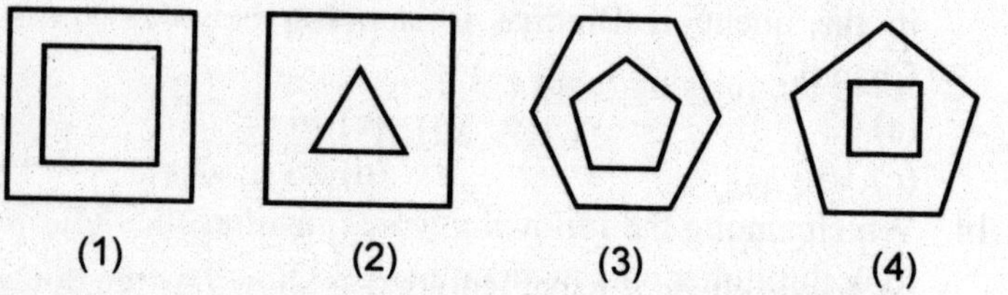

9. The first two letters of the following four-letter word are missing. Find out the missing letters to form a word.

___ ___ AF

10. MANAGE is composed of MAN and AGE, neither of which has any connection with MANAGE. Below are given two three-letter words which combine to form a six-letter word. The three-letter words are defined but not the six-letter word. Find the six-letter word. For example: Male child + Trap = SONNET

Section of a journey + Final part = __________ (Caption)

11. Which figure in the lower row should replace the question mark so that C and the chosen figure maintain the same relationship as A and B?

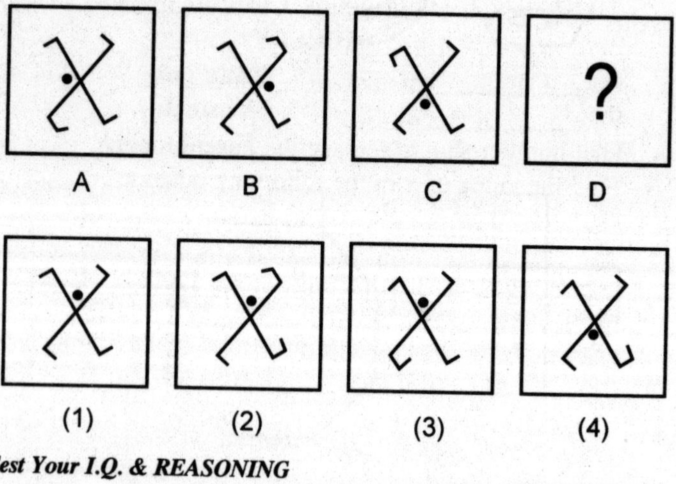

12. If BAT is 17 and CAN is 10 then find the value of DAM.
(a) 6 (b) 8
(c) 10 (d) 12

13. In a queue of girls to see the movie *Munna Bhai MBBS*, Ankita is 9th from the back and Chanda's place is 8th from the front then what would be the minimum number of girls standing in the queue if Bindiya is standing between Ankita and Chanda?
(a) 12 (b) 14
(c) 16 (d) 18

14. Which among the following words justifies the definition 'to look through a narrow opening'?
(a) Ogle (b) Gaze
(c) Peep (d) Sneak

15. Which among the four options should occupy the position indicated by a question mark to continue the sequence?

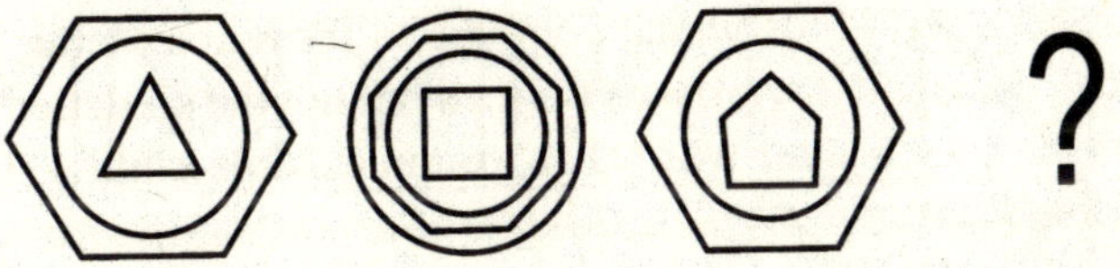

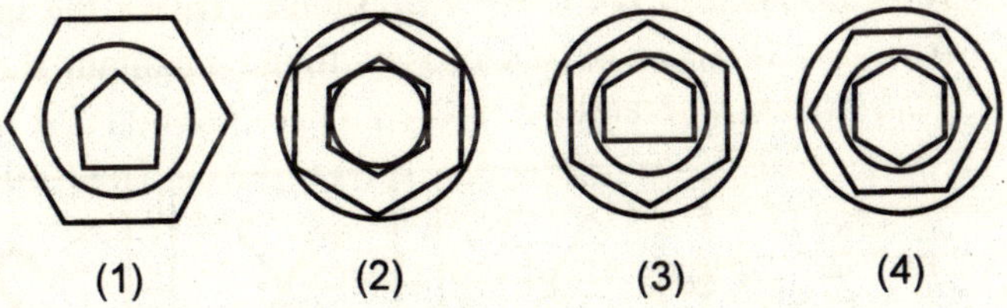

16. What number should replace the question mark?

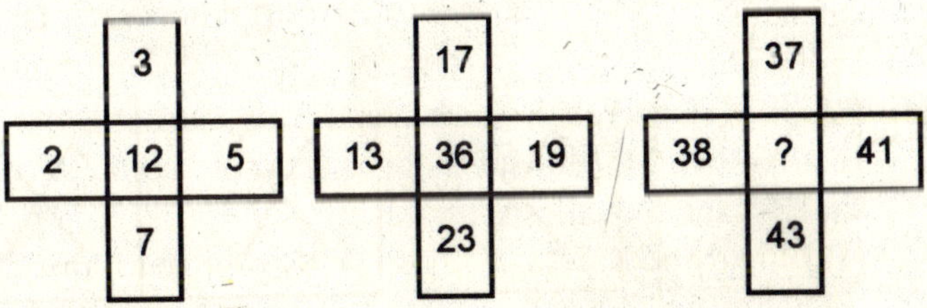

17. Insert a three-letter word in the blank spaces which completes the first word and starts the second?

LAY(__ __ __)AGE

18. Which among the following African countries is different from others?

SENEGAL
MOROCCO
BOTSWANA
BURUNDI

19. Select the alternative whose alphabet when placed at the missing spaces complete the following sequence?

αβ __ __ γα __ β __ γ __ β

(a) ββββα (b) βββαβ
(c) αβββγ (d) βββαγ

20. Select the correct figure among the four options to complete the first figure to make it symmetrical?

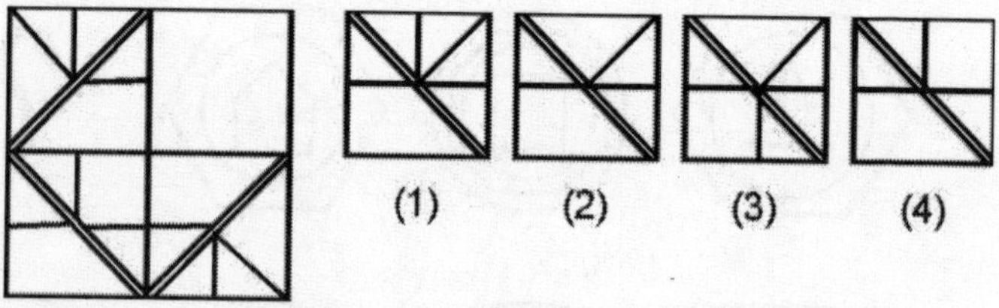

21. Which key word should replace the question mark so as to make a two-word phrase from the list of words that follows, i.e. [?] : BAG, MARSHAL, CONDITIONING (? is AIR)

[?] COLD/FACTOR/SENSE

22. The following seven-letter word contains HAD at its centre. Fill up the blanks to spell a name of a month in Hindu calendar.

__ __ H A D __ __

23. Rahim is shorter than Ahmed but not as short as Daler. Daler is taller than Etmad who is not as short as Fahim. Who is the shortest and the tallest?

(a) Etmad and Rahim (b) Etmad and Ahmed
(c) Fahim and Ahmed (d) Ahmed and Fahim

24. Which among the four options should occupy the position indicated by a question mark to continue the sequence?

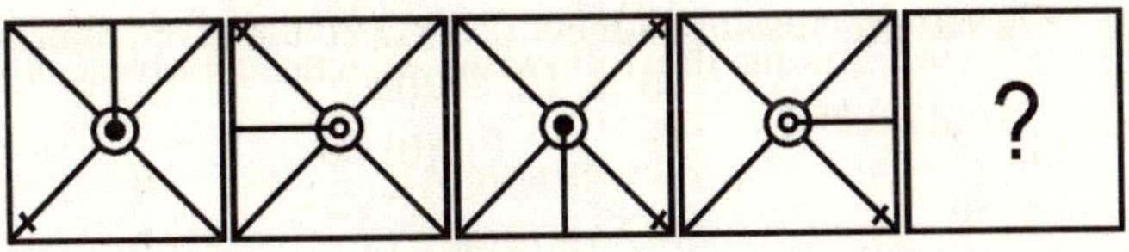

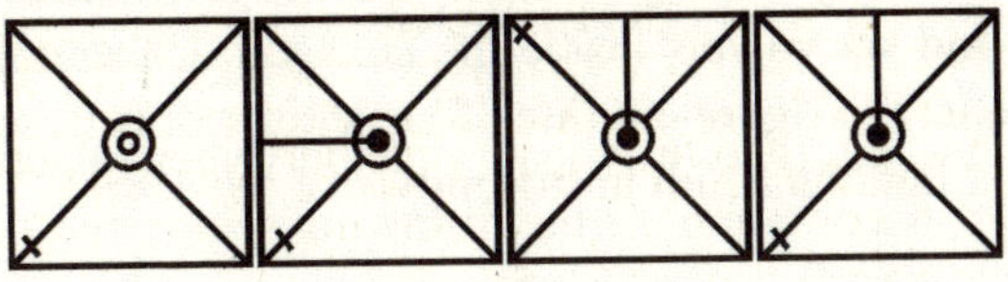

(1) (2) (3) (4)

25. Can you find out the missing number in this series?

37, 10, 82
29, 11, 47
96, 15, 87
42, ?, 15

❑

TEST-8

1. Choose the missing number ("?") from the given alternatives?

   0, 4, 18, ?, 100

   (a) 24 (b) 36

   (c) 48 (d) 64

2. In the following star figure there are six consonants at the vertices and six vowels inside the hexagon. Unscramble the twelve letters to figure out three four-letter words to spell the name of a famous Hindi horror movie of the sixties?

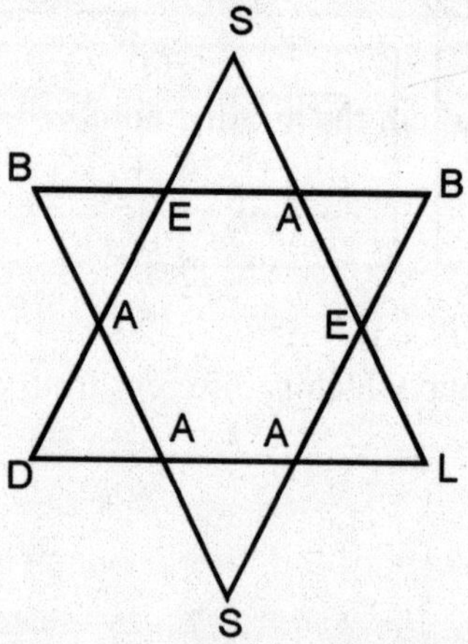

3. How many rhombuses are there in the following figure?

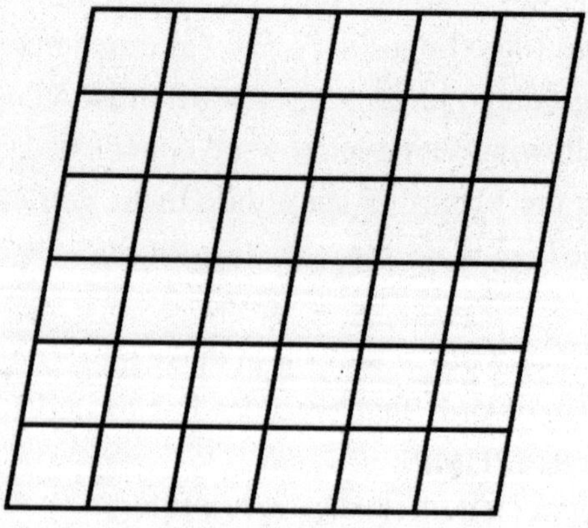

4. Which of the four alternatives is exactly the mirror image of the object placed in front of a plane mirror AB?

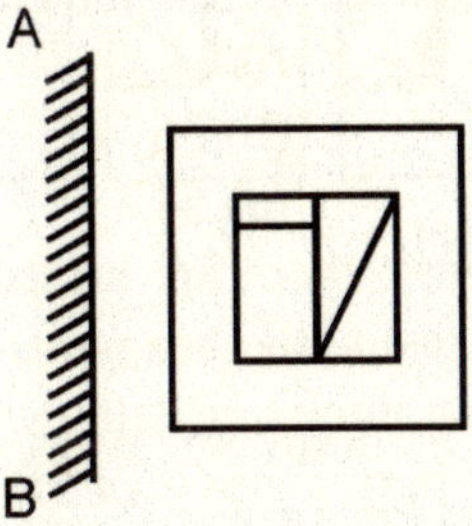

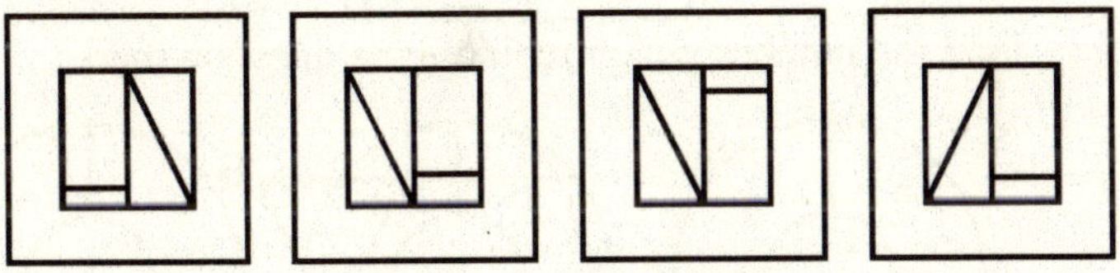

(1) (2) (3) (4)

5. Find the group which is different from others?

(a) NZ (b) FZ

(c) XZ (d) DZ

6. In an alien language 'Natasha is beautiful' is spoken as 'dingo mingo lingo'. 'Beautiful becomes actress' is spoken as 'lingo ringo jingo'. 'Actress becomes star' is spoken as 'jingo ringo bingo'. How is 'Natasha is star' spoken in that language?

(a) jingo ringo lingo (b) dingo mingo lingo

(c) ringo dingo jingo (d) dingo mingo bingo

7. The following seven-letter word contains NUM at its centre. Fill up the blanks to spell the Hindu god of devotion and courage?

__ __ N U M __ __

8. Put the key word in the box to make a two-word phrase from the list of words that precede. For example: AIR/FILTER/PETROL [PUMP]

FOUNDATION/KIDNEY/STEPPING [?]

9. Select the correct figure among the four options to complete the first figure to make it symmetrical?

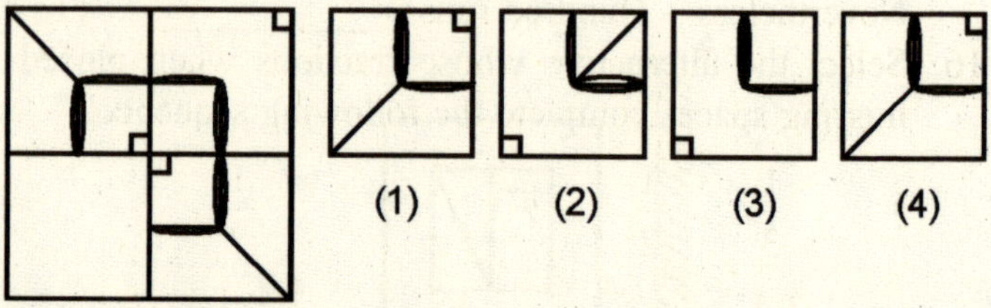

(1) (2) (3) (4)

10. The first three letters of the following word are missing. Find out the missing letters to form a word?

___ ___ ___ IKH

11. Find the number which replaces the question mark?

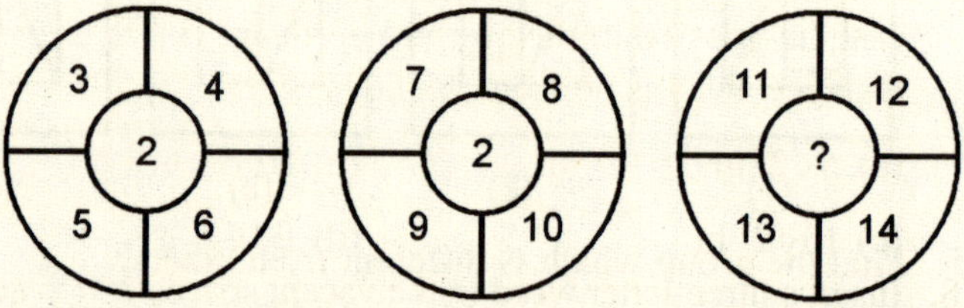

12. Which three-letter word should be inserted within the parenthesis to form two new words?

O (___ ___ ___) E
C (___ ___ ___) E

13. How many meaningful words can you make from the following set of letters?

AEGINR ______ ______ ______ ______ ______

14. Which among the following figures is different from others?

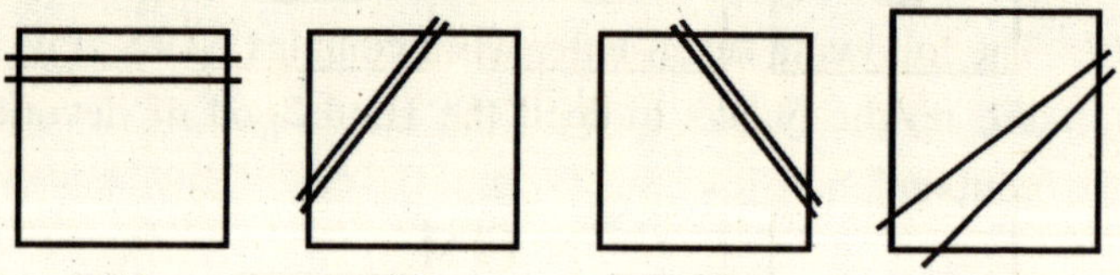

(1) (2) (3) (4)

15. SONNET is composed of SON and NET, neither of which has any connection with SONNET. Below are listed some pair of words, each of them has a three-letter word as its meaning. The two three-letter words combine to form a

six-letter word which is defined. Find the six-letter word. For example: Male child + Trap = SONNET?

Nevertheless + Hundred runs = __________ (To fasten)

16. Select the alternative whose fractions when placed at the missing spaces complete the following sequence?

$$? \quad \frac{1}{3} \quad \frac{1}{2} \quad ? \quad ? \quad \frac{1}{2} \quad ? \quad ? \quad \frac{1}{2}$$

(a) $\frac{1}{2}\frac{1}{4}\frac{1}{3}\frac{1}{2}\frac{1}{3}$ (b) $\frac{1}{4}\frac{1}{3}\frac{1}{2}\frac{1}{4}\frac{1}{2}$

(c) $\frac{1}{4}\frac{1}{3}\frac{1}{2}\frac{1}{4}\frac{1}{3}$ (d) $\frac{1}{4}\frac{1}{2}\frac{1}{2}\frac{1}{4}\frac{1}{3}$

17. Bachchan goes 20 m to the south of his house, then turn to east, he goes 10 m then turn to north to go 30 m. How much distance away is he from his housc?

(a) $5\sqrt{2}$ m (b) $10\sqrt{2}$ m

(c) $15\sqrt{2}$ m (d) $20\sqrt{2}$ m

18. Insert a three-letter word in the vacant spaces which complete the first word and starts the second?

FLAT(_ _ _)FOLD

19. Which figure in the lower row should replace the question mark so that C and the chosen figure maintain the same relationship as A and B?

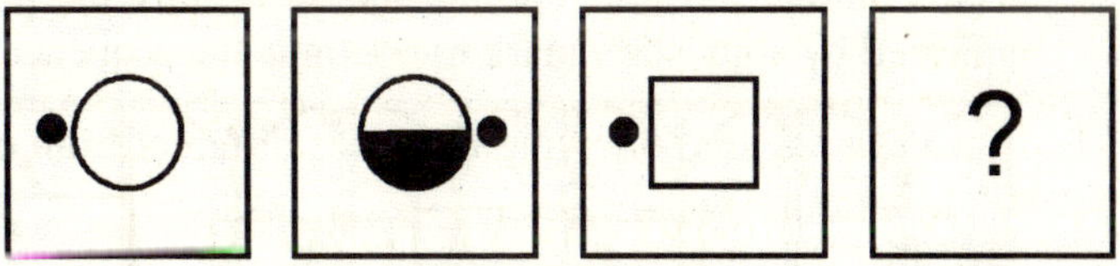

A B C D

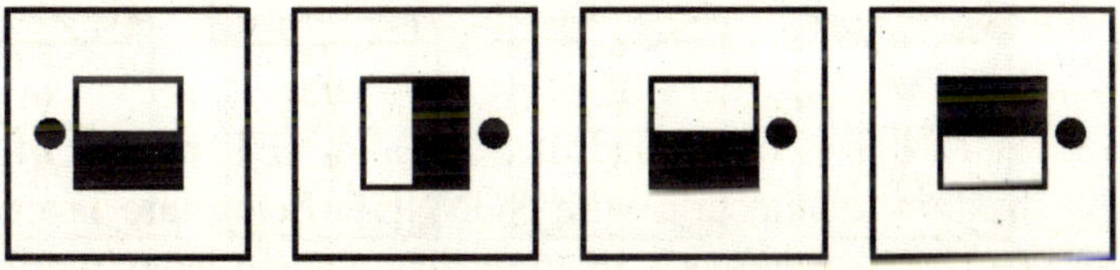

(1) (2) (3) (4)

20. Find a single word that defines both the words. For example: Quick bird would be Swift?
Training vehicle ____________

21. Which letter should be placed before and after the following word so that new words are formed which spell the same—forward and backward?

__ I __

22. A square sheet of paper is folded as shown by the dotted lines and then holes are punched or a cut on the corner is made. Which option suggests its look when it is unfolded?

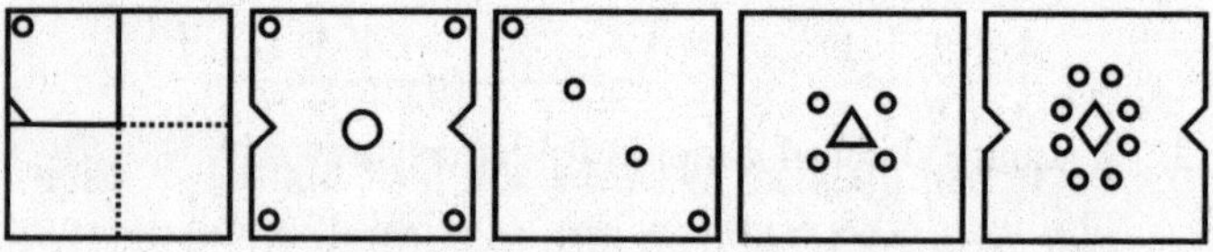

(1) (2) (3) (4)

23. POTASH is composed of POT and ASH, neither of which has any connection with POTASH. Below are listed some pair of words, each of them has a three-letter word as its meaning. The two three-letter words combine to form a six-letter word which is defined. Find the six-letter word. For example: Male child + Trap = SONNET

Because + Self = ____________ (Precede)

24. How can you add eight 8's together so they add up to exactly one thousand?

25. Which among the four options should occupy the position indicated by a question mark to continue the sequence?

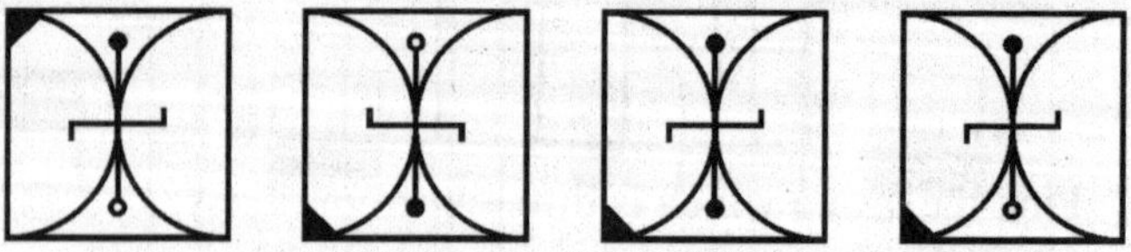

(1) (2) (3) (4)

TEST-9

1. Find the angle which replaces the question mark?

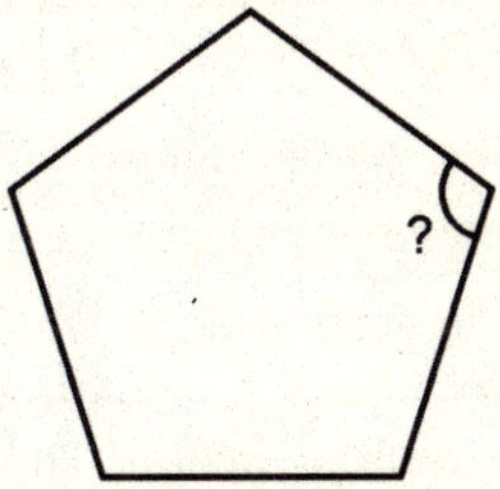

2. A square sheet of paper is folded as shown by the dotted lines and then holes are punched as shown in the diagram. Which option suggests its look when it is unfolded?

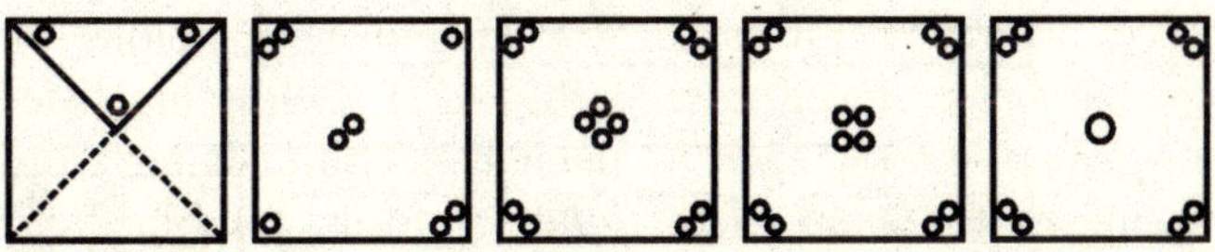

(1) (2) (3) (4)

3. How many squares are there in the following figure?

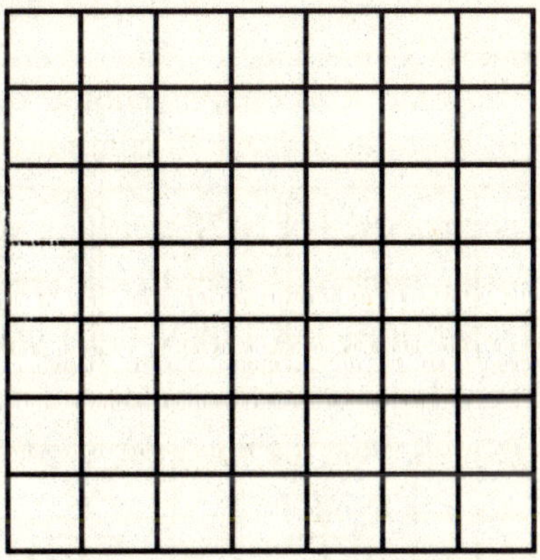

4. Find the group which is different from others.
   (a) QCU (b) NCW
   (c) PDT (d) SAT

5. Uddhava's wife Abha is the aunt of Bhumika who's cousin is Phizo and Phizo is the only child of Uddhava. How is Phizo related to Abha?
   (a) Son (b) Daughter
   (c) Uncle (d) Mother
6. If 45229 is the phone number of DEVI then what is SRIDEVI's phone number?
   (a) 1198945229 (b) 9119845229
   (c) 9118945229 (d) 1918945229
7. Which among the four options should occupy the position indicated by a question mark to continue the sequence?

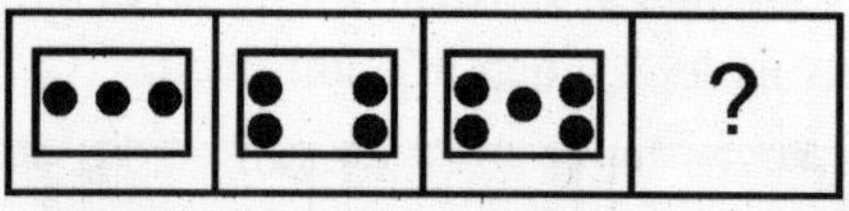

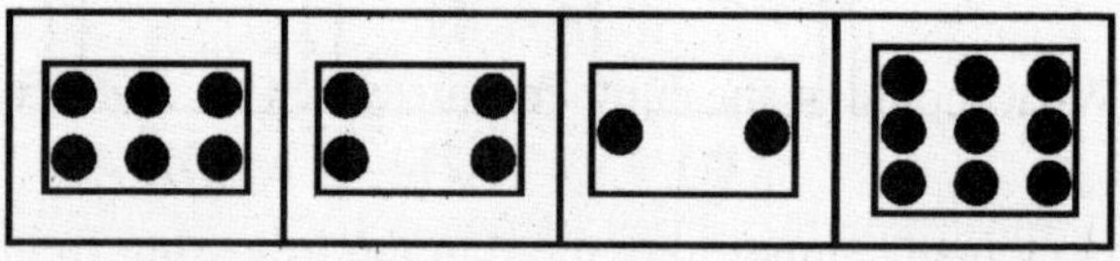

(1) (2) (3) (4)

8. If one hundred is coded as 'C', how is coded one thousand?
   (a) D (b) P
   (c) T (d) M
9. NOTICE is composed of NOT and ICE, neither of which has any connection with NOTICE. Below are listed some pair of words, each of them has a three-letter word as its meaning. The two three-letter words combine to form a six-letter word which is defined. Find the six-letter word. For example: Male child + Trap = SONNET
   Moist + Of a female = ____________ (Male sheep)
10. Insert a three-letter word in the blank spaces which completes the first word and starts the second?

MOR(__ __ __)GET

11. Which figure in the lower row should replace the question mark to maintain the same relationship as the first two figures?

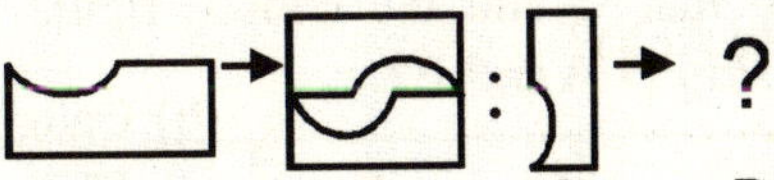

A B C D

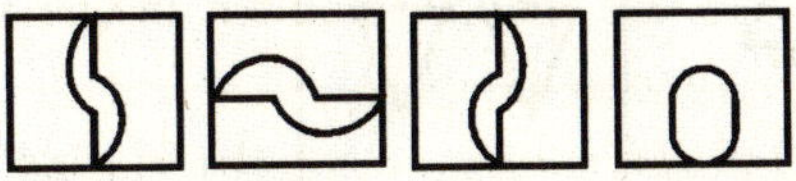

(1) (2) (3) (4)

12. Which among the following words is different from others?

DYNAMO
SHANDY
WAR-CRY
SCANTY

13. The following seven-letter word contains ETN at its centre. Fill up the blanks to spell the name of an Asian country?

__ __ E T N __ __

14. What should be the number represented by the question mark?

8 5 4 9 1 7 6 10 3 2 ?

15. In the following series of numbers how many such 3's are followed by even number and preceded by odd number?

7313494328793273186324031362321398632736

(a) Three (b) Four
(c) Five (d) Six

16. What number should replace the question mark?

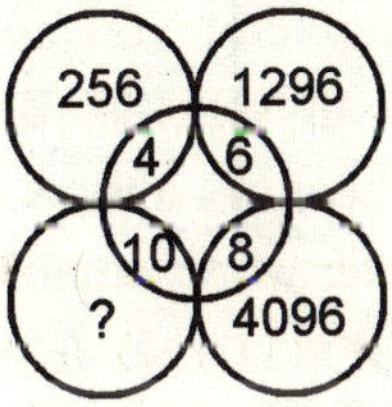

17. Find a single word that defines both the words. For example: Quick bird would be Swift.

Hard company ________

18. Which bird is hidden in the following sentence?

Why do you bluff in chess?

19. Shuffling the letters in ANTHER, guess the capital city?

20. Which figure in the lower row should replace the question mark so that C and the chosen figure maintain the same relationship as A and B?

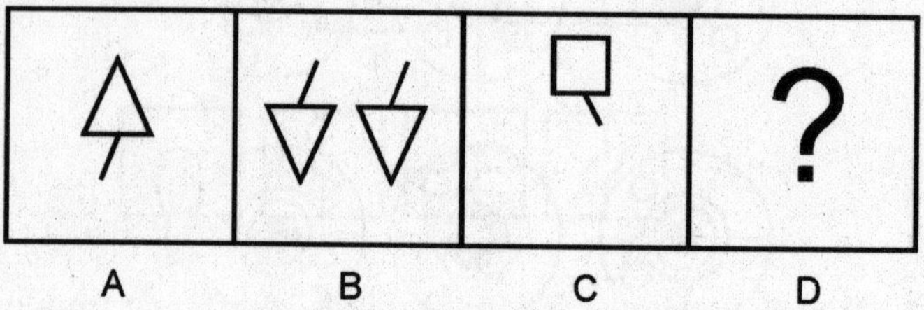

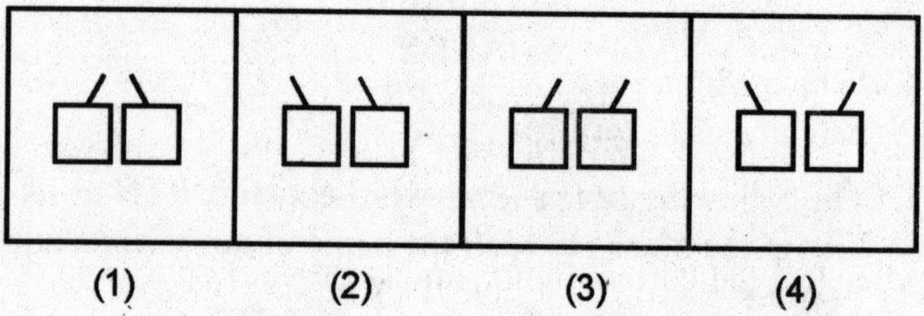

21. Find the number which replaces the question mark?

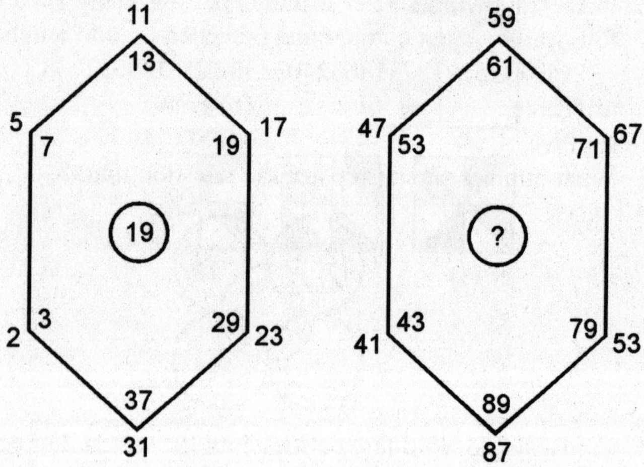

22. Unscramble the letters of the following word to make a new one.

SPOILT ___________

23. Which among the four options should occupy the position indicated by a question mark to continue the sequence?

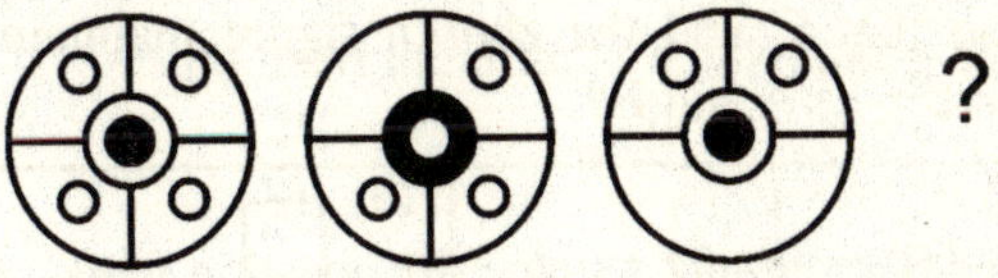

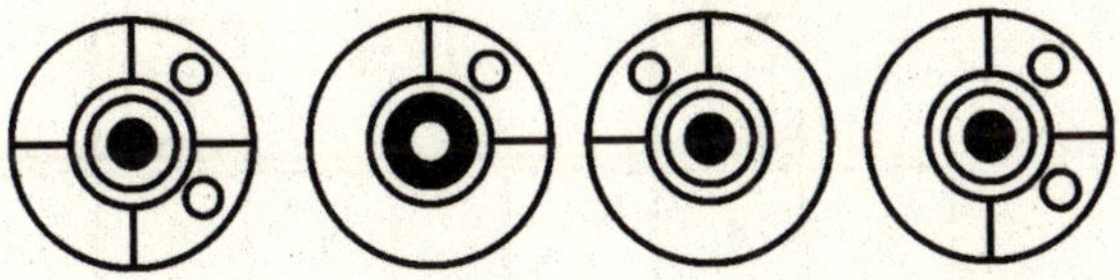

(1) (2) (3) (4)

24. Which three-letter word should be inserted within the parenthesis to form two new words?

Y (___ ___ ___) N
W (___ ___ ___) Y

25. Select the correct figure among the four options to complete the first figure to make it symmetrical?

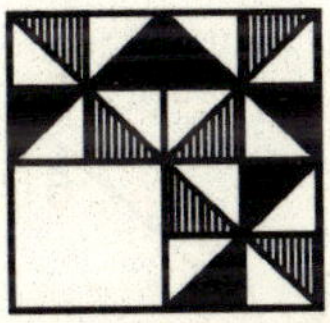

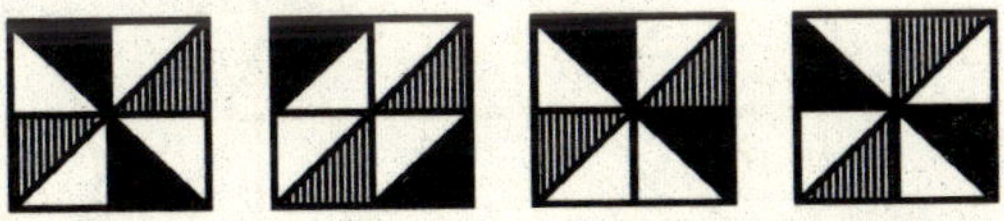

(1) (2) (3) (4)

❑

TEST-10

1. Find the group which is different from others?
   (a) FJ (b) DI
   (c) OT (d) UZ
2. What number should replace the question mark?

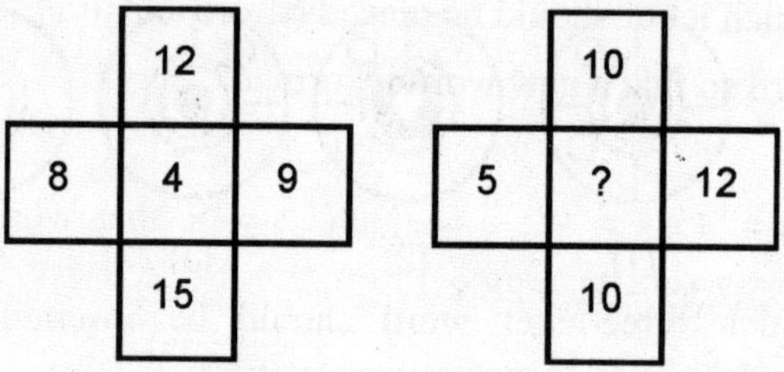

3. Choose the missing number ("?") from the given alternatives?
   1, 3, 9, ?, 33, 51, 73
   (a) 11 (b) 13
   (c) 17 (d) 19
4. A square sheet of paper is folded twice as shown by the dotted lines (A and B) and then holes are punched so that its final shape looks like the figure C. Which option suggests its look when it is unfolded?

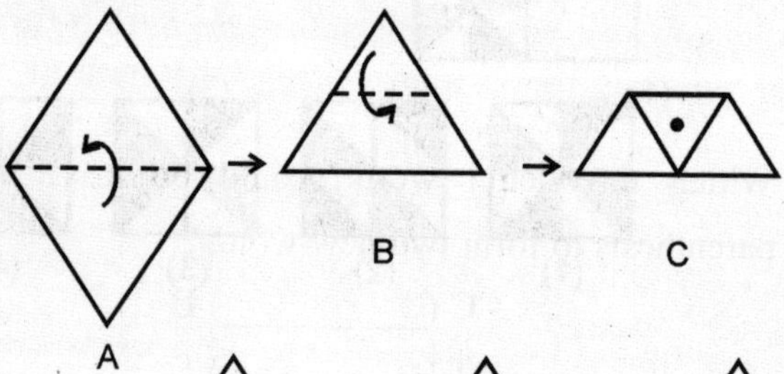

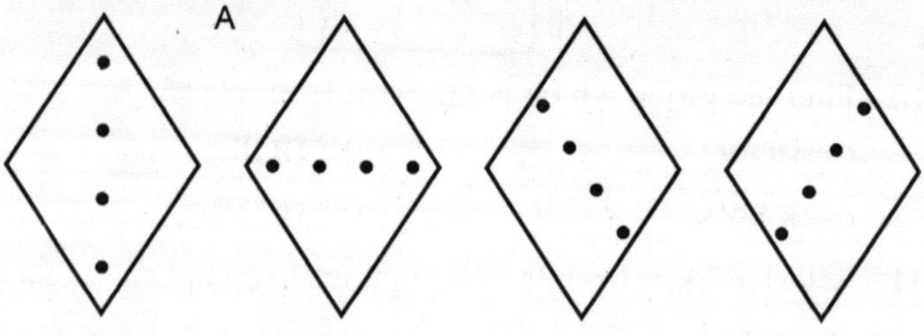

(1) (2) (3) (4)

5. Select the alternative whose alphabet when placed at the missing spaces complete the following series.

ψ __ ψ ω __ χ ψ ψ __ ω ω __ ψ__

(a) ψ ω ψ ω χ (b) ψ ω ψ ψ χ

(c) ψ ω ψ χ ψ (d) ψ ω ψ χ ω

6. Which letter should be placed before and after the following word so that a new word is formed?

__USE__

7. If x = '+'; + = '–'; – = '÷', and ÷ = '×' then what is the value of 95 ? 19 ÷ 11 + 28 × 17 ?

(a) 22 (b) 33

(c) 44 (d) 55

8. Which among the following figures is different from others?

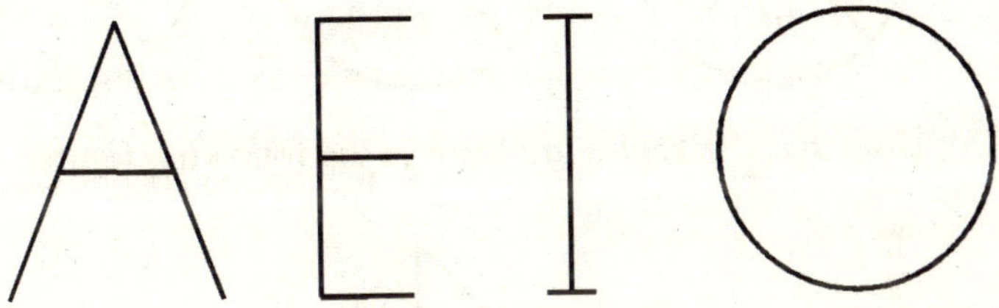

(1) (2) (3) (4)

9. Which three-letter word should be inserted within the parenthesis to form two new words?

C (__ __ __) B

T (__ __ __) P

10. Find the group which is different from others.

(a) BOPC (b) DQRE

(c) KXYM (d) HUVI

11. Select a figure from the four options to complete the sequence above?

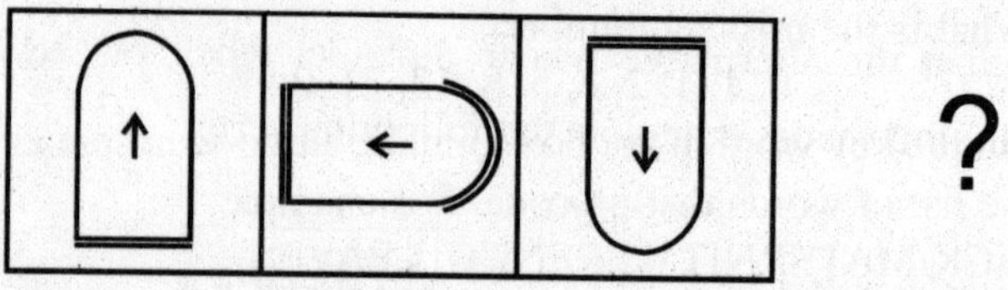

(1) (2) (3) (4)

12. What number should replace the question mark?

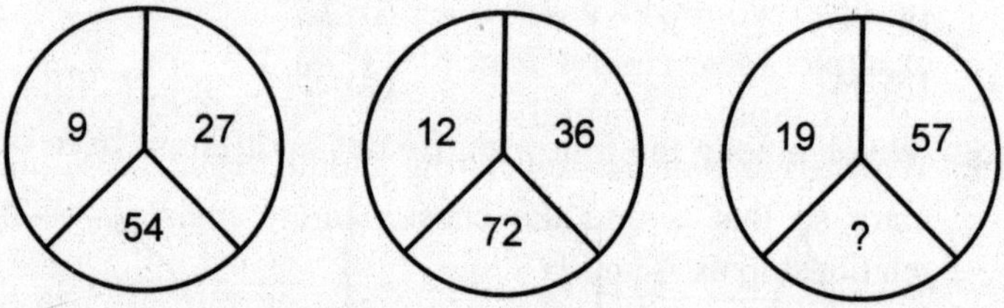

13. How many triangles are there in the following figure?

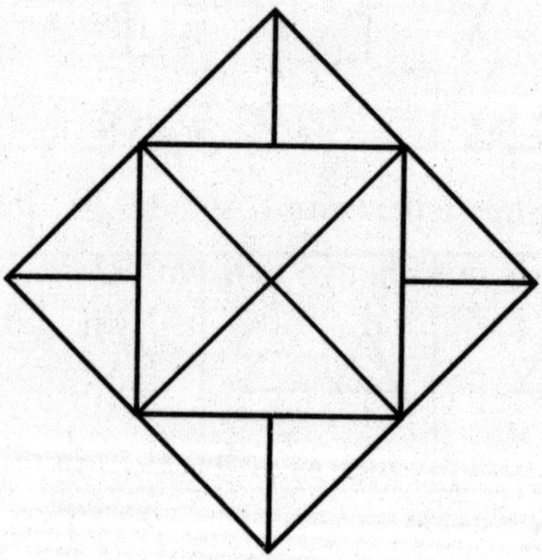

14. The first two letters of the following five-letter word are missing. Find out the missing letters to form a word?

___ ___ VOY

15. What is the missing number:

0, 1, 1, 2, 3, 5, 8, 13, 21, 34 ?

16. Put the key word in the box to make a two-word phrase from the list of words that precede. For example:

SICK/MATERNITY/FRENCH [LEAVE]

ZERO/LUNCH/ELEVENTH [ ]

17. Unscramble the following set of letters and spell the name of an animal.

ACHILT

18. WARDEN is composed of WAR and DEN, neither of which has any connection with WARDEN. Below are listed some pair of words, each of them has a three-letter word as its meaning.. The two three-letter words combine to form a six-letter word which is defined. Find the six-letter word. For example: Male child + Trap = SONNET

Spoil + Bashful = __________ (Wet)

19. Which figure in the lower row should replace the question mark so that C and the chosen figure maintain the same relationship as A and B?

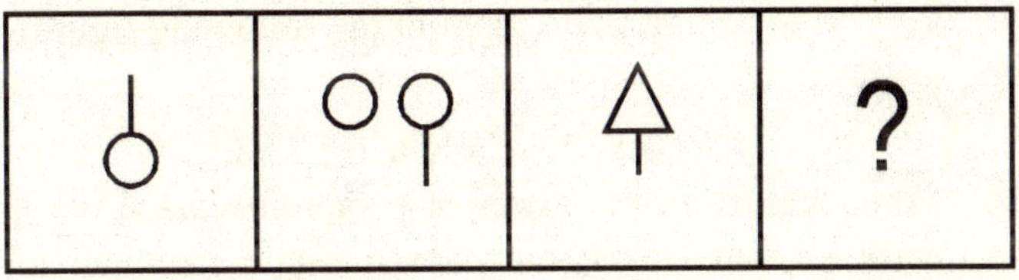

A B C D

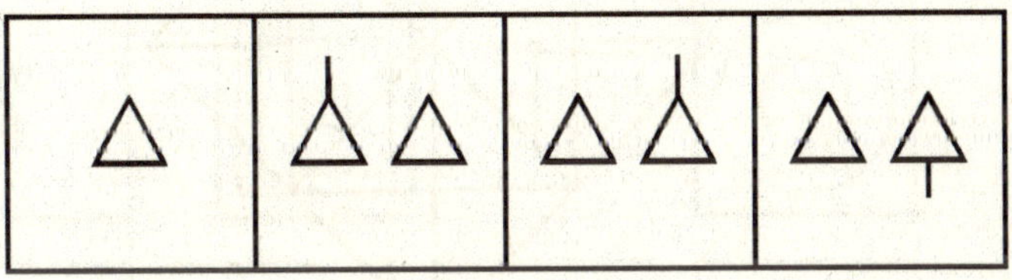

(1) (2) (3) (4)

20. Find a single word that defines both the words. For example: Quick bird would be swift?

Conceal skin = ________

21. The numbers inside each triangle follow certain arithmetical rule. Compare the figures and find out the number represented by the question mark?

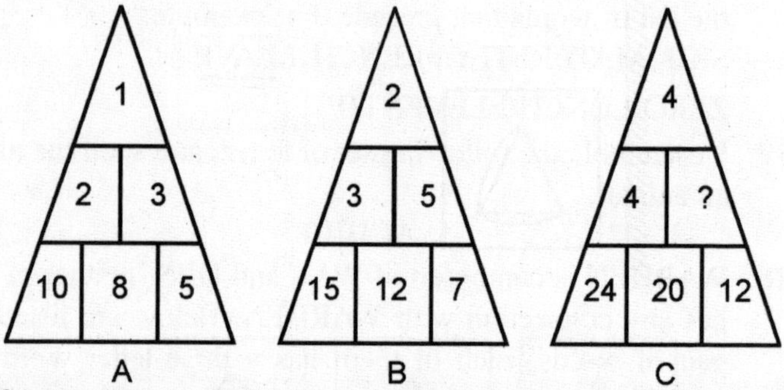

22. If 'sa re ga' stands for 'Lata is singer'; 'ga ma pa' stands for 'singer sings songs'; 'pa dha ni' stands for 'songs are melodious', then what will be the code for 'Lata sings melodious songs'?

(a) sa pa ni ma (b) sa ni ma pa
(c) sa ma pa ni (d) sa ma ni pa

23. Which KEY WORD should replace the question mark so as to make a two-word phrase from the list of words that follows? i.e. ____?____:BAG, MARSHAL, CONDITIONING (? is AIR)

____?___ CYCLE/INSURANCE/STYLE

24. Which figure in the lower row should replace the question mark so that C and the chosen figure maintain the same relationship as A and B?

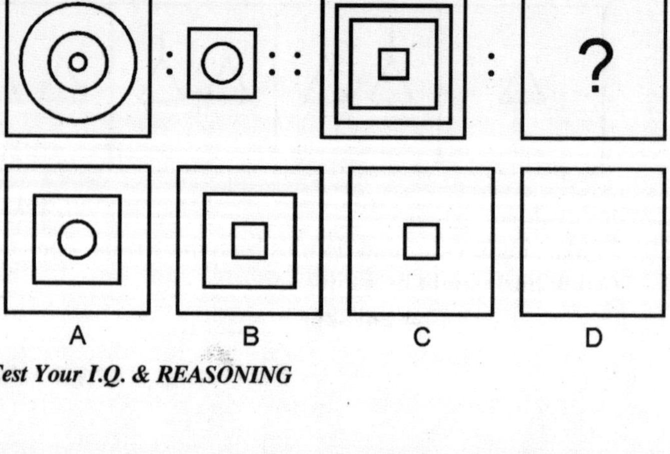

25. Which of the four alternatives is exactly the mirror image of the object placed in front of a plane mirror?

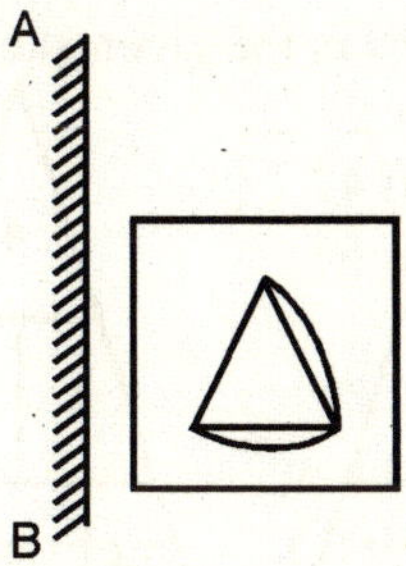

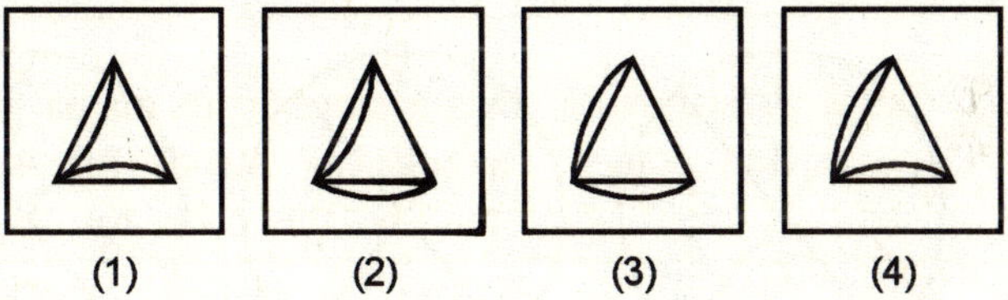

❑

TEST-11

1. Choose the missing number ("?") from the given alternatives?

   3, 7, 14, 23, 36, ?

   (a) 43 (b) 47
   (c) 49 (d) 53

2. Find the missing letters ("?")?

   y, l, t, g, o, b, ?, ?

   (a) j, u (b) k, u
   (c) i, v (d) w, j

3. What fraction should replace the question mark?

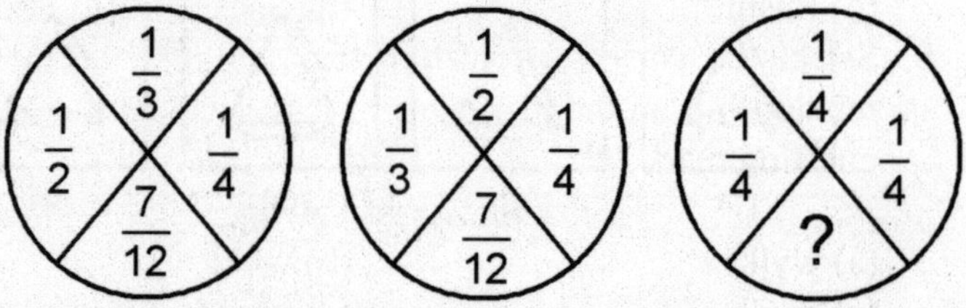

4. Which figure in the lower row should replace the question mark so that C and the chosen figure maintain the same relationship as A and B?

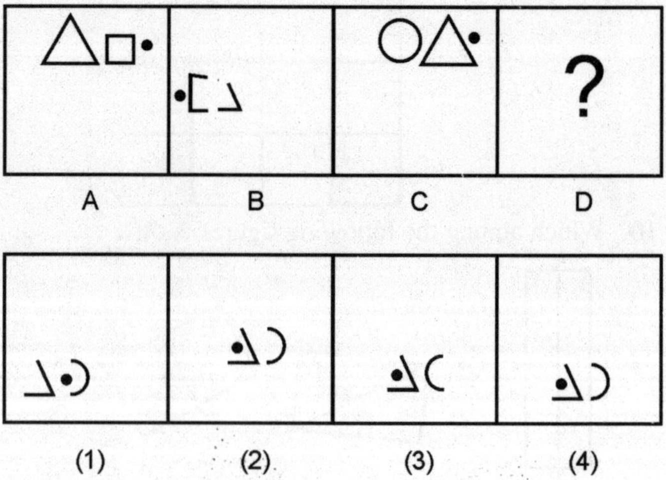

5. Find the group which is different from others?

(a) JVL (b) AND

(c) CPF (d) FSI

6. Select the alternative whose alphabet when placed at the missing spaces complete the following series.

__ y __ x __ y x __ x y __ yxy

(a) xxyyx (b) xxyxy

(c) yxyxy (d) xxyyy

7. Rashi and Shashi are fair. Madhu and Sudha are dark. Rashi and Madhu are tall. Who is tall and fair?

(a) Madhu (b) Sudha

(c) Rashi (d) Shashi

8. Select the correct alternative that will maintain the same relationship on the two signs "::", if it is substituted for the question mark "?".

xzkm: ?:: vxik: uwhj

(a) wyjk (b) wykl

(c) wyik (d) wyjl

9. How many squares are there in the following figure?

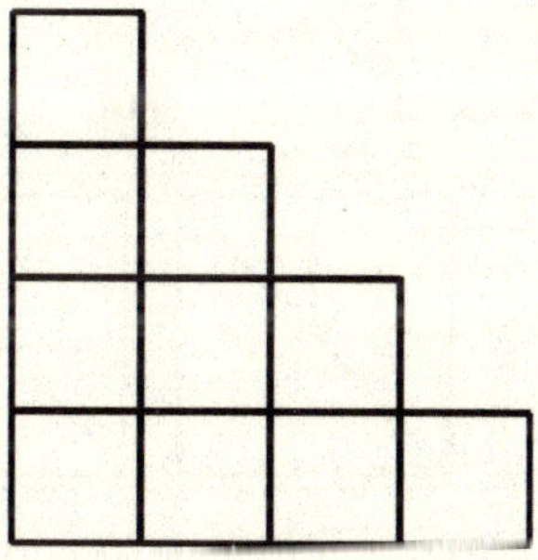

10. Which among the following figures is different from others?

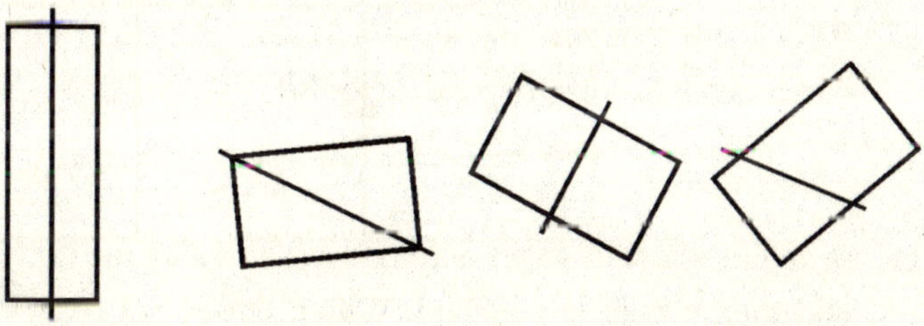

(1) (2) (3) (4)

11. The following nine-letter word contains IRK at its centre. Fill in the blanks to spell the name of one of the best actors of Hindi films?

___ ___ ___ I R K ___ ___ ___

12. Put the key word in each box to make a two-word phrase from the list of words that follow. For example: [MILK] BAR/TOOTH/SHAKE

[ ] RUSH/MEDAL/COAST

13. The first two letters of the following word are missing. Find out the missing letters to form a word.

___ ___ YAK

14. Select the correct figure among the four options to complete the first figure to make it symmetrical?

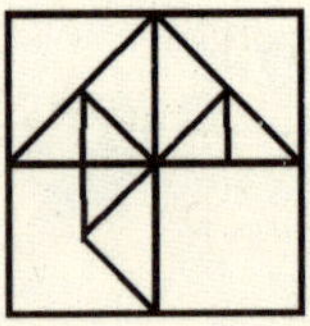

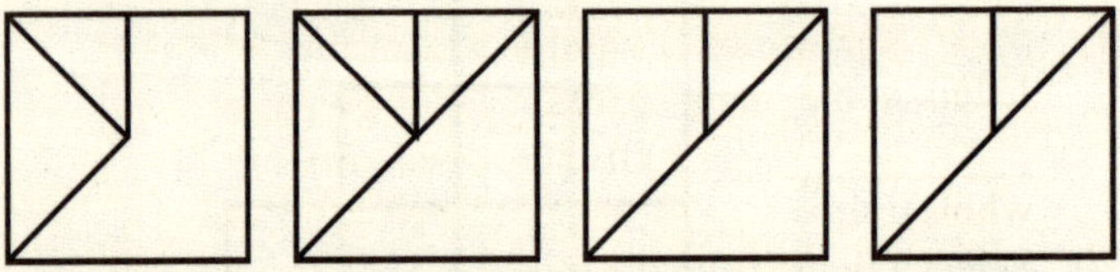

(1) (2) (3) (4)

15. Which three-letter word should be inserted within the parenthesis to form two new words?

C (___ ___ ___) T

M (___ ___ ___) N

16. A square sheet of paper is folded as shown by the dotted lines and then a hole is punched. Which option suggests its look when it is unfolded?

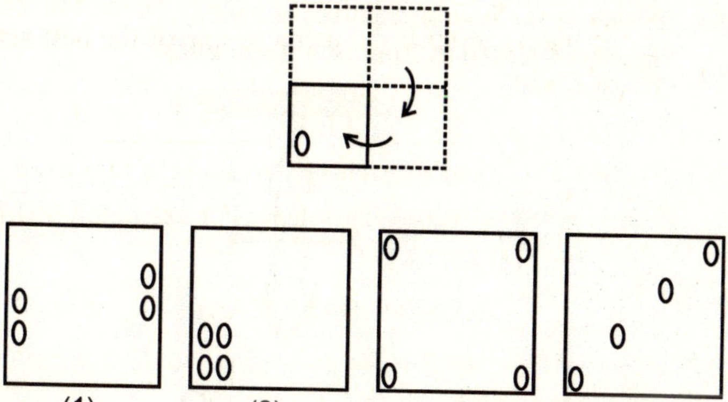

(1) (2) (3) (4)

17. Unscramble the letters of the following word to make a new one?

REGION ____________

18. TIPTOP is composed of TIP and TOP, neither of which has any connection with TIPTOP. Below are listed some pair of words, each of them has a three-letter word as its meaning. The two three-letter words combine to form a six-letter word which is defined. Find the six-letter word. For example: Male child + Trap = SONNET

Seated + Jar = ____________ (A planet)

19. Make a seven-letter word to match the definition by putting letters in the blank spaces. Clue is given.

___ ___ ___ ___ AGE (Proposals offered or accepted as a whole)

20. Select a figure from the four options to complete the sequence above.

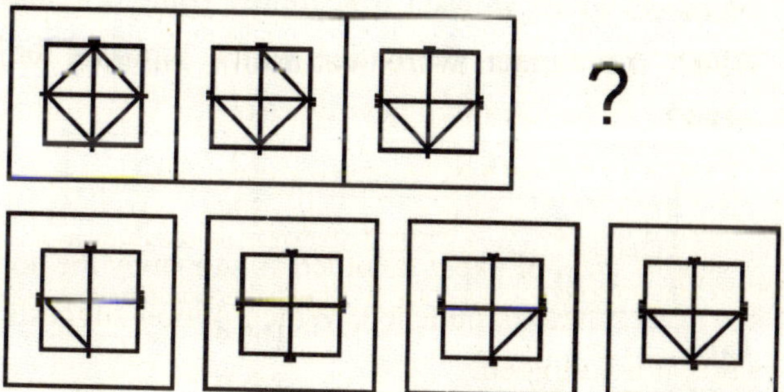

(1) (2) (3) (4)

21. Which of the four alternatives is exactly the mirror image of the object placed in front of a plane mirror?

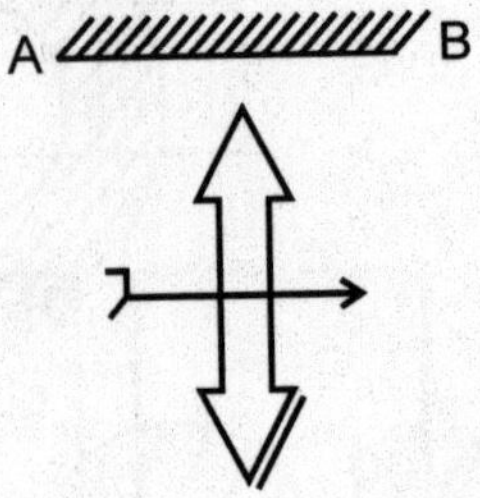

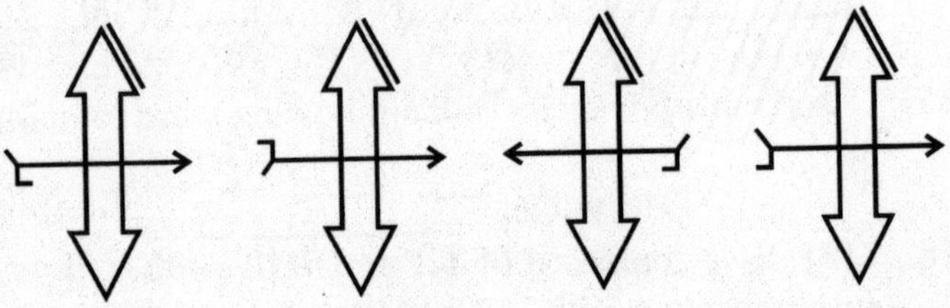

(1) (2) (3) (4)

22. Find a single word that defines both the words. For example: Quick bird would be Swift?

Chief cleric = ________

23. Which among the following words is different from others?

ZEALOTRY

DISCOVER

DISJUNCT

RIDICULE

24. Numbers given in each row follow some arithmetical rule. Select the correct alternative which replaces the question mark?

2	3	5
2	4	4
2	2	?

(a) 2 (b) 4

(c) 6 (d) 8

25. Among the four alternatives A, B, C, D, which replaces the question mark?

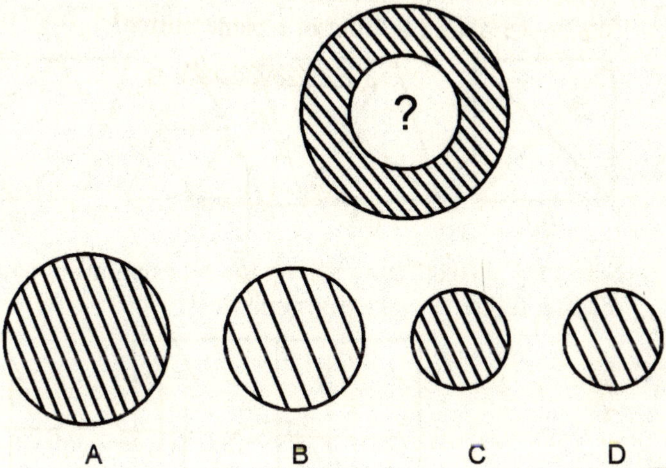

TEST-12

1. Which among the following figures is different from others?

(a) (b) (c) (d)

2. Select the correct figure among the four options to complete the first figure to make it symmetrical?

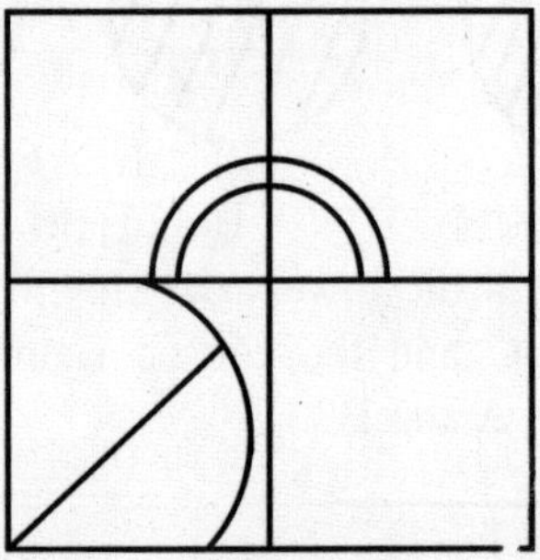

(1) (2) (3) (4)

3. Fractions given in each row follow some arithmetical rule. Select the correct alternative which replaces the question mark?

1/2	2/3	4/3
6/7	6/7	?
3/7	4/7	8/7

(a) 4/7 (b) 5/7
(c) 6/7 (d) 8/7

4. Choose the missing numbers ("?") from the given alternatives?

9, 3, 17, 15, 25, 27, 33, ?, ?

(a) 39, 39
(b) 39, 41
(c) 41, 39
(d) 41, 41

5. Find the group which is different from others?
(a) MAZ
(b) XAH
(c) UBN
(d) TCT

6. The given pattern of numbers follow some arithmetical rule. Select the correct alternative which replaces the question mark.

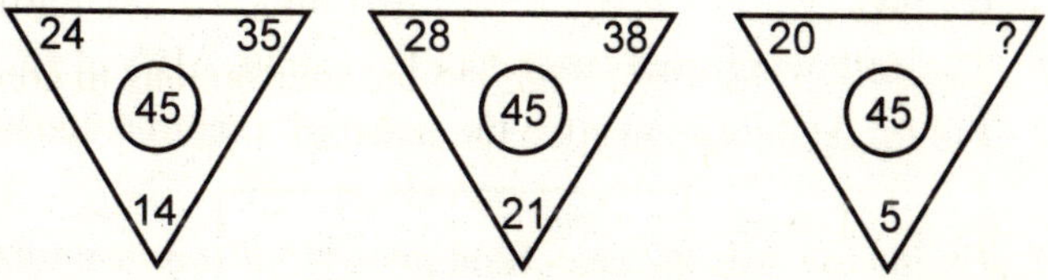

(a) 15
(b) 20
(c) 25
(d) 30

7. Which figure in the lower row should replace the question mark so that C and the chosen figure maintain the same relationship as A and B?

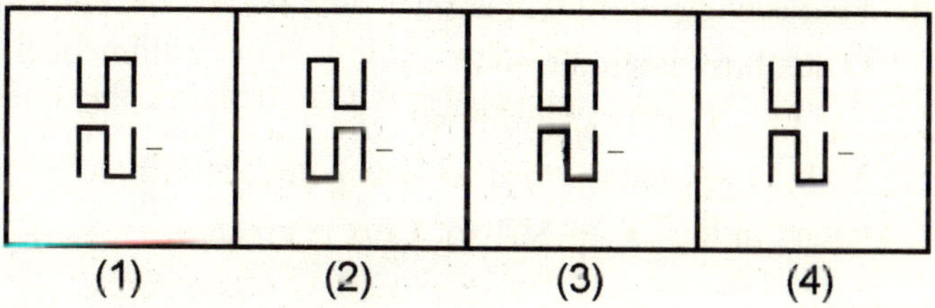

8. Which among the following words is different from others?

RUNNER
BRANCH
CRUNCH
GERUND

9. Insert a three-letter word in the blank spaces which completes the first word and starts the second?

MODE(__ __ __)LISH

10. The age of a father is 32 years and that of his son is 8 years. In how many years his father will be three times as old as his son?

(a) Three (b) Four
(c) Five (d) Six

11. The following nine-letter word contains AHA at its centre. Fill up the blanks to spell the name of a famous Indian city?

___ ___ ___ A H A ___ ___ ___

12. Facing towards the east, Ram goes 90 m and then turns right 20 m; he again turns right for 30 m. He then turns in north direction for 100m. How far is he from the starting point?

(a) 80 m (b) 100 m
(c) 120 m (d) 140 m

13. Which among the following figures is different from others?

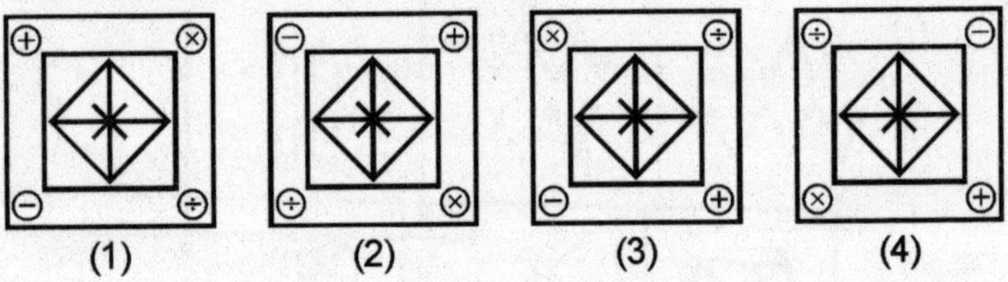

(1) (2) (3) (4)

14. Find a single word that defines both the words. For example: Quick bird would be swift.

Lovely punishment __________

15. Make a six-letter word to match the definition by putting letters in the vacant spaces. Clue is given.

___ ___ ___ LET = Glass cup

16. How many triangles are there in the following figure?

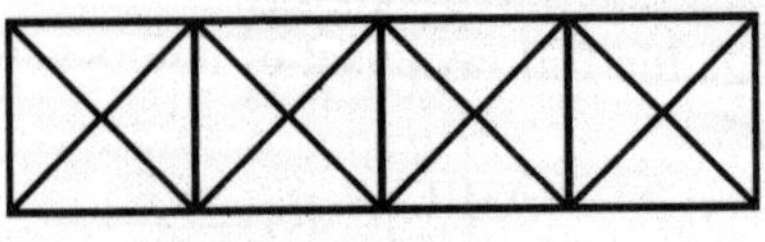

17. A square sheet of paper is folded as shown by the dotted lines and then a hole is punched at the corner. Which option suggests its look when it is unfolded?

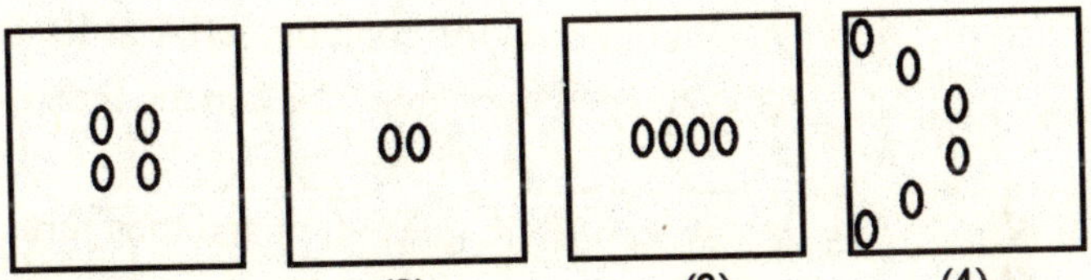

(1) (2) (3) (4)

18. Apply your intelligence to fill in the blank spaces so that the three words have the same five letters?

B ___ E ___ ___

___ ___ K ___ ___

___ R A ___ ___

19. Select a figure from the four options to complete the sequence above.

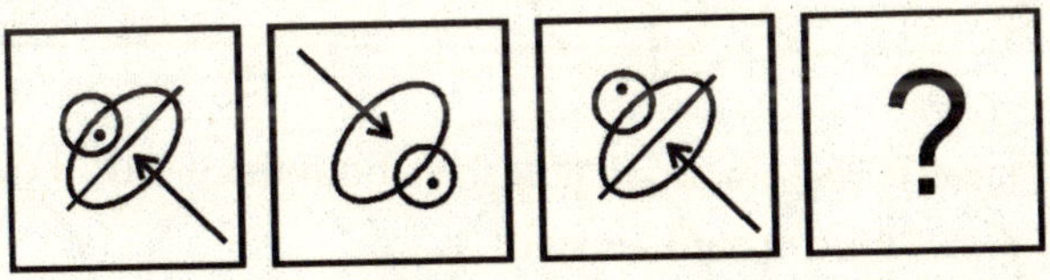

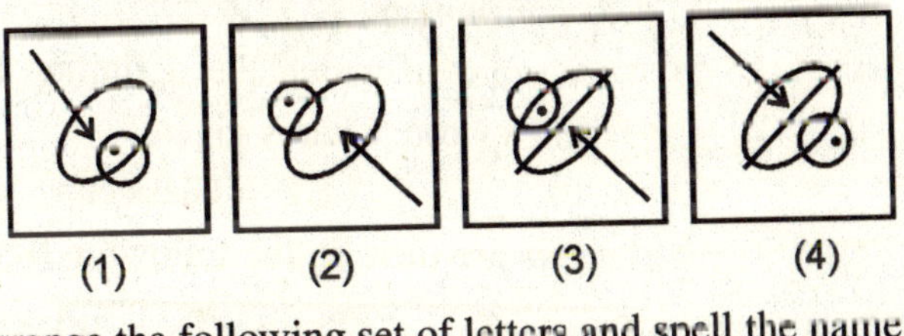

(1) (2) (3) (4)

20. Rearrange the following set of letters and spell the name of a country?

ABILRZ = ________

21. If 36 × 49 = 13 and 4 × 144 = 14, then what is the value of 1 × 196?
(a) 15 (b) 16
(c) 17 (d) 18

22. The following nine-letter word contains ARA at its centre. Fill up the blanks to spell the name of a famous tabla player?
___ ___ ___ A R A ___ ___ ___

23. What number should replace the question mark?

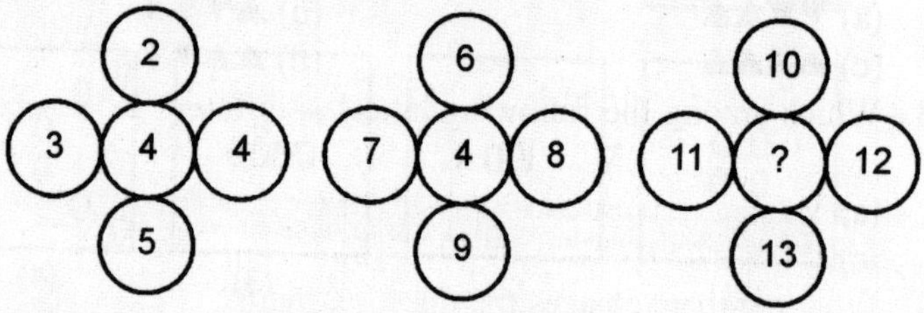

24. If BADE is 40 and CAFÉ is 90 then what is EACH equals to?
(a) 80 (b) 100
(c) 120 (d) 140

25. Select the correct figure among the four options A, B, C, D, to complete the first figure to make it symmetrical?

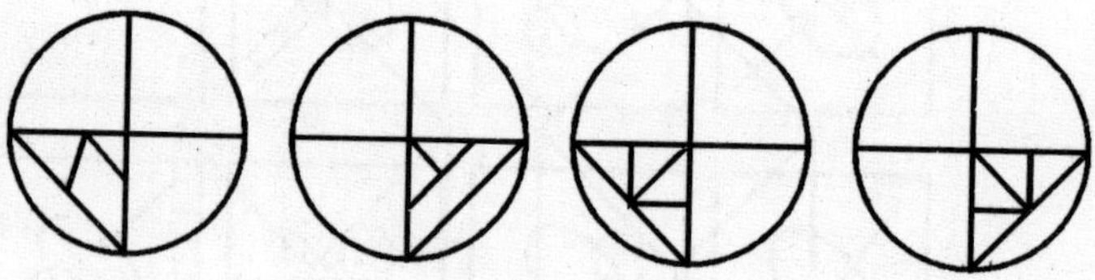

A B C D

❑

TEST-13

1. Find the group which is different from others?
   (a) QGL (b) PDJ
   (c) TDL (d) XBN
2. Select the alternative whose symbols when placed at the missing spaces complete the following sequence?
   ?▲▼▼?▲?▼▲▲?▼
   (a) ▼▼▲▲ (b) ▲▼▼▲
   (c) ▲▲▲▲ (d) ▲▲▼▼
3. Which among the following letters is different from others?
   V I L T Y
   (a) V (b) I
   (c) L (d) T
4. What number replaces the question mark?

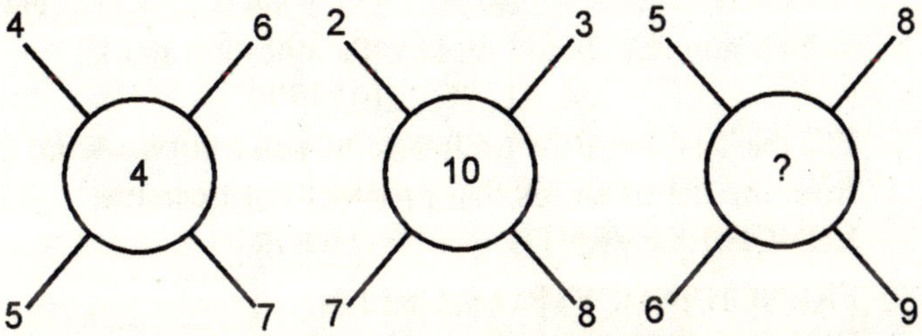

5. Two positions of a dice are shown below. Which number will appear on the face opposite to the face with number 4?

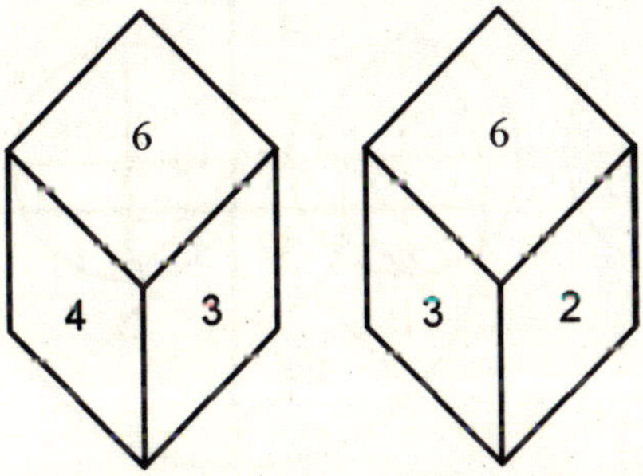

6. Among the following words, which suits the following definition?
   Offspring of white and negro?

(a) Liger (b) Mulatto
(c) Tigon (d) Brat

7. A square sheet of paper is folded as shown by the dotted lines and then holes are punched or a cut on the corner is made. Which option suggests its look when it is unfolded?

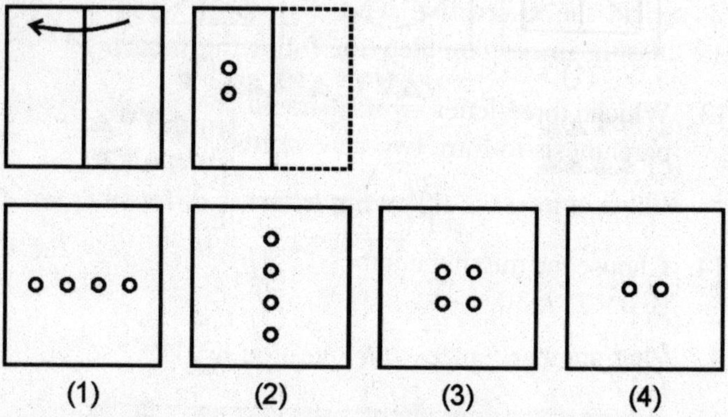

8. Which number should replace the question mark?

24, 41, 75, 126, ?, 279

9. Put the key word in each box to make a two-word phrase from the list of words that precede. For example: ZERO/LUNCH/ELEVENTH [HOUR]

FRENCH/INDUSTRIAL/GREEN [ ]

10. Find the missing number.

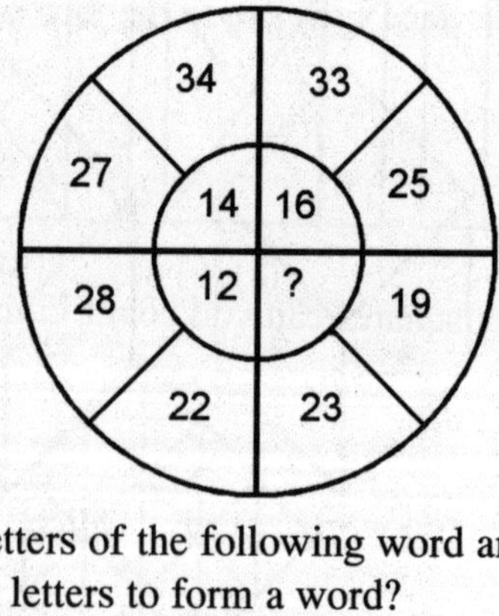

11. The first two letters of the following word are missing. Find out the missing letters to form a word?

__ __ NUE

12. Which among the following figures is different from others?

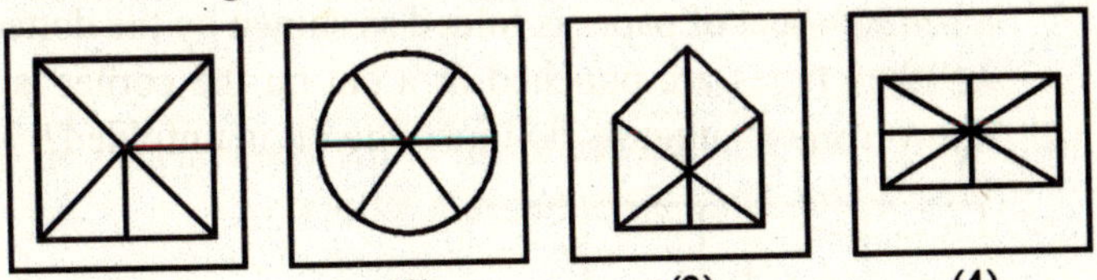

(1) (2) (3) (4)

13. Which three-letter word should be inserted within the parenthesis to form two new words?

B (___ ___ ___) E

T (___ ___ ___) E

14. Choose the missing number ("?") from the given alternatives?

2, 6, 12, ?, 30

(a) 18 (b) 20

(c) 22 (d) 24

15. Which of the four alternatives is exactly the mirror image of the object placed in front of a plane mirror AB?

A 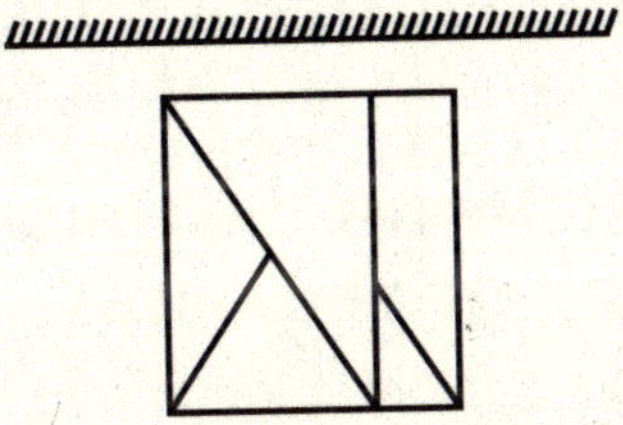 B

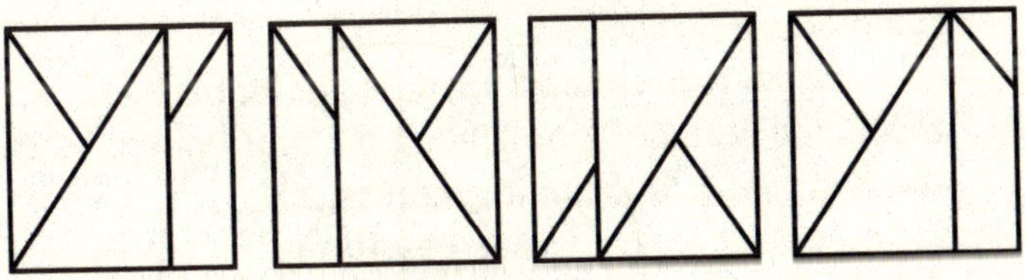

(1) (2) (3) (4)

16. How many squares can you count in the following figure?

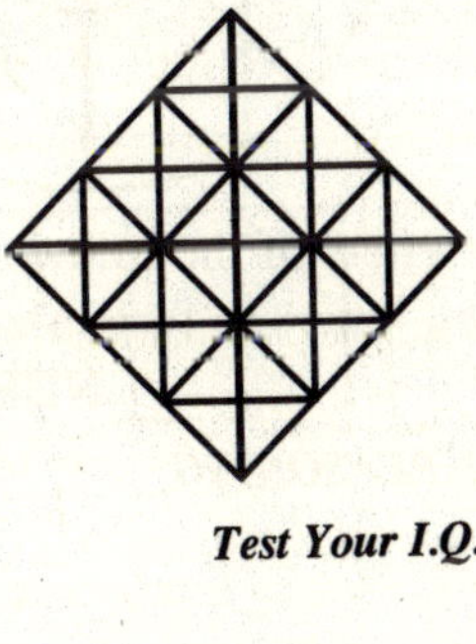

17. Make three meaningful seven-letter words from the following set of letters?

ACDEILT __________ __________ __________

18. Apply your intelligence to fill in the blank spaces so that the three words have the same five letters?

__ T __ __ E

S __ __ __ L

__ __ A __ __

19. Which figure in the lower row should replace the question mark so that C and the chosen figure maintain the same relationship as A and B?

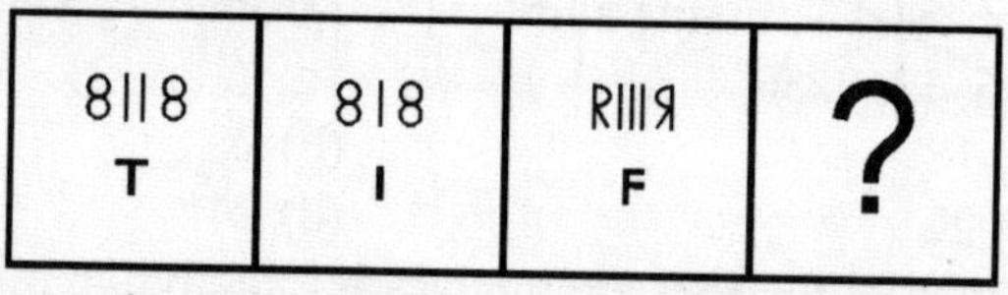

A B C D

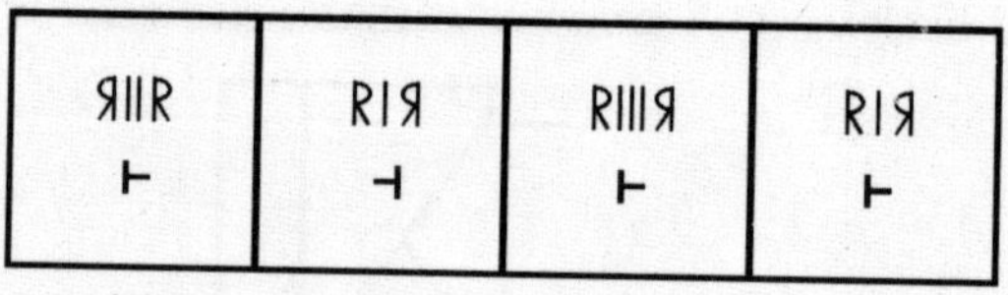

(1) (2) (3) (4)

20. Find out the name of a World Cup cricketer hidden in the following sentence?

Is he really sharp? Error is not on his part.

21. Select the correct figure among the four options to complete the first figure to make it symmetrical?

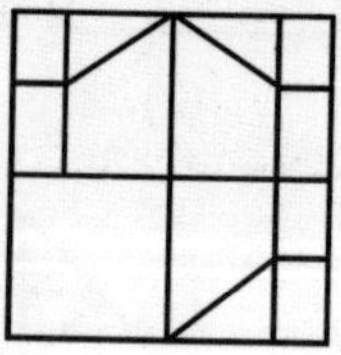

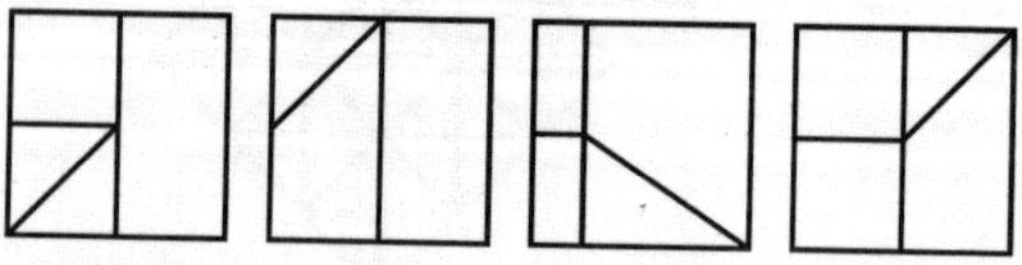

(1) (2) (3) (4)

22. Find a single word that defines both the words. For example: Quick bird would be Swift.

Smooth apartment = ________

23. Insert a 3-letter word in the blank spaces which complete the first word and starts the second.

PARA (__ __ __) RIFY

24. Which among the following figures is different from others?

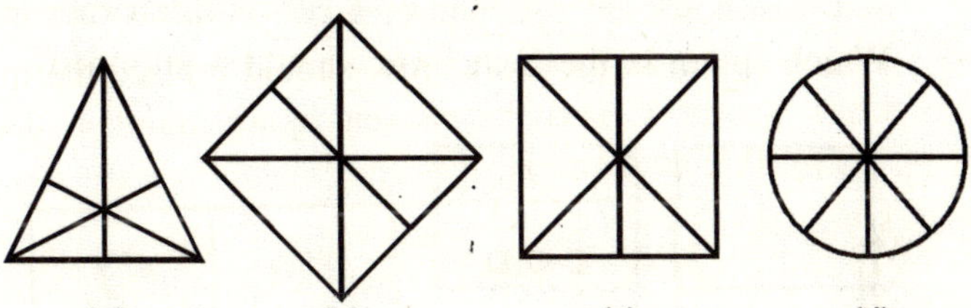

(a) (b) (c) (d)

25. Which letter should be placed before and after the following word so that a word is formed which spells the same—forward and backward?

__ EFE __

❑

TEST-14

1. Choose the missing number ("?") from the given alternatives?

   0, 7, 26, 63, ?

   (a) 122 (b) 123
   (c) 124 (d) 125

2. A square sheet of paper is folded as shown by the dotted lines and then holes are punched or a cut on the corner is made. Which option suggests its look when it is unfolded?

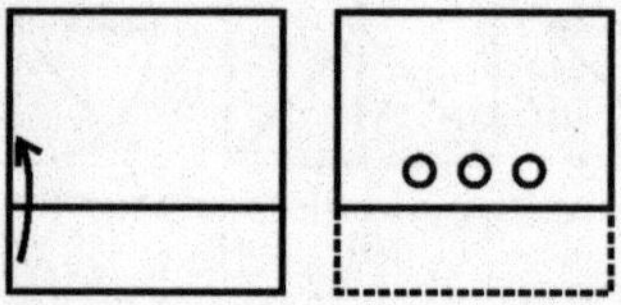

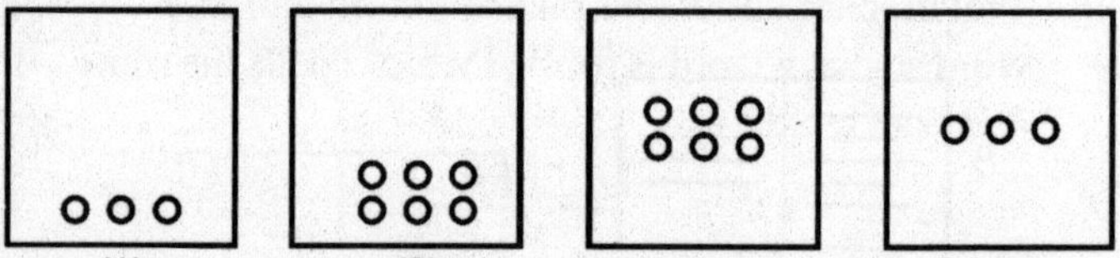

(1) (2) (3) (4)

3. Using the letters C I I K L L N N O O O O O T T U, complete this grid with valid words. Letter 'O' is given as a clue. The grid reads the same across and down?

			O
		O	
	O	O	
O			O

4. What will be the next number in this sequence?

   3872, 2387, 7238, 8723, ?

5. Which word best suits the definition as given below:
   A humorous verse in a five line jingle?

   (a) Stave (b) Stich
   (c) Iamb (d) Limeric

6. Find the group which is different from others.

(a) APCN (b) GVIT

(c) DSFQ (d) JYLX

7. Which among the following words is different from others?

YUCCA

WRONG

URGED

VIRUS

8. Which letter should be placed before and after the following word so that a word is formed which spells the same—forward and backward?

__ ENE __

9. Which figure in the adjoining row should replace the question mark so that C and the chosen figure maintain the same relationship as A and B?

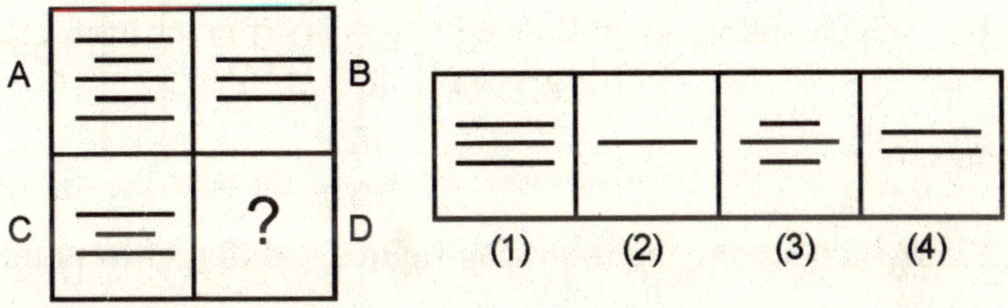

10. The following eleven-letter word contains ROB at its centre. Fill in the blanks to spell the name of a famous West Indian fast bowler?

___ ___ ___ ___ R O B ___ ___ ___ ___

11. Make a seven-letter word to match the definition by putting letters in the blank spaces. Clue is given.

___ ___ ___ ___ AGE (Act of great violence)

12. Which key word should replace the question mark so as to make a two-word phrase from the list of words that follows, i.e. ____?____: BAG, MARSHAL, CONDITIONING (? is AIR)

____?___ SCHOOL/TIME/HOLIDAY

13. Which among the following words is different from others?

VAST
TAXI
CODE
RICH

14. Select the correct figure among the four options to complete the first figure to make it symmetrical?

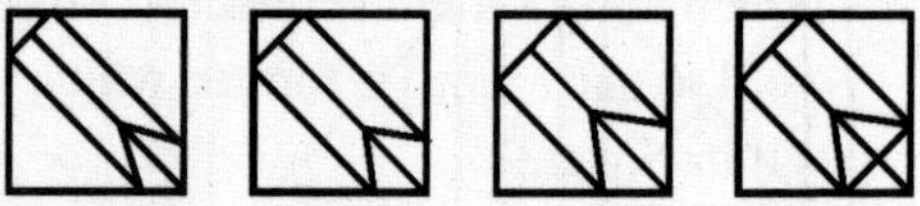

(1) (2) (3) (4)

15. Which word describes the fear of reptiles?

(a) Herpetophobia (b) Arachnophobia
(c) Zoophobia (d) Serpentophobia

16. Which among the following letters is different from others?

S P O R T

(a) S (b) P
(c) R (d) T

17. Which among the following figures is different from others?

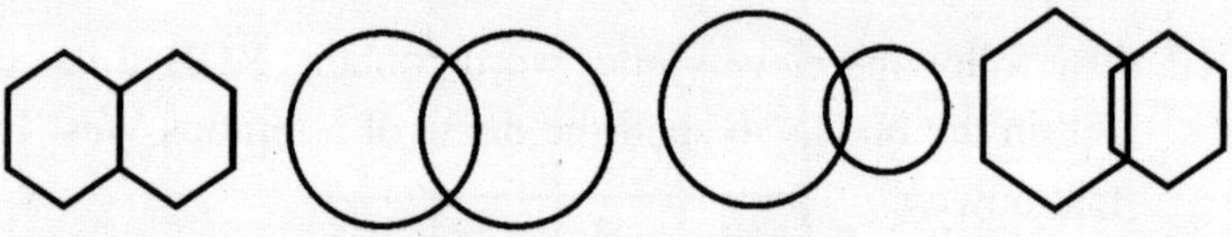

(1) (2) (3) (4)

18. Insert a three-letter word in the blank spaces which complete the first word and starts the second?

BAND(__ __ __)LESS

19. Apply your intelligence to fill in the blank spaces so that the three words have the same five letters?

___ I ___ ___ R
___ ___ D ___ ___
___ ___ A ___ N

20. Select a figure from the four options to complete the sequence above?

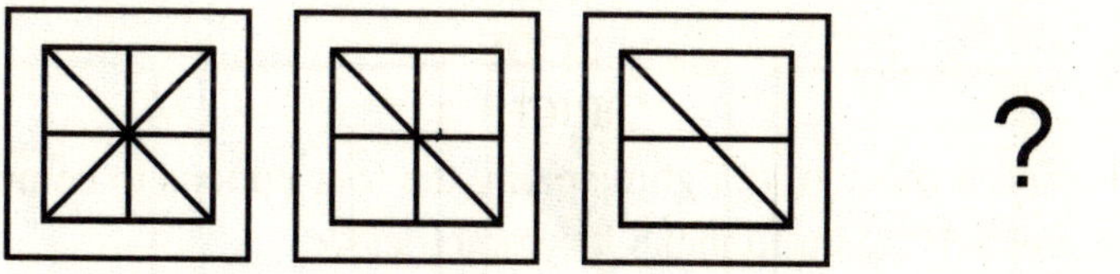

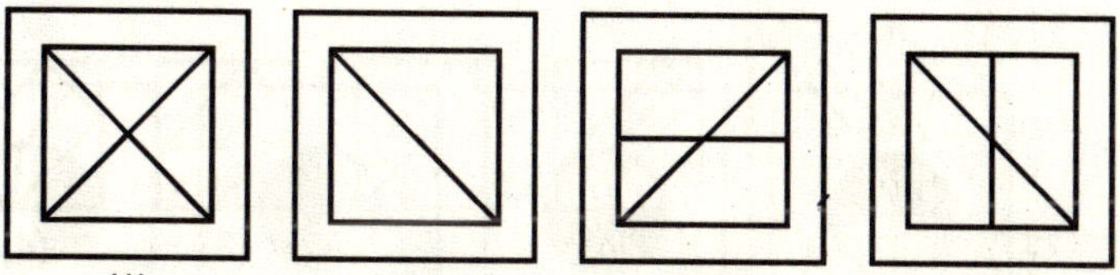

(1) (2) (3) (4)

21. If A = +, B = ÷, C = × and D = –, find the valuc of

½ C2B½A½D¼?

22. How many meaningful words can you make from the following set of letters?

CEORST _______ _______ ______ ______

23. What number should be placed at the question mark?

3	2	9	10
7	8	9	8
10	10	10	10
7	5	9	?

24. Which three-letter word should be inserted within the parenthesis to form two new words?

T (___ ___ ___) K

P (___ ___ ___) E

25. Which figure in the lower row should replace the question

mark so that C and the chosen figure maintain the same relationship as A and B?

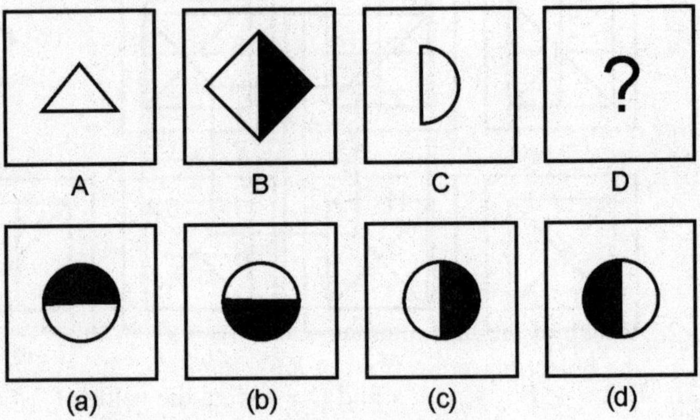

❑

TEST-15

1. What number should replace the question mark?

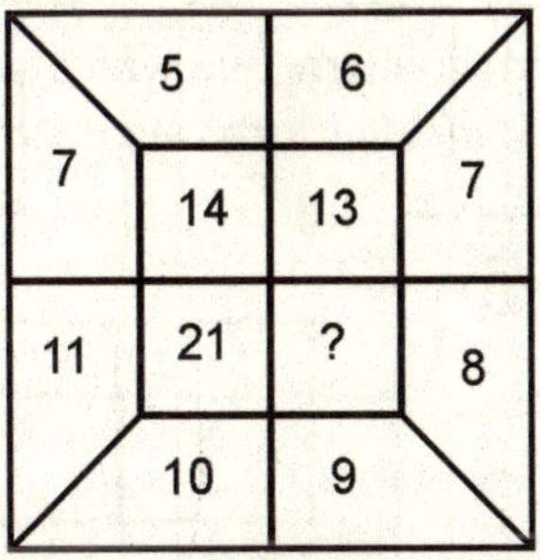

2. Which of the four alternatives is exactly the mirror image of the object placed in front of a plane mirror AB?

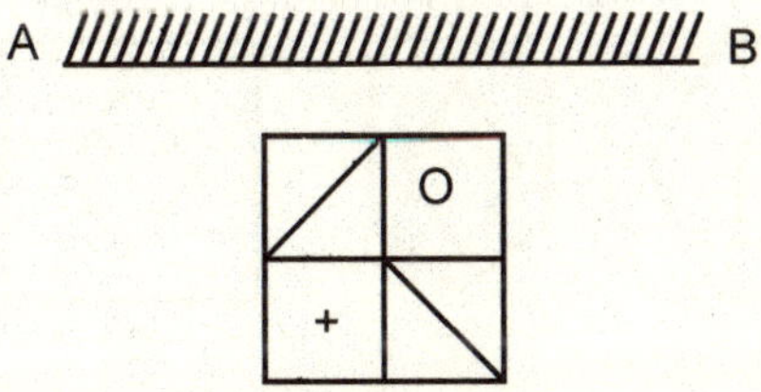

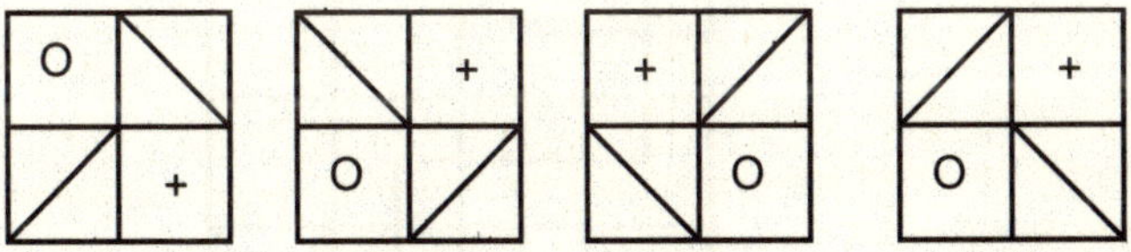

(1) (2) (3) (4)

3. Select the alternative whose alphabet when placed at the missing places complete the series.

_α _β_γα _αβ _γ

(a) αββαβ (b) ααγαβ
(c) ααβαβ (d) ααβαα

4. If NEW YORK is coded as MFXZPQL, how will FLORIDA be coded?

(a) DKPQJCB (b) DKPQJBC
(c) DKPQKBC (d) DKPQLCB

5. Which three-letter word should be inserted within the parenthesis to form two new words?

P (___ ___ ___) O
D (___ ___ ___) I

6. Select the correct alternative which when substituted for the question mark maintains the symmetry?

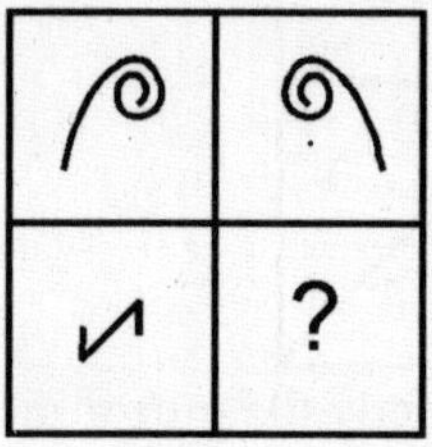

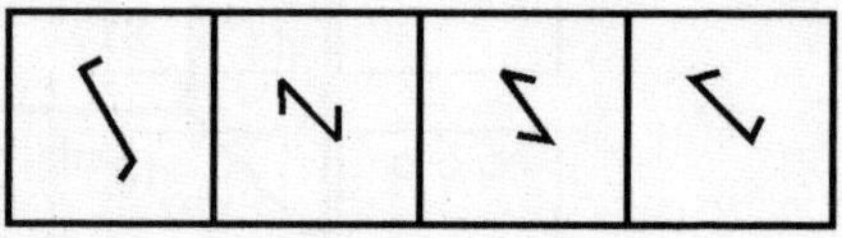

(1) (2) (3) (4)

7. Which among the following figures is different from others?

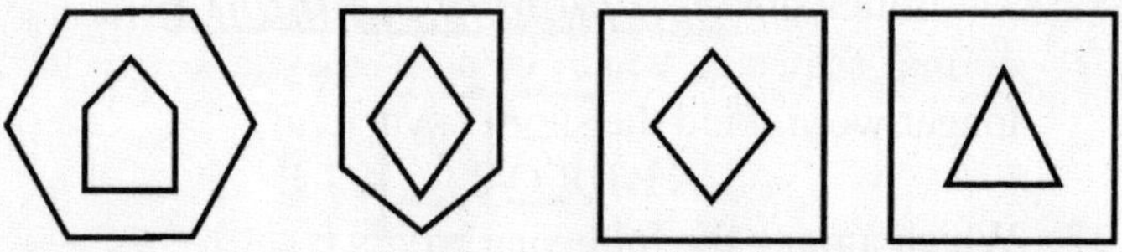

(1) (2) (3) (4)

8. How many squares can you count in this figure?

9. The first three letters of the following word are missing. Find out the missing letters to form a word?

___ ___ ___ MAX

10. Which among the following words is different from others?

SITOSE
GIGOLO

CHROME

PINOLE

11. A square sheet of paper is folded as shown by the dotted lines and then holes are punched or a cut on the corner is made. Which option suggests its look when it is unfolded?

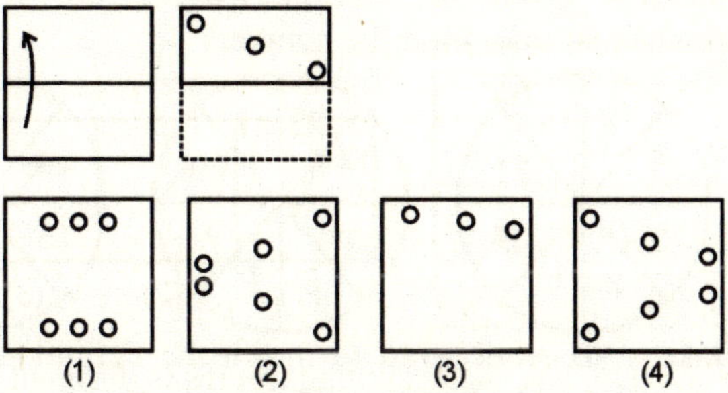

12. The following word carries a shorter word within it in the normal sequence which conveys the same meaning as the longer word. Find the shorter synonym?

APPROPRIATE

13. Which among the following words is different from others?

ACCEPT

ACCOST

ACCUSE

ACCENT

ACCESS

14. Select the correct figure among the four options to complete the first figure to make it symmetrical.

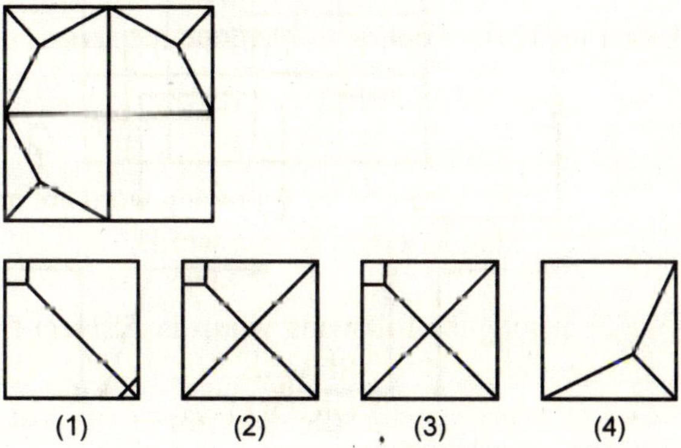

15. Which key word should replace the question mark so as to make a two-word phrase from the list of words that follows? i.e. ____?____: BAG, MARSHAL, CONDITIONING (? is AIR)

____?___ AGE/BLOCK/DISORDER

16. Numbers given in the following figure follow some arithmetical rule. Find the number?

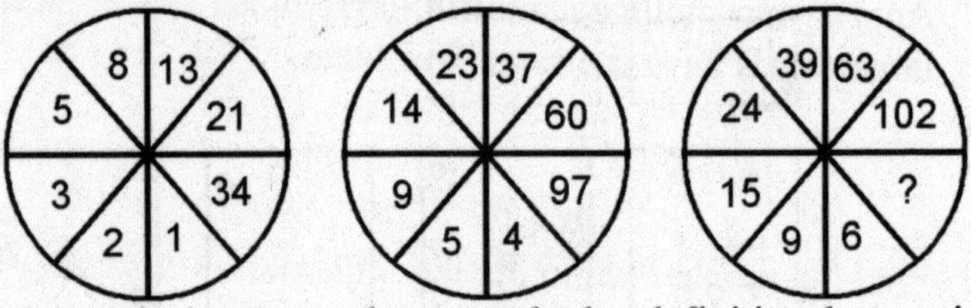

17. Make a six-letter word to match the definition by putting letters in the blank spaces. Clue is given.

___ ___ ___ KER = Pedler

18. Which figure in the adjacent row should replace the question mark to maintain the same relationship?

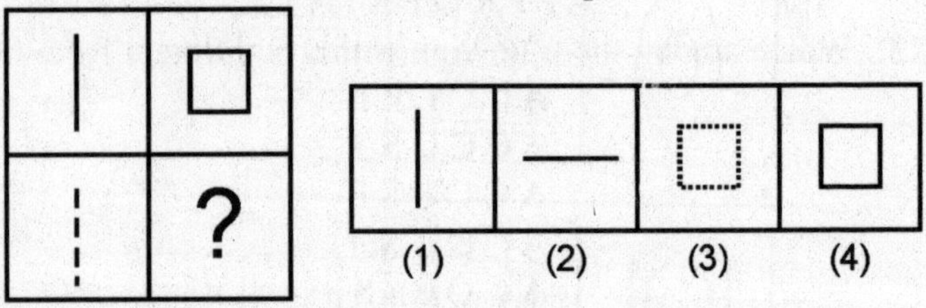

19. The first three letters of the following word are missing. Find out the missing letters to form a word?

___ ___ ___ IAC

20. Select the correct option to continue the series?

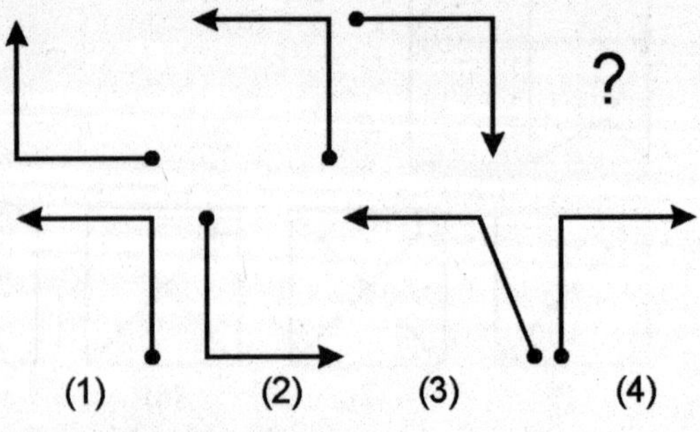

21. Observe the following word and find its synonym within this word?

DELIBERATE

22. Unscramble the following letters and make three seven-letter words?

AELPRST ____________

____________ ____________

23. Apply your intelligence to fill in the blank spaces so that the three words have the same five letters.

___ ___ ___ P ___

___ H___ S ___

___ ___ A ___ E

24. Find the number which replaces the question mark?

289, 324, 361, ?

25. Which among the four options should occupy the position indicated by a question mark to continue the sequence?

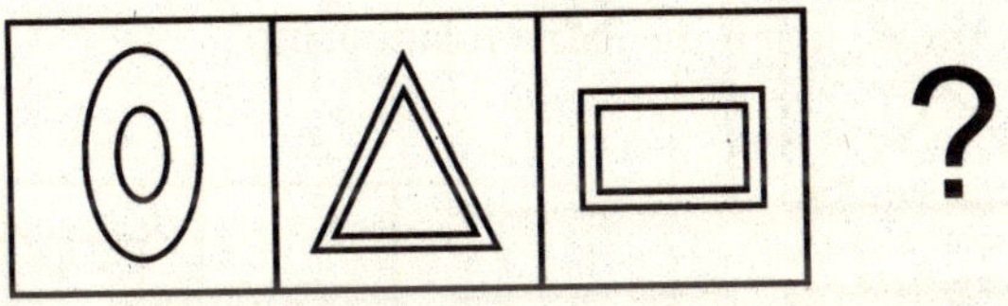

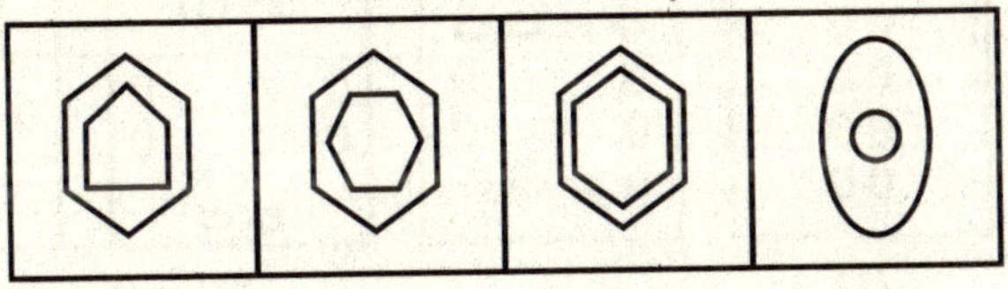

(1) (2) (3) (4)

TEST-16

1. Choose the missing number ("?") from the given alternatives.

   1, 7, 17, 31, 49, ?

   (a) 61 (b) 71

   (c) 81 (d) 91

2. Which among the following 'alphanumeric words' is odd one out?

   100HI5050I

   5050A1000A

   BU5050

   50A1000B

3. A square sheet of paper is folded twice as shown by the dotted lines and then two holes are punched on the corner of a triangle. Which option suggests its look when it is unfolded?

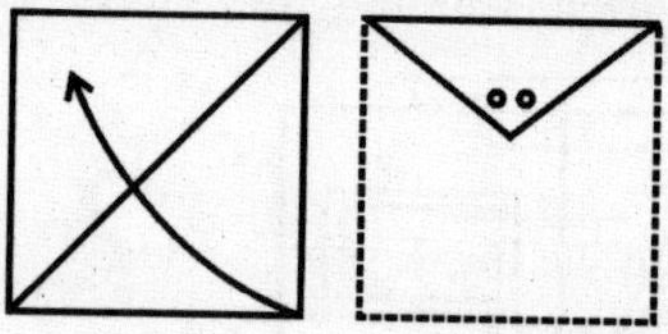

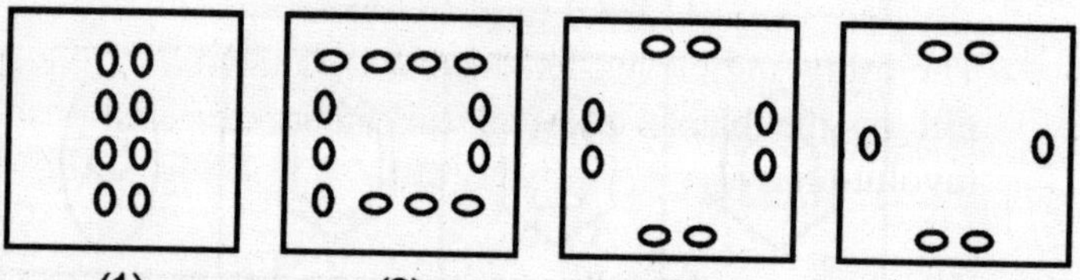

(1) (2) (3) (4)

4. If you count from 1 to 100, how many 9's will you pass on the way?

5. Numbers given in each row follow some arithmetical rule. Select the correct alternative which replaces the question mark?

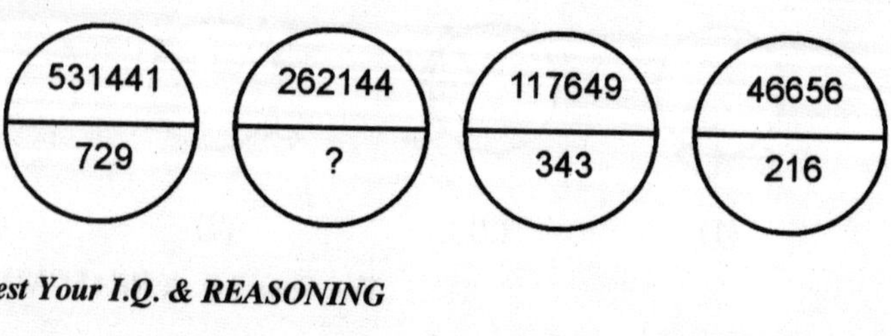

6. Which figure in the lower row should replace the question mark so that C and the chosen figure maintain the same relationship as A and B?

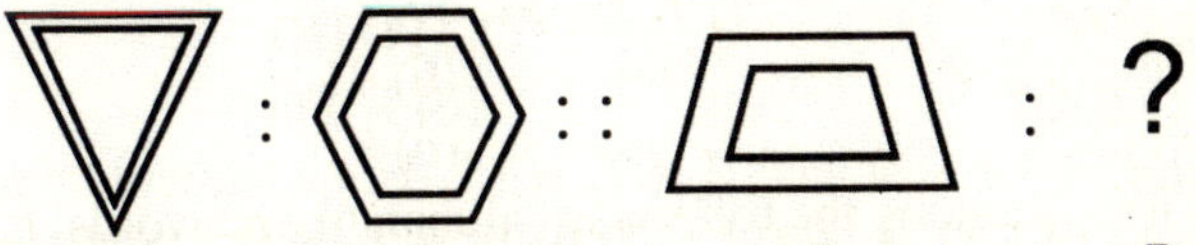

A B C D

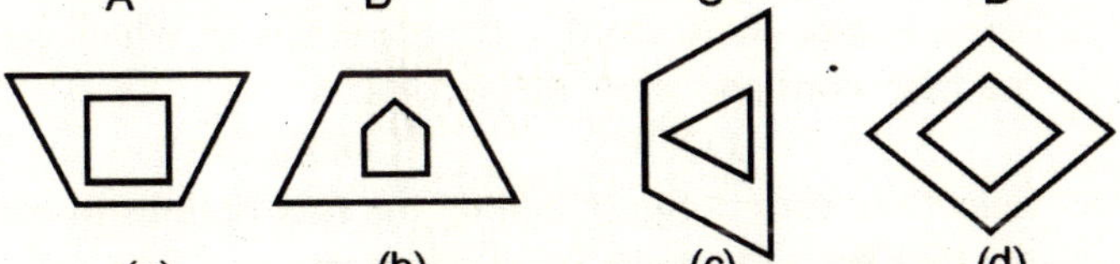

(a) (b) (c) (d)

7. Apply your intelligence to fill in the blank spaces so that the three words have the same five letters?

___ O ___ ___ ___

___ T ___ ___ E

___ N S ___ ___

8. Insert a three-letter word in the blank spaces which complete the first word and starts the second?

LONG(___ ___ ___)SHOT

9. The following eleven-letter word contains ATS at its centre. Fill up the blanks to spell the name of a famous Indian revolutionary?

___ ___ ___ ___ A T S ___ ___ ___ ___

10. Which among the following words is different from others?

ALMOST
BEGILD
ACORUS
AGNOSY

11. Which among the following figures is different from others?

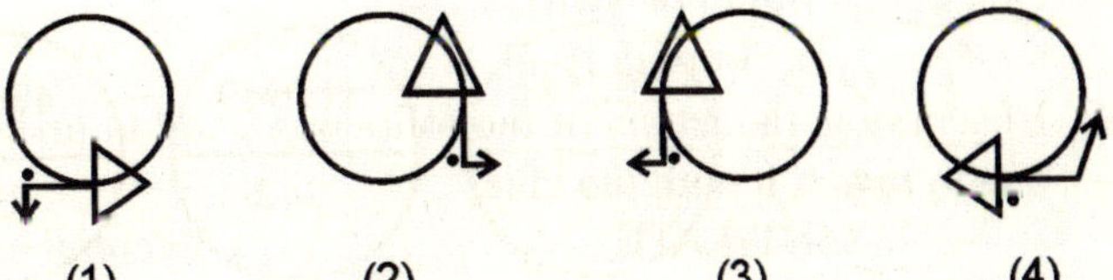

(1) (2) (3) (4)

12. Select the correct alternative that will maintain the same relationship on the two signs "::", if it is substituted for the question mark "?".

TSQR: XWUV:: EDBC: ?

(a) HIFG (b) IFHG
(c) IHGI (d) IHFG

13. If 42 × 73 = 24 and 21 × 72 = 15, then what will be 63 × 43?
14. If LOWEST is coded as TOWELS, how is LISTEN coded?
15. Insert a three-letter word in the blank spaces which complete the first word and starts the second?

LOOK(__ __ __)LOOK

16. Select the correct figure among the four options to complete the first figure to make it symmetrical.

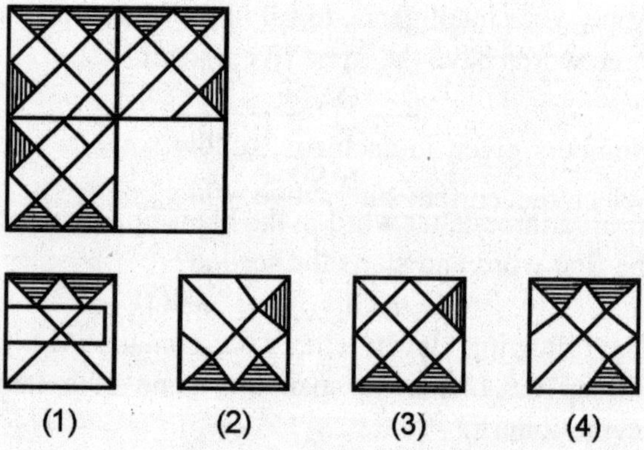

17. Which key word should replace the question mark so as to make a two-word phrase from the list of words that follows? i.e. ____?____: BAG, MARSHAL, CONDITIONING (? is AIR)

____?____ SPRING, LINE, DOG

18. Find a single word that defines both the words. For example: Quick bird would be swift.

Smooth level = ________

19. Unscramble the letters of the following word to make a new one to match it with the clue?

MUTILATE ______________ = Eventful

20. Which of the four alternatives is exactly the mirror image of the object placed in front of a plane mirror AB?

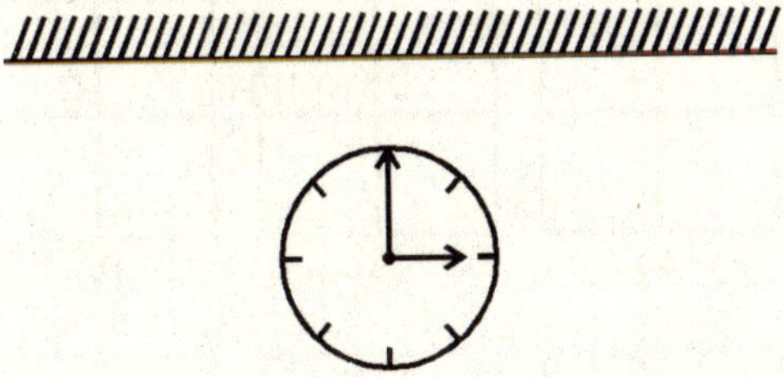

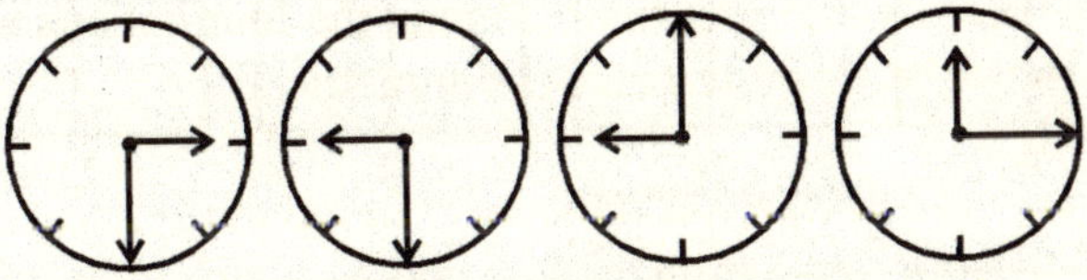

(1) (2) (3) (4)

21. Numbers given in each row follow some arithmetical rule. Select the correct alternative which replaces the question mark?

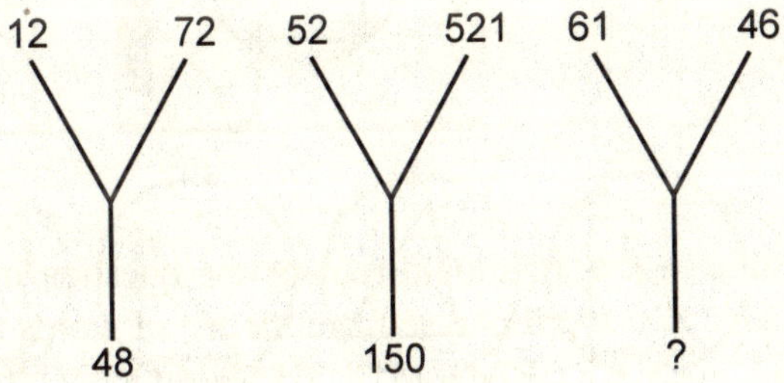

22. Which three-letter word should be inserted within the parenthesis to form two new words?

S (___ ___ ___) D

U (___ ___ ___) D

23. The first three letters of the following word are missing. Find out the missing letters to form a word.

___ ___ ___ FEW

24. Which among the four options should occupy the position indicated by a question mark to continue the sequence?

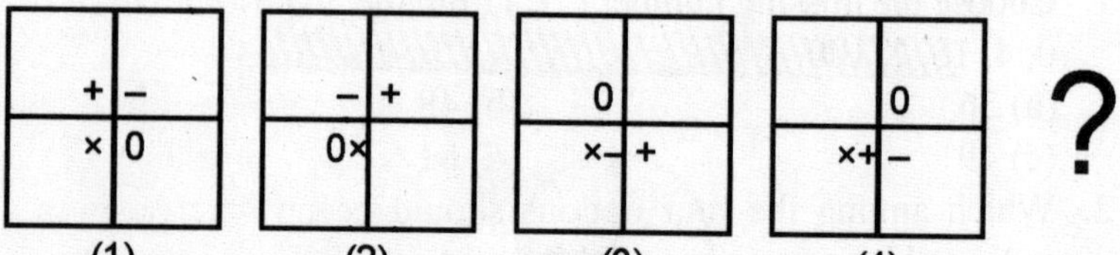

(1) (2) (3) (4)

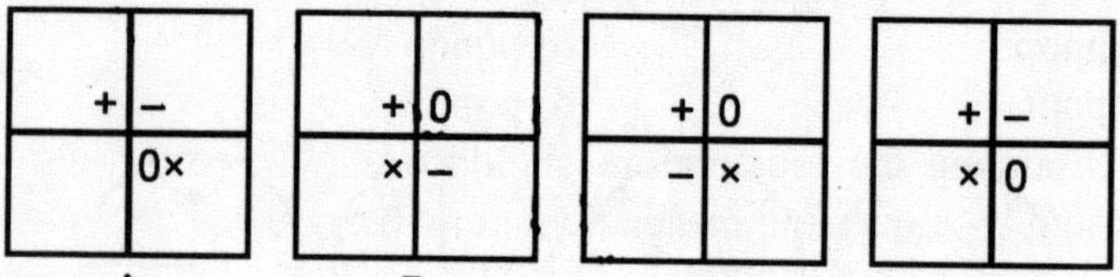

A B C D

25. Select a figure from the four options which is the mirror image of the object in front of the plane mirrror?

(1) (2) (3) (4)

TEST-17

1. Choose the missing number ("?") from the given alternatives?
   0, 4, 18, ?, 100
   (a) 36 (b) 48
   (c) 49 (d) 81
2. Which among the four options should occupy the position indicated by a question mark to continue the sequence?
   qp_ _rq_ _ qrq_
   (a) qpppp (b) pqpqp
   (c) qpqpr (d) pqppp
3. Which among the four options should occupy the position indicated by a question mark to continue the sequence?

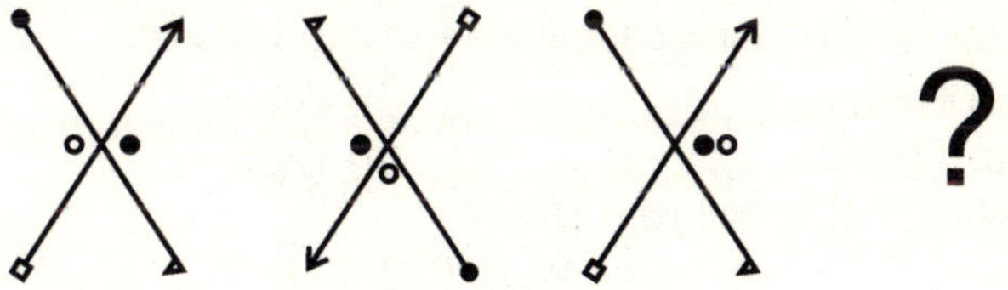

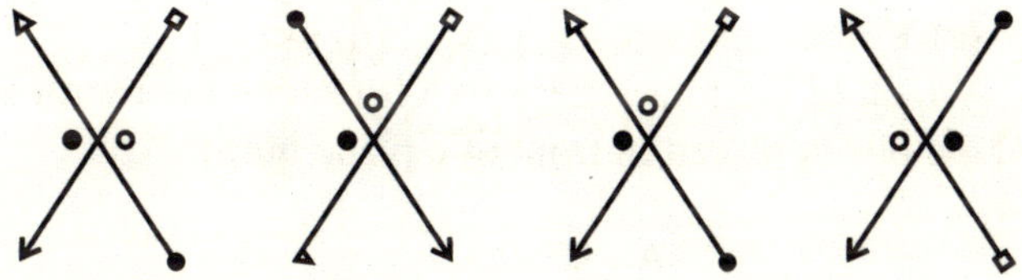

A B C D

4. Put the key word in the box to make a two-word phrase from the list of words that precede. For example:
   ZERO/LUNCH/ELEVENTH [HOUR]
   NATURAL/SOCIAL/EARTH [ ]
5. Which alphabet replaces the question mark?

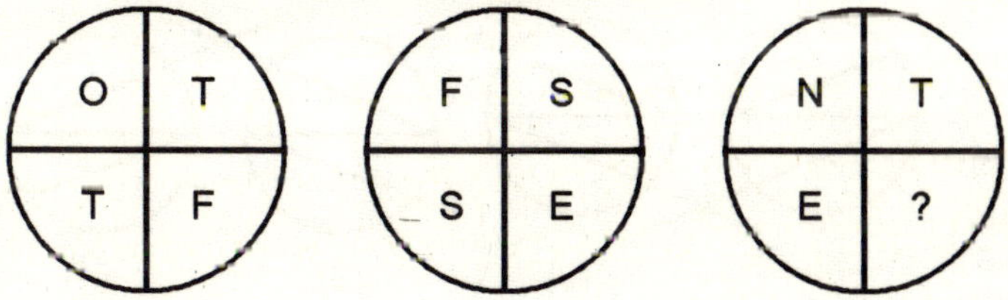

6. Select a figure from the four options to complete the sequence above?

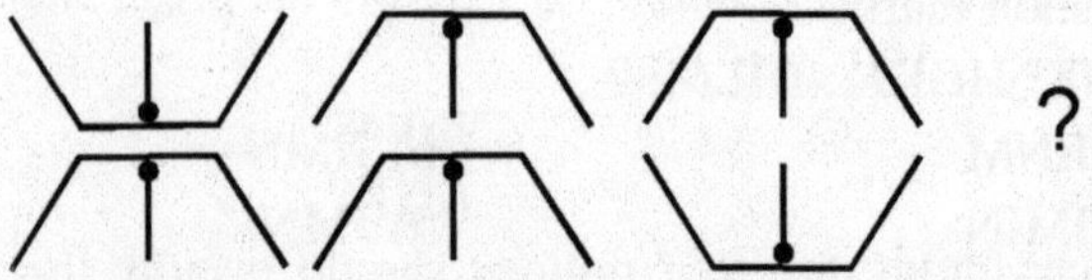

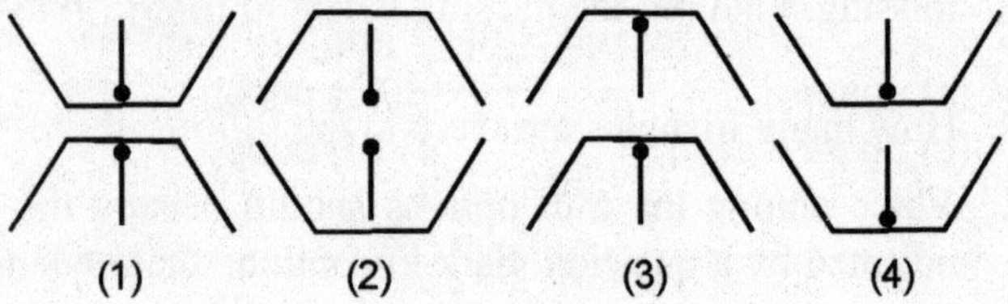

7. How is the first wedding anniversary called?

(a) Pearl (b) Pottery

(c) Plastic (d) Paper

8. What will be the next letter?

Q, W, E, R, T, ?

(a) U (b) I

(c) Y (d) O

9. Which of the four alternatives is exactly the mirror image of the object placed in front of a plane mirror AB?

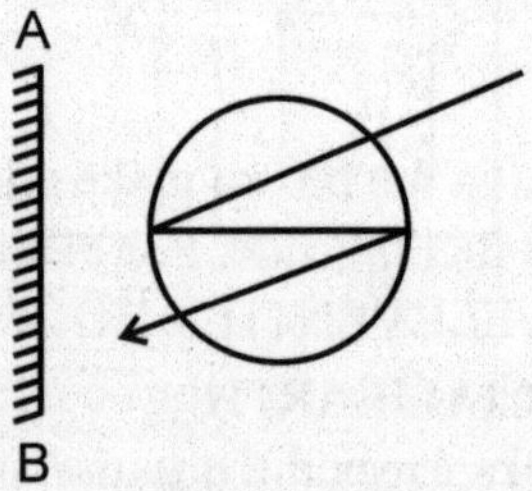

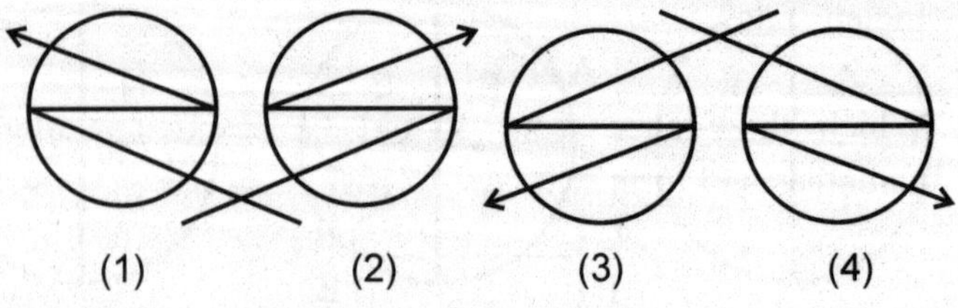

10. Select the correct alternative that will maintain the same relationship on the two signs "::", if it is substituted for the question mark "?".

GFJK: HGKL:: IHLM: ?

(a) JINM (b) JIMN

(c) JMIN (d) JMNI

11. The first two letters of the following four-letter word are missing. Find out the missing letters to form a word?

__ __ LC

12. How many triangles are there in the following figure?

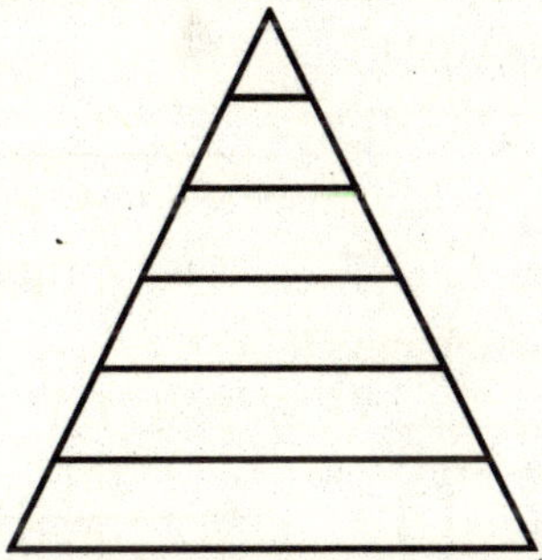

13. Which among the following figures is different from others?

(1) (2) (3) (4)

14. The following eleven-letter word contains ANE at its centre. Fill up the blanks to spell the name of the capital city of an Indian state?

__ __ __ __ ANE __ __ __ __

15. Which three-letter word should be inserted within the parenthesis to form two new words?

C (__ __ __) E

P (__ __ __) E

16. Find the number which replaces the question mark?

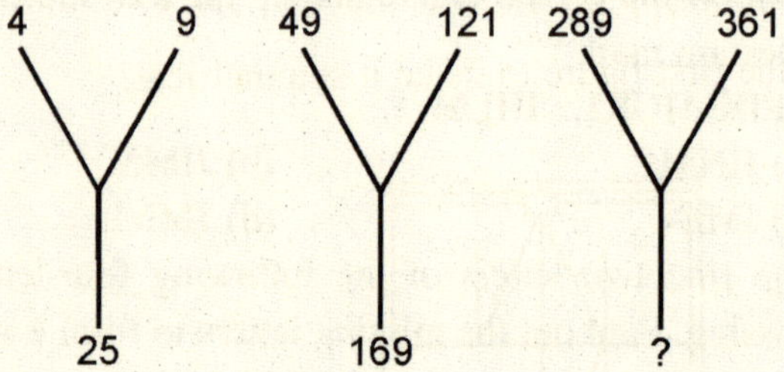

17. A clue is preceded by the meaning of a word which has the same letters as the clue. Write its anagram, e.g. (Nakedness): UNTIDY = NUDITY

(Estimate) : CONKER =__________

18. Which figure in the adjacent row should replace the question mark so that C and the chosen figure maintain the same relationship as A and B?

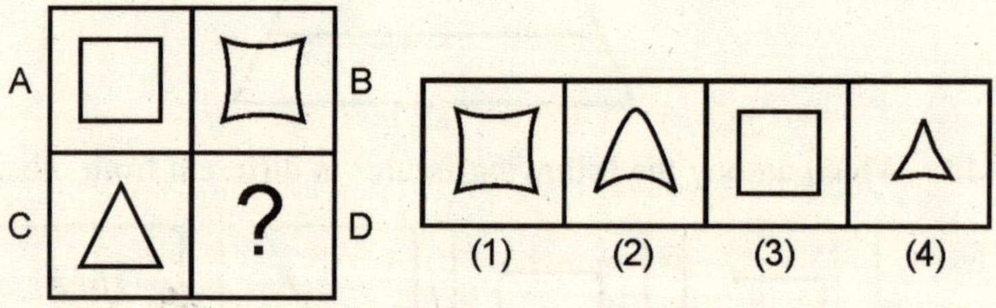

19. SATURN (a planet) is composed of SAT and URN, neither of which has any connection with SATURN. Below are given two three-letter words which combine to form a six-letter word. The three-letter words are defined but not the six-letter word. Find the six-letter word. For example: Our star + Barren = SUNDRY

Friend + Expert = __________ (Castle)

20. Which letter should be placed before and after the following letter so that new words are formed which spell the same—forward or backward?

__ O __

21. Select the correct figure among the four options to complete the first figure to make it symmetrical?

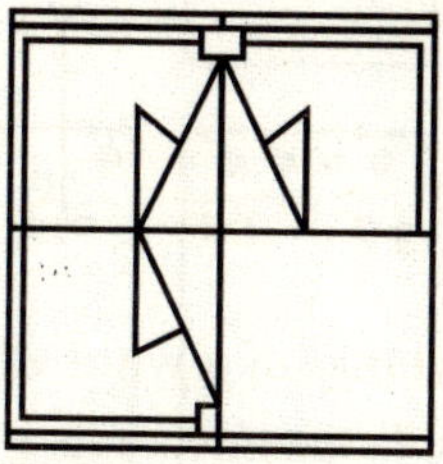

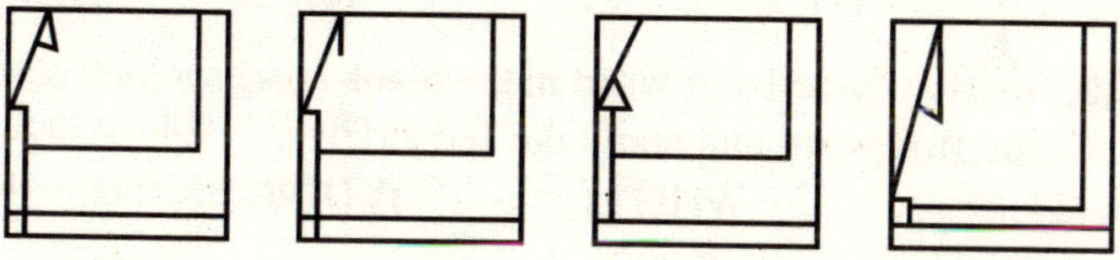

(1) (2) (3) (4)

22. Find a single word that defines both the words. For example: Quick bird would be swift.

Hit branch ____________

23. Which among the following words is different from others?

CITADEL

DECRIAL

DELTAIC

DIALECT

EDICTAL

24. A square sheet of paper is folded as shown by the dotted lines and then holes are punched or a cut on the corner is made. Which option suggests its look when it is unfolded?

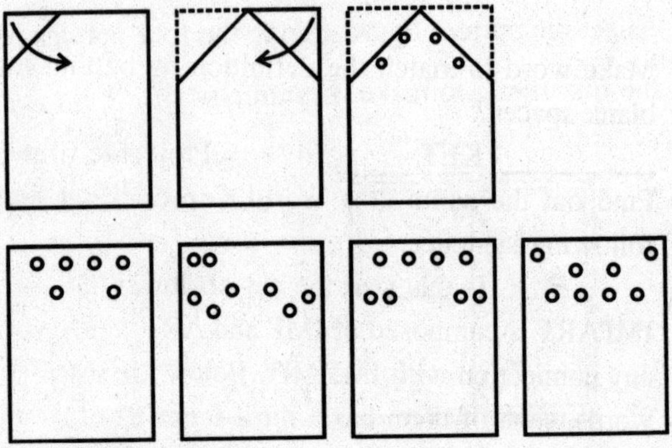

(1) (2) (3) (4)

25. Insert a three-letter word in the blank spaces which completes the first word and starts the second?

WHITE(__ __ __)VOUS

❑

TEST-18

1. Make word to match the definition by putting letters in the blank spaces?

   ___ ___ ___ KET = Projectile firework

2. Find out the name of a World Cup cricketer hidden in the following sentence.

   Is this year the cut-off lower?

3. IMPART is composed of IMP and ART, neither of which has any connection with IMPART. Below are listed some pair of words, each of them has a three-letter word as its meaning.. The two three-letter words combine to form a six-letter word which is defined. Find the six-letter word. For example: Male child + Trap = SONNET

   Negative + Frozen water = ___________ (Intimation)

4. Apply your intelligence to fill in the blank spaces so that the three words have the same five letters?

   A ___ ___ R ___

   ___ ___ T ___ ___

   ___ AT ___ ___

5. Find the number which replaces the question mark?

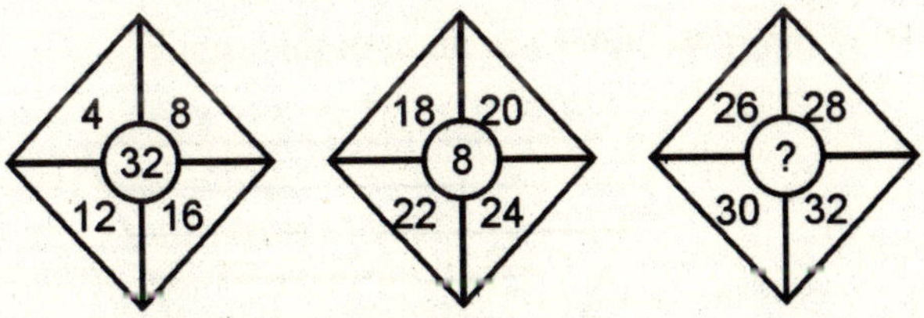

6. A square sheet of paper is folded as shown by the dotted lines and then holes are punched or a cut on the corner is made. Which option suggests its look when it is unfolded?

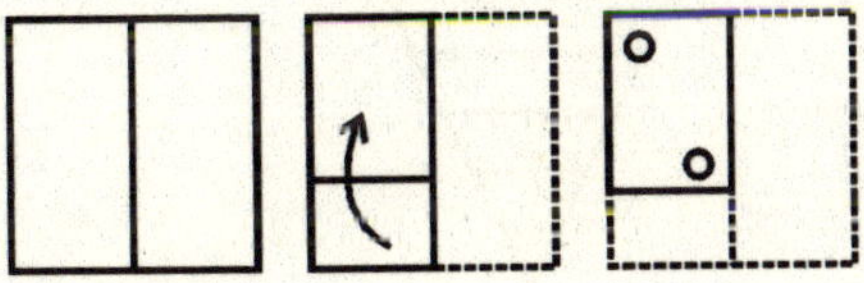

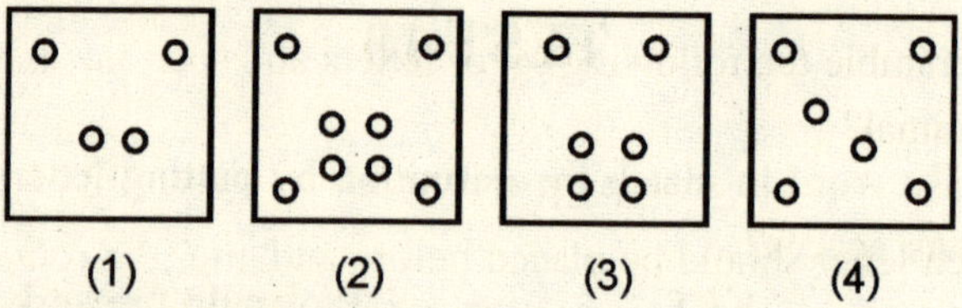

7. Which among the four options should occupy the position indicated by a question mark to continue the sequence?

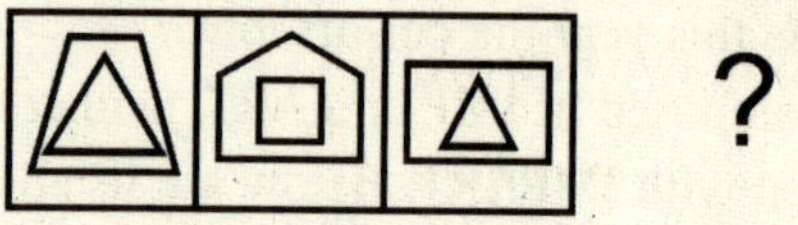

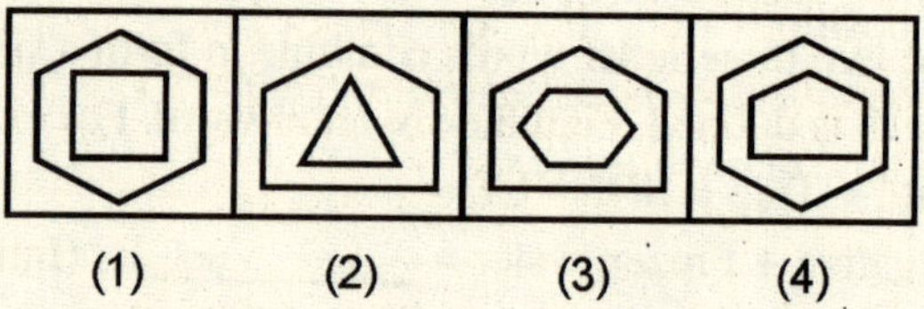

8. Which among the following figures is different from others?

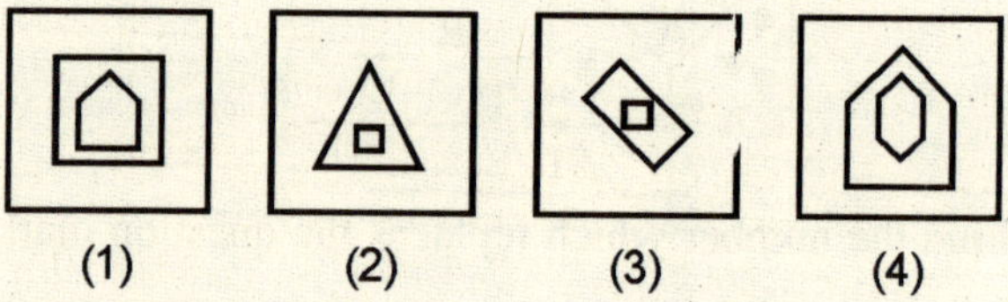

9. How many triangles are there in this figure?

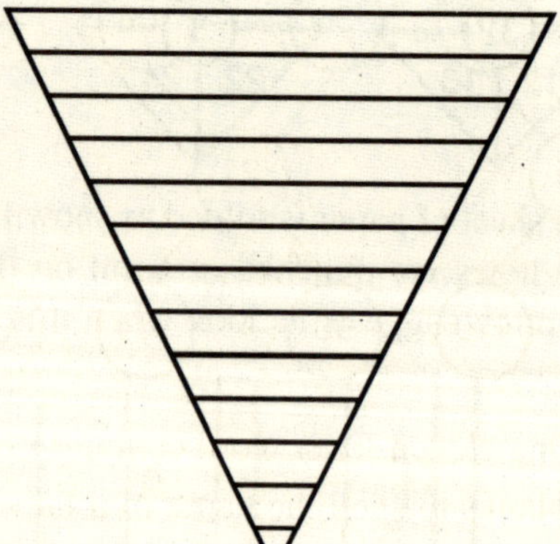

10. Unscramble the following set of letters and spell the name of an animal?

ALRSUW

11. Which letter should be placed before and after the following word so that a new word is formed?

–ABLE–

12. Which three-letter word should be inserted within the parenthesis to form two new words?

G (___ ___ ___) D

P (___ ___ ___) K

13. Two positions of a dice are shown below. When the face showing six dots is on the bottom, the top of the dice will show how many black dots?

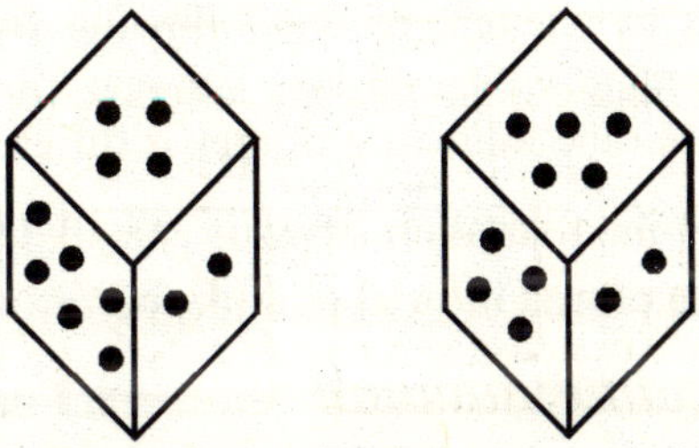

14. What numbers should replace the question mark?

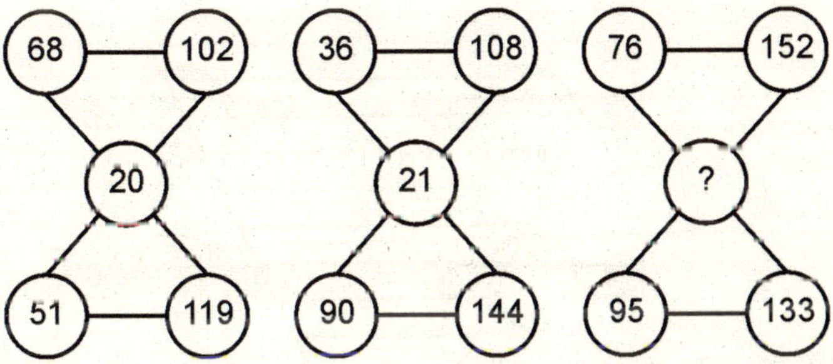

15. The following eleven-letter word contains ODA at its centre. Fill in the blanks to spell the name of a famous explorer?

___ ___ ___ ___ O D A ___ ___ ___ ___

16. Select the correct figure among the four options to complete the first figure to make it symmetrical?

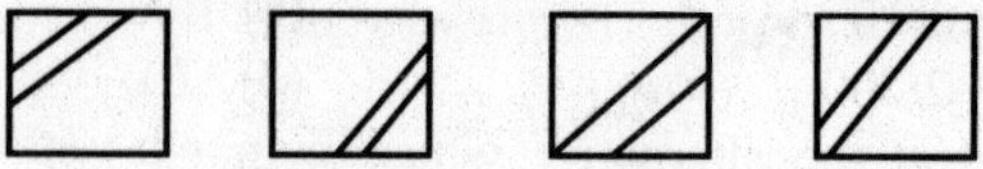

(1) (2) (3) (4)

17. What is the next number in this series?

3, 1, 4, 1, 5, 9, 2, 6, 5, ?

18. The first two letters of the following five-letter word are missing. Find out the missing letters to form a word?

___ ___ RGO

19. Which of the four alternatives is exactly the mirror image of the object placed in front of a plane mirror?

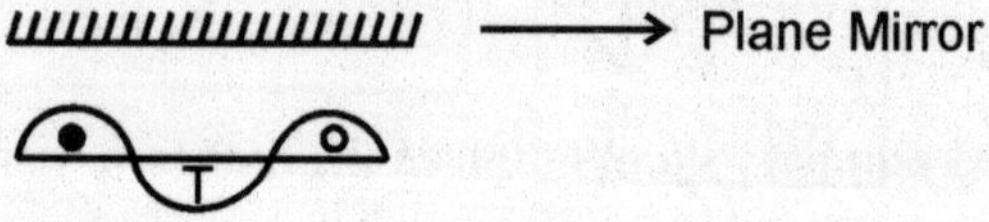

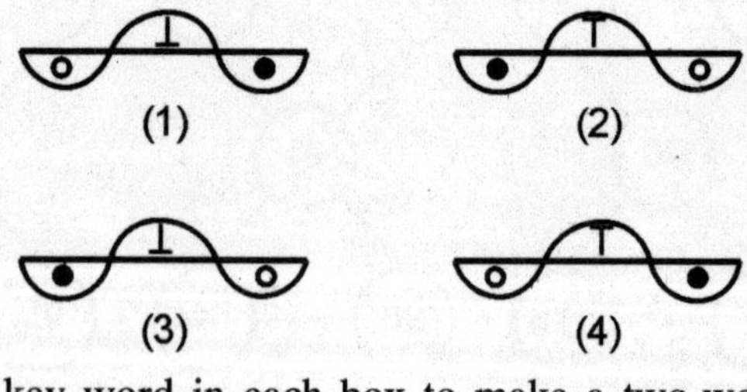

(1) (2)

(3) (4)

20. Put the key word in each box to make a two-word phrase from the list of words that precede. For example:

FRENCH/INDUSTRIAL/GREEN REVOLUTION

HOT/PLUMB/GOAL ________

21. Find the missing letter ("?")

d, ?, d, q

(a) p (b) q
(c) o (d) r

22. Which digit should be removed from 123456789 so that the remaining eight digits when multiplied by 9 or its multiples yields the similar digits nth times?

23. Find out the number which is different from others.

(a) 1/10 (b) 10/100
(c) 2/200 (d) 5/50

24. Select the alternative whose symbols when placed at the missing spaces complete the following sequence?

_ ♣♥ _ _ ♣ _ ♦

(a) ♦♣♥♠ (b) ♠♣♥♦
(c) ♣♣♥♥ (d) ♠♣♥♥

25. Which figure in the lower row should replace the question mark so that C and the chosen figure maintain the same relationship as A and B?

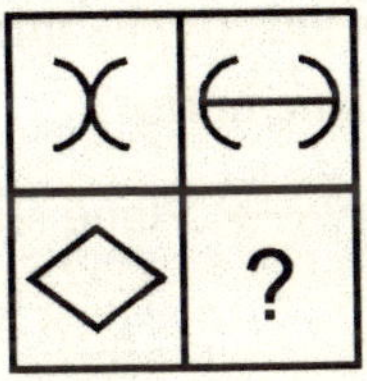

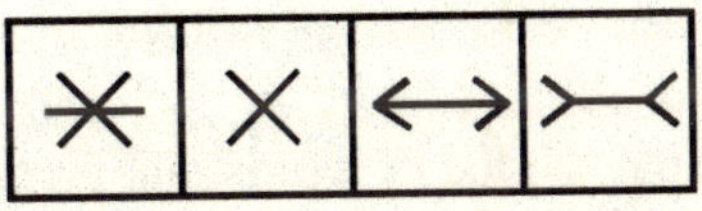

(1) (2) (3) (4)

❑

TEST-19

1. Find the number which is different from others?
   (a) 5/8 (b) 7/9
   (c) 11/13 (d) 17/19
2. Find the number which replaces the question mark?

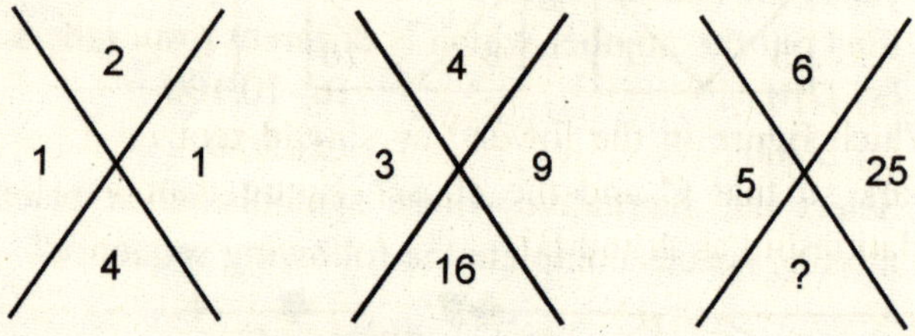

3. Which among the following figures is different from others?

(1) (2) (3) (4)

4. Put the key word in each box to make a two-word phrase from the list of words that precede. For example:
   ZERO/LUNCH/ELEVENTH HOUR
   BACK/REVOLVING/NEXT
5. What comes next in this sequence?
   1979 1987 1993 1997 ?
6. Select the correct alternative that will maintain the same relationship on the two signs "::", if it is substituted for the question mark "?".
   ZXUV: TROP::PNKL: ?
   (a) IFDE (b) JHFE
   (c) JGEF (d) JHEF
7. The letter EILNST when rearranged form LISTEN, SILENT, and TINSEL. In the following groups rearrange the letters to form anagrams. Clues are given?
   ADERRT

(a) ____________ Impede
(b) ____________ Merchant
(c) ____________ Brazilian pelican

8. Find the number which replaces the question mark?

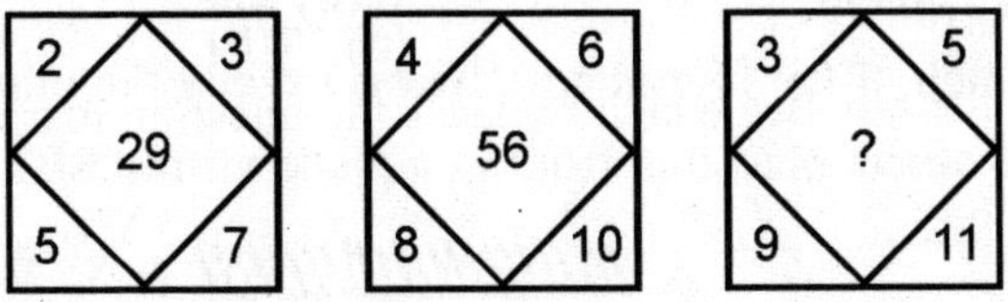

9. Which figure in the lower row should replace the question mark so that C and the chosen figure maintain the same relationship as A and B?

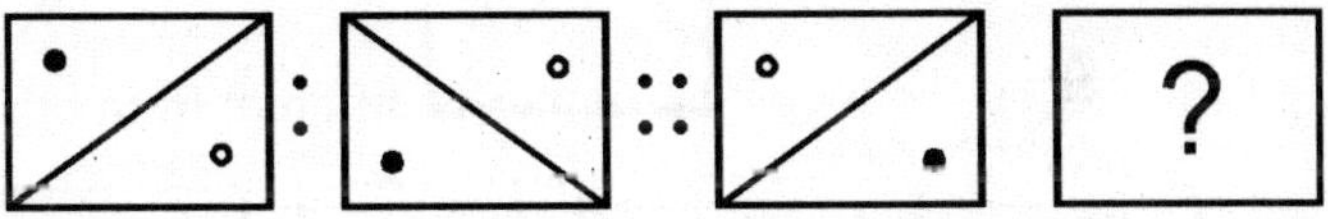

A B C D

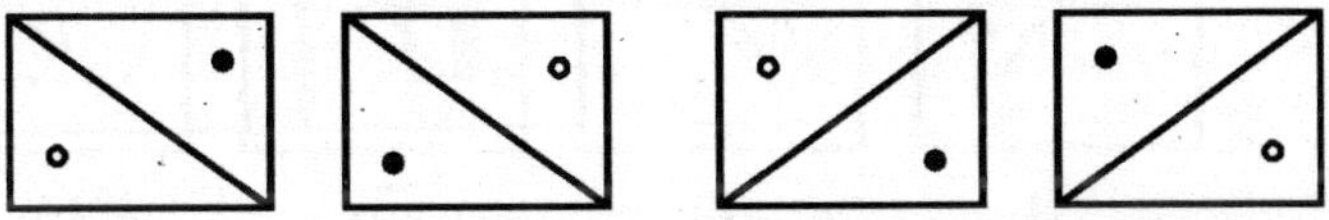

(a) (b) (c) (d)

10. Heteronyms are two words or phrases having the same spelling but different meanings and different pronunciations. Find the four-letter pair of heteronyms for each of the clue?

Air in motion/Meander

11. CUTLET is composed of CUT and LET, neither of which has any connection with CUTLET. Below are listed some pair of words, each of them has a three-letter word as its meaning. The two three-letter words combine to form a six-letter word which is defined. Find the six-letter word. For example: Male child + Trap = SONNET

Conclude + Hearing organ = ____________ = (Captivate)

12. Make word to match the definition by putting letters in the blank spaces?

___ ___ ___ ___ MENT = Body of troops under a Colonel.

13. Which among the following words aptly describes the definition: 'Sorrow expressed in cries'?

(a) Dole (b) Mourn

(c) Lament (d) Rue

14. Which of the four alternatives is exactly the mirror image of the object placed in front of a plane mirror AB?

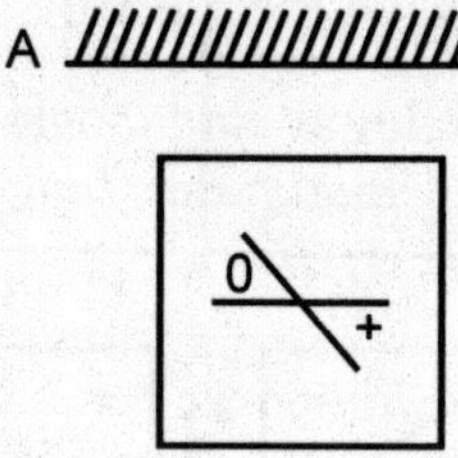

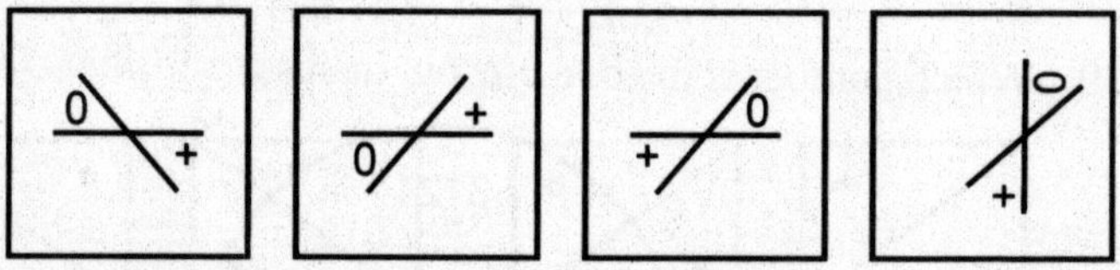

(1) (2) (3) (4)

15. Find a single word that defines both the words. For example: Quick bird would be swift.

At-home alliance__________

16. Which among the following words is different from others?

ABDUCT

BEHEAD

BECAME

BLEACH

BRANCH

CAMBER

17. A square sheet of paper is folded as shown by the dotted lines and then holes are punched or a cut on the corner is made. Which option suggests its look when it is unfolded?

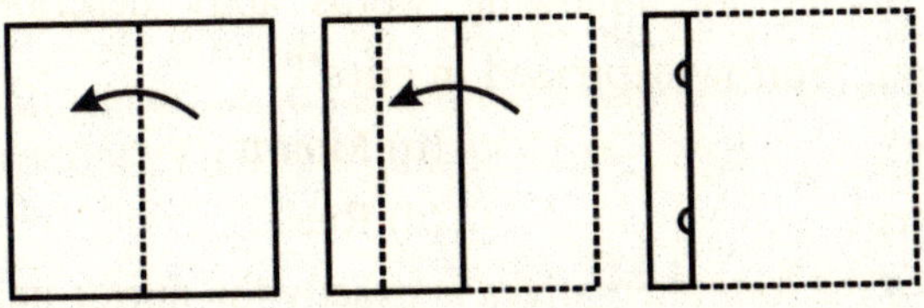

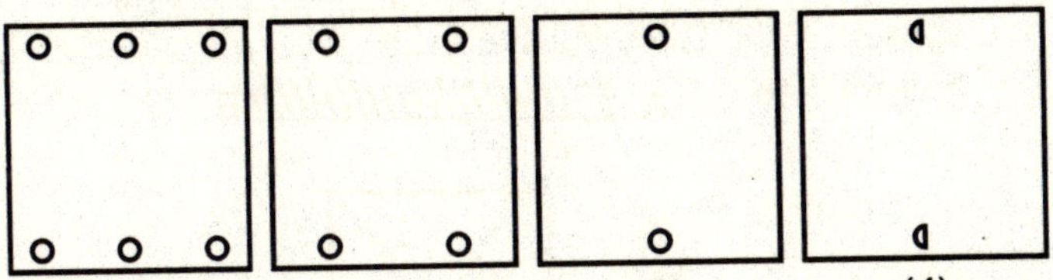

(1) (2) (3) (4)

18. Insert a three-letter word in the blank spaces which complete the first word and starts the second.

GALL(_ _ _)HILL

19. Which number is the odd one out inside the following figure?

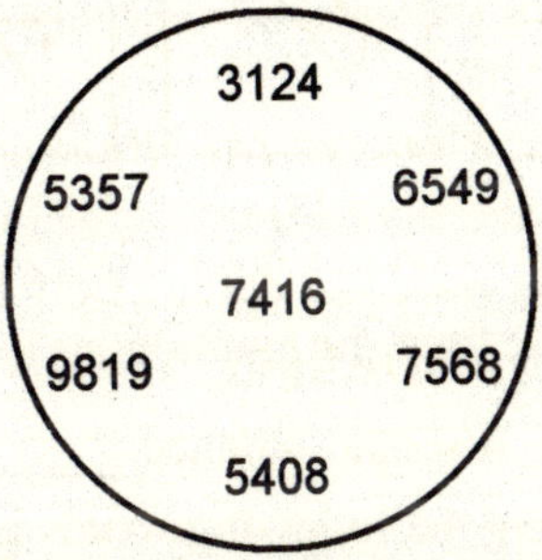

20. The following word carries a shorter word within it in the normal sequence which conveys the same meaning as the longer word. Find the shorter synonym?

ILLUMINATED

21. Select the correct figure among the four options to complete the first figure to make it symmetrical?

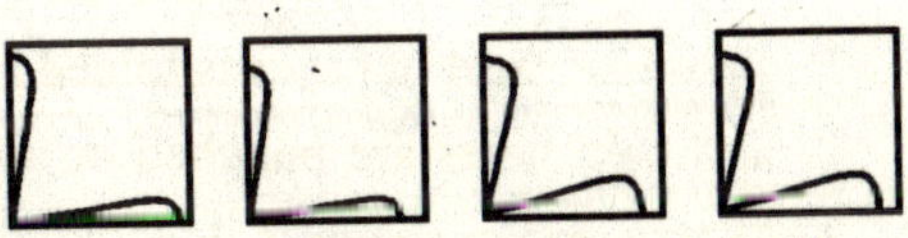

(1) (2) (3) (4)

22. Which key word should replace the question mark so as to make a two-word phrase from the list of words that follows, ie. ____?____: BAG, MARSHAL, CONDITIONING (? is AIR)

____?___ SHOT, JUMP, BEACH

23. Two positions of a dice are shown below. Which number will appear on the face opposite to the face with number 1 at the bottom?

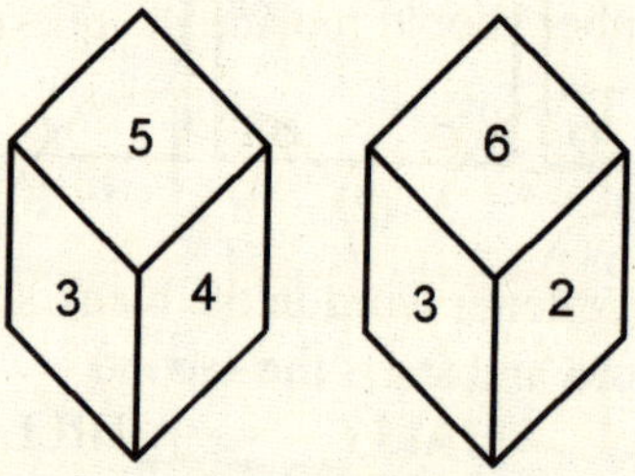

24. Select the correct alternative which when substituted for the question mark maintain the same relationship on both the sides of the sign "::"?

Ajitpal Singh: Hockey:: Ajit Wadekar: ?

(a) Billiards (b) Football

(c) Shooting (d) Cricket

25. Select a figure from the four options to complete the sequence above?

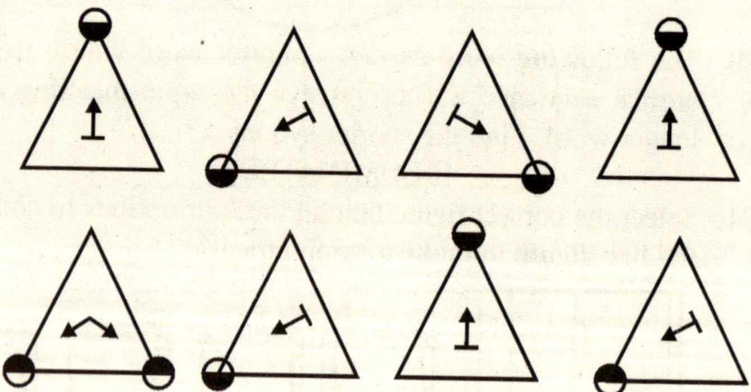

(1) (2) (3) (4)

TEST-20

1. Select the correct alternative that will maintain the same relationship on the two signs "::", if it is substituted for the question mark "?".

byy: cxx:: dww: ?

(a) att (b) auu

(c) avv (d) azz

2. What number should replace the question mark?

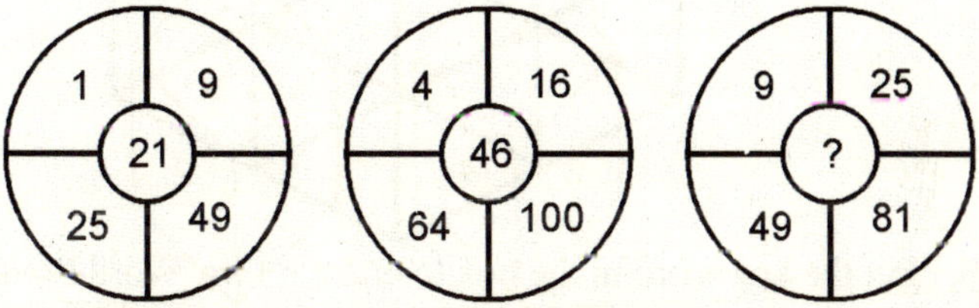

3. The first three letters of the following four six-letter capital city of well-known country is written below. Fill the blank spaces to find these city?

___ ___ ___ ANA

4. Which among the four options should occupy the position indicated by a question mark to continue the sequence?

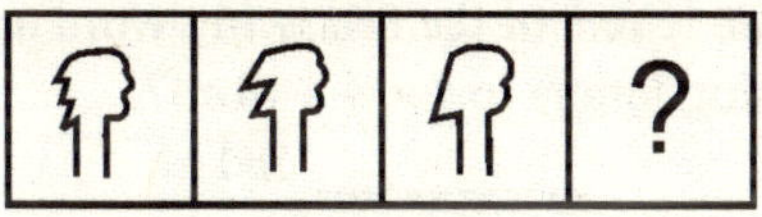

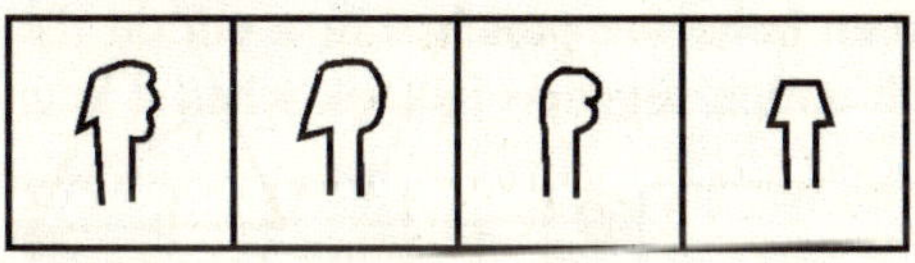

(1) (2) (3) (4)

5. Which among the following figures is different from others?

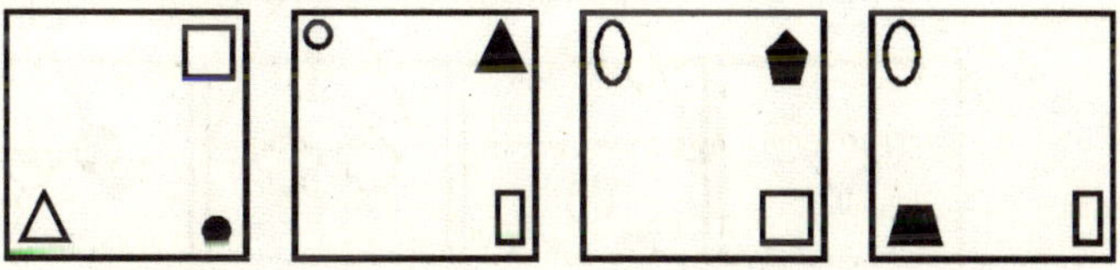

(1) (2) (3) (4)

6. Arrange the following group of letters into a familiar bird?

ARABIA MILD FIR

7. How many triangles can you count in this figure?

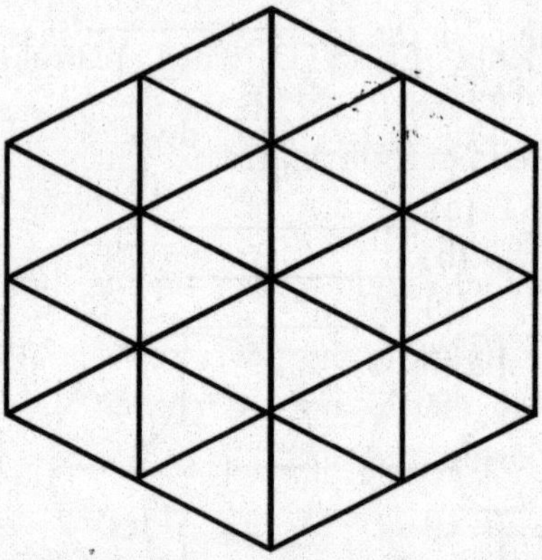

8. Put the key word in the box to make a Two-Word Phrase from the list of words that follow. For example: [GOLD] RUSH/MEDAL/COAST

[   ] SPOT/SALOON/QUEEN

9. The following eleven-letter word contains ROB at its centre. Fill in the blanks to spell the name of an Indian state?

___ ___ ___ ___ RAK ___ ___ ___ ___

10. The first three letters of the following word are missing. Find out the missing letters to form a word?

___ ___ ___ IFT

11. A square sheet of paper is folded as shown by the dotted lines and then holes are punched or a cut on the corner is made. Which option suggests its look when it is unfolded?

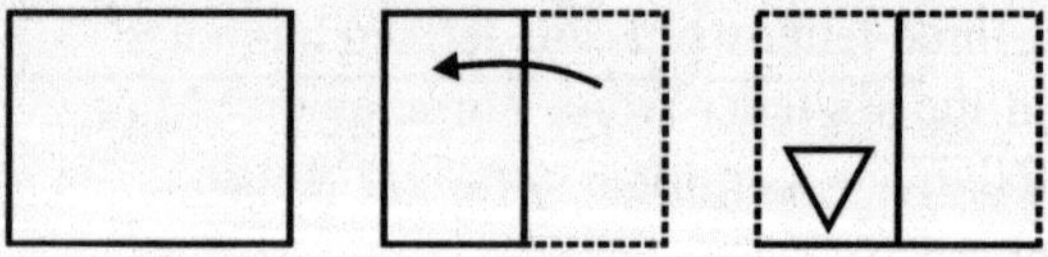

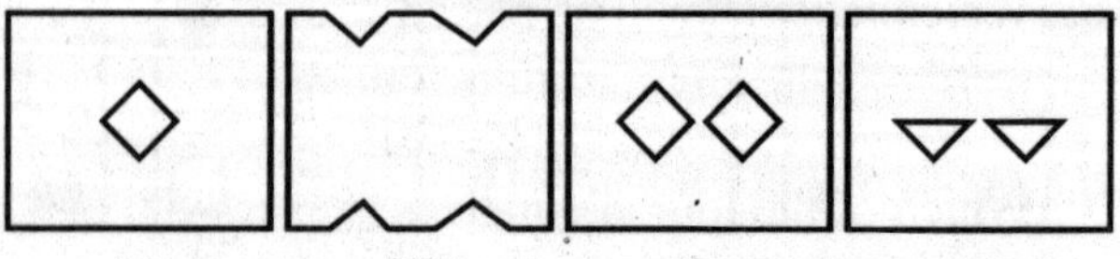

(1) (2) (3) (4)

12. Which three-letter word should be inserted within the parenthesis to form two new words?

D (___ ___ ___) E

G (___ ___ ___) H

13. The letter ELRSTU when rearranged form LUSTRE; RESULT and RUSTLE. In the following groups rearrange the letters to form anagrams. Clues are given.

EIPRST (a) __________ Paster

(b) __________ Fairy

(c) __________ Band

14. Which figure in the lower row should replace the question mark so that C and the chosen figure maintain the same relationship as A and B?

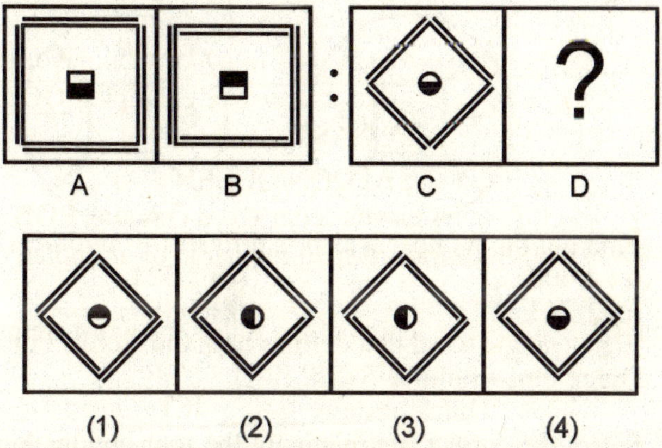

15. NAPKIN is composed of NAP and KIN, neither of which has any connection with NAPKIN. Below are given two three-letter words which combine to form a six-letter word. The three-letter words are defined but not the six-letter word. Find the six-letter word. For example: Male child + Trap = SONNET

Peak + Cover = __________ (A-One)

16. Which letter should be placed before and after the following word so that a new word is formed?

__ EVIVE __

17. Which of the four alternatives is exactly the mirror image of the object placed in front of a plane mirror?

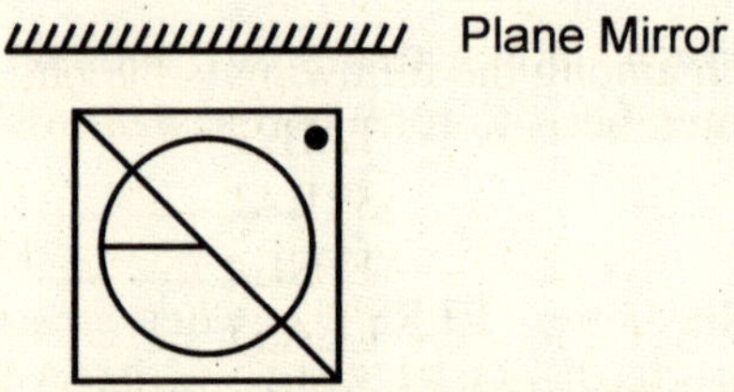

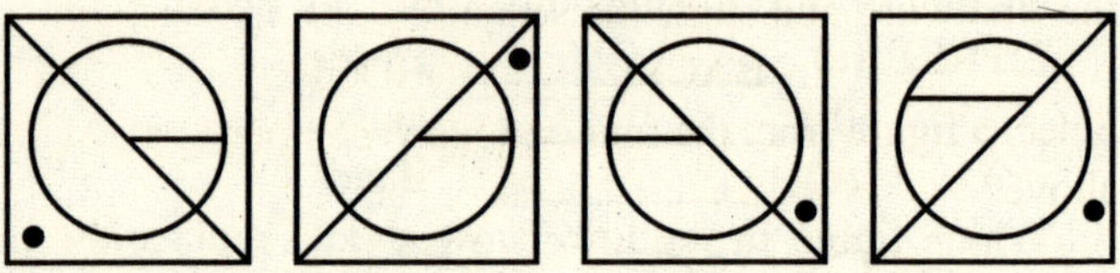

(1) (2) (3) (4)

18. What number should replace the question mark?

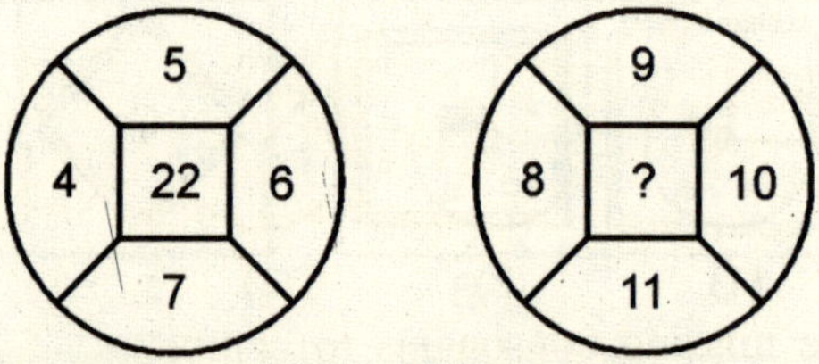

19. Find out the number which is different from others?

(a) 1/400 (b) 1/324

(c) 1/343 (d) 1/49

20. Find a single word that defines both the words. For example: Quick bird would be Swift.

Quick abstain ___________

21. Select the correct figure among the four options to complete the first figure to make it symmetrical?

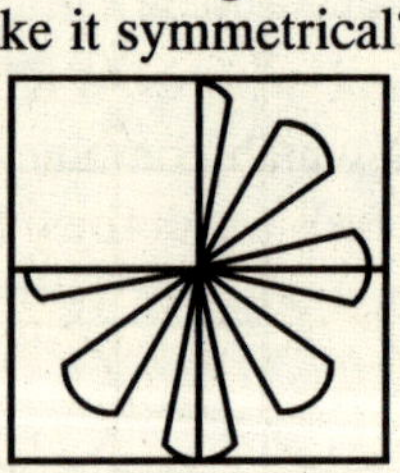

(1) (2) (3) (4)

22. Which among the following is the odd one out?

TAILS
STEAL
TESLA
LEAST

23. Insert a three-letter word in the blank spaces which complete the first word and starts the second?

BACK(__ __ __)BOOK

24. Select a figure from the four options to complete the sequence above?

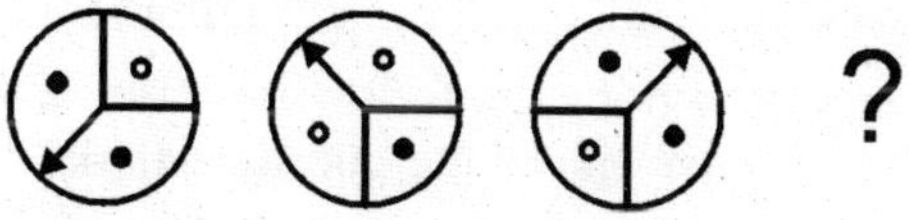

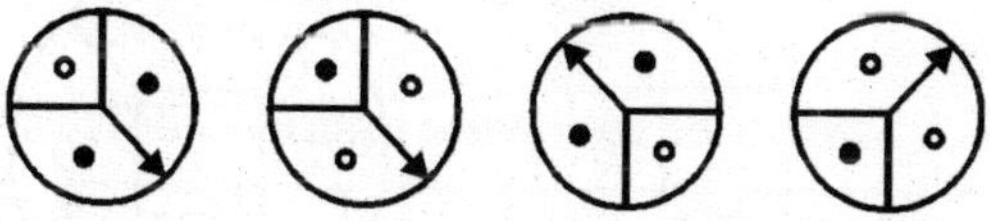

(1) (2) (3) (4)

25. Insert the missing consonants to complete a magic square where all words read the same across and down The consonants are:

D D N R R R R S S S T T W?

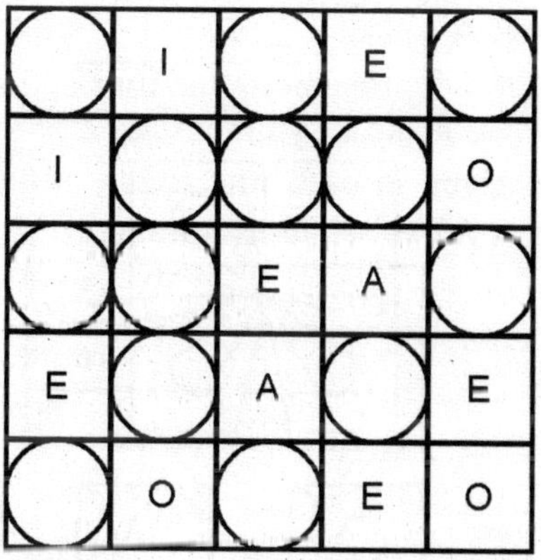

TEST-21

1. Find the next two numbers of the series?

   1 2 3 4 5 7 9 11 13 16 ? ?

2. Which group of letters is different from others?

   (a) KOH (b) TXQ

   (c) OSM (d) EIB

3. Which word is odd one out?

   (a) AFFIRE (b) HANOI

   (c) PRIMA (d) OPINE

4. Which number among the following series is wrong?

   19, 28, 37, 73, 85, 82, 91

   (a) 37 (b) 73

   (c) 85 (d) 91

5. Which among the following figures is different from others?

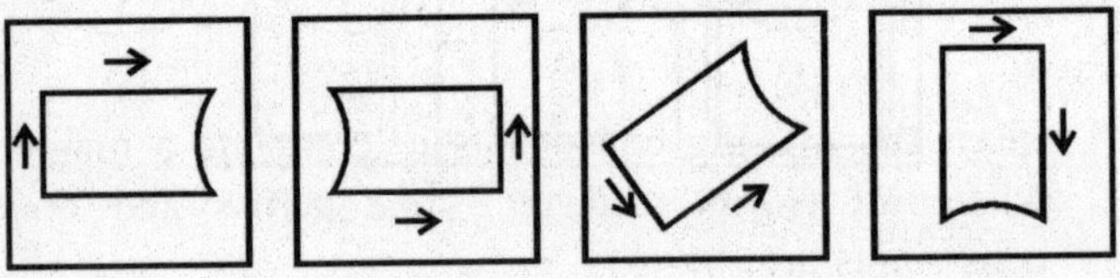

(1) (2) (3) (4)

6. Which among the following letters is different from others?

   K H W A Z A

   (a) K (b) H

   (c) W (d) Z

7. Numbers given in each row follow some arithmetical rule. Select the number which is missing?

6	6	15
8	6	16
6	8	?

   (a) 17 (b) 18

   (c) 19 (d) 20

8. Find the group which is different from others.

   (a) rkin (b) pigl

   (c) nfdj (d) ohfk

9. Insert a three-letter word in the blank spaces which completes the first word and starts the second?

TAIL(_ _ _)LESS

10. Which figure in the lower row should replace the question mark so that C and the chosen figure maintain the same relationship as A and B?

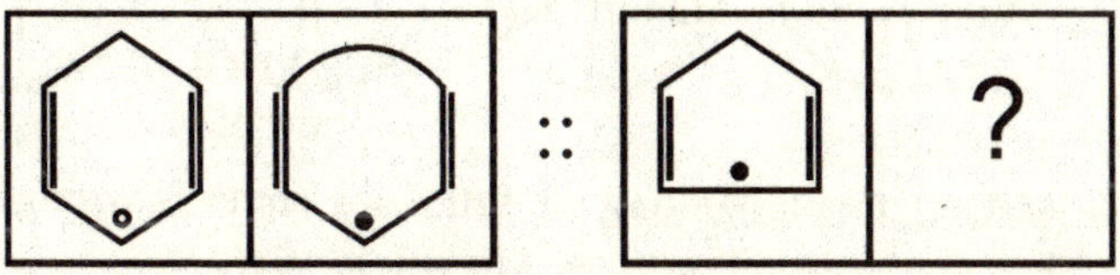

A B C

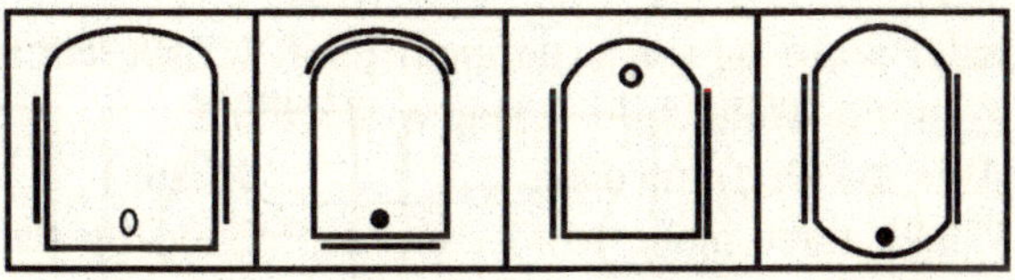

(1) (2) (3) (4)

11. Make word to match the definition by putting letters in the blank spaces.

__ __ __ __ANT __________ (Employee)

12. What number should replace the question mark?

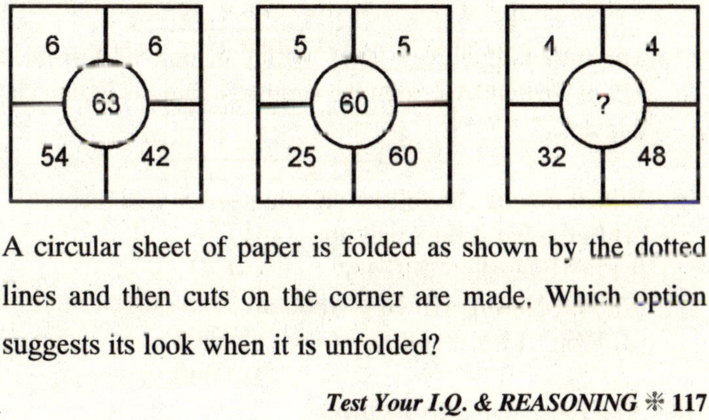

13. A circular sheet of paper is folded as shown by the dotted lines and then cuts on the corner are made. Which option suggests its look when it is unfolded?

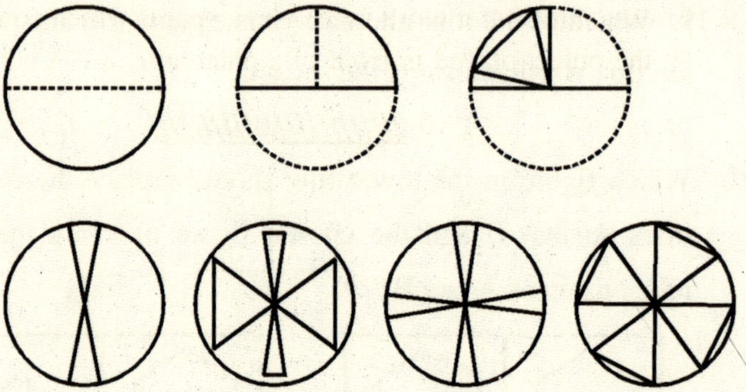

(1) (2) (3) (4)

14. MIDGET is composed of MID and GET, neither of which has any connection with MIDGET. Below are listed some pair of words, each of them has a three-letter word as its meaning. The two three-letter words combine to form a six-letter word which is defined. Find the six-letter word. For example: Male child + Trap = SONNET
Able to+ Performed = ___________ (Frank)
15. Which three-letter word can be prefixed by the following group of letters to form different words?
AY CE GE GO TE TH TY UM
16. What numbers should replace the question marks?

5	9	10	6
7	3	8	12
2	6	13	9
4	5	?	?

17. The following eleven-letter word contains SHA at its centre. Fill in the blanks to spell the name of a famous Indian classical dancer.
___ ___ ___ ___ SHA___ ___ ___ ___
18. Which among the following sentences is odd one out?
(a) Pull a bat, I hit a ball up.
(b) Is Malayalam difficult?
(c) 'Not New York,' Roy went on.
(d) Won't love revolt now?

19. Which of the four alternatives is exactly the mirror image of the object placed in front of a plane mirror?

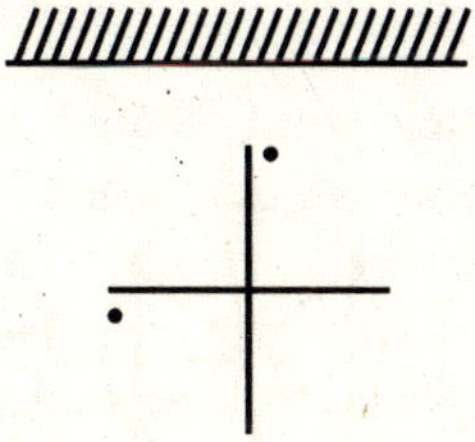

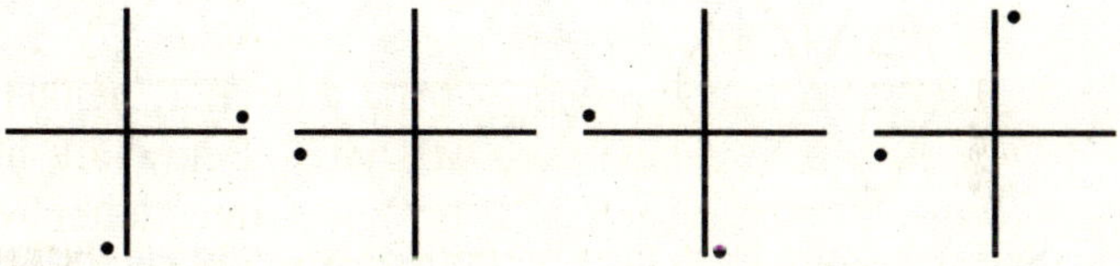

(1) (2) (3) (4)

20. Select the correct figure among the four options to complete the first figure to make it symmetrical?

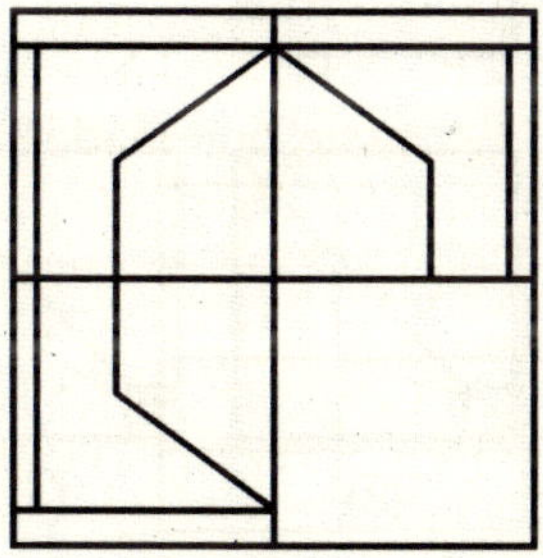

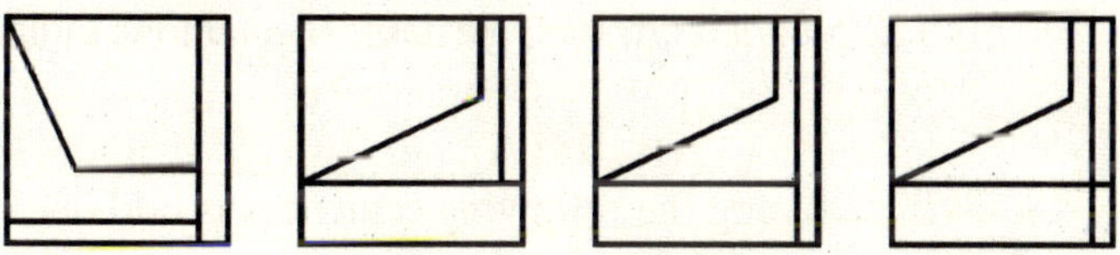

(1) (2) (3) (4)

21. Shuffle the letters in capitals and guess the answer?

Which imp LIVED backward?

22. How many meaningful words can you make from the following set of letters?
ADERRW

_______ _______

_______ _______

23. Which three-letter word should be inserted within the parenthesis to form two new words?

G (___ ___ ___) T

T (___ ___ ___) K

24. What number replaces the question mark?

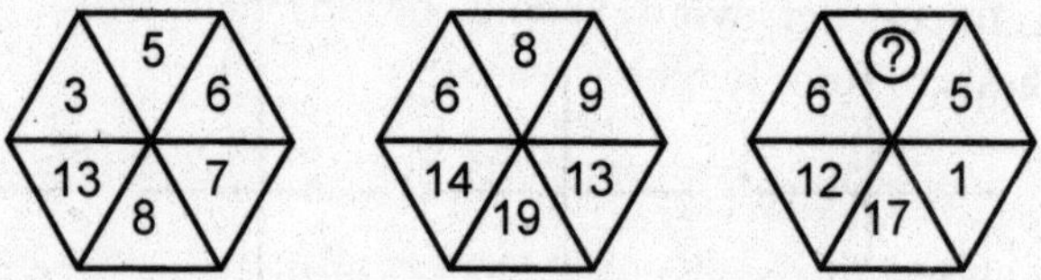

25. Select a figure from the four options to complete the sequence above.

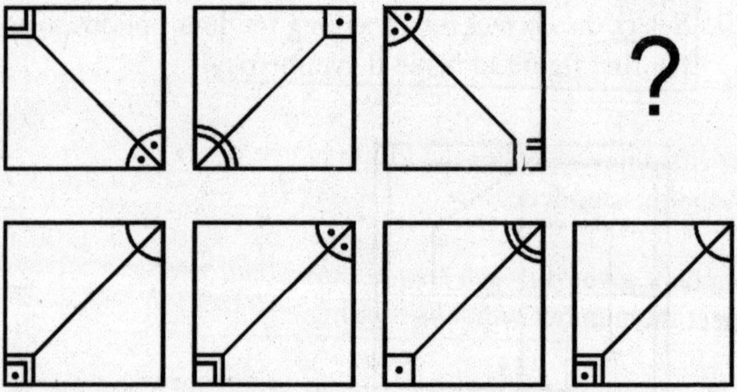

(1) (2) (3) (4)

TEST-22

1. What number should replace the question mark?

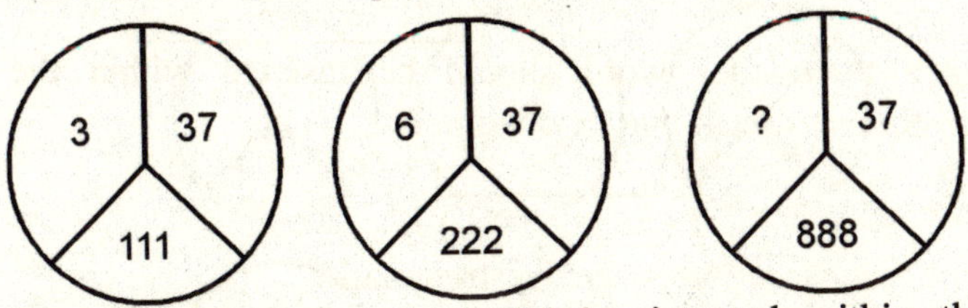

2. Which three-letter word should be inserted within the parenthesis to form two new words?

I (___ ___ ___) E
W (___ ___ ___) H

3. Which among the following figures is different from others?

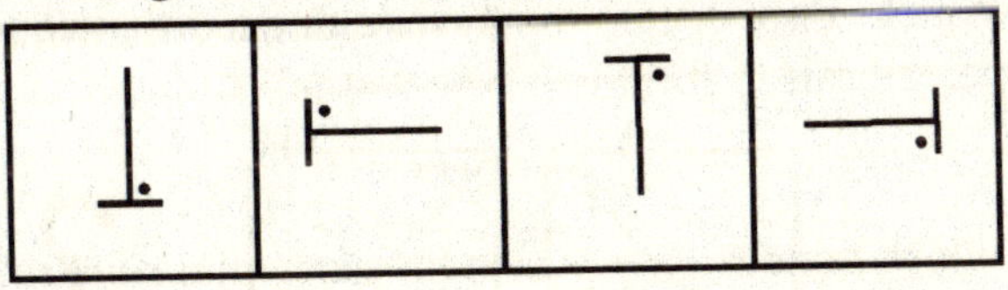

(1) (2) (3) (4)

4. The first three letters of the following word are missing. Find out the missing letters to form a word.

___ ___ ___ RTZ

5. Numbers given in each row follow some arithmetical rule. Select the number which is missing.

33	5	4
26	4	5
?	4	3

(a) 22 (b) 24
(c) 26 (d) 28

6. Which word is odd one out?

(a) SAVES (b) SPEAK
(c) GLASS (d) ASSAM

7. The first three letters of the following word are missing. Find out the missing letters to form a word.

___ ___ ___ RGY

8. A circular sheet of paper is folded as shown by the dotted lines and then holes are made. Which option suggests its look when it is unfolded?

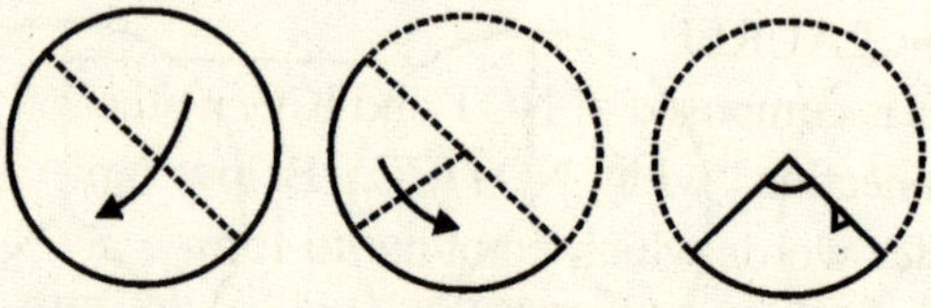

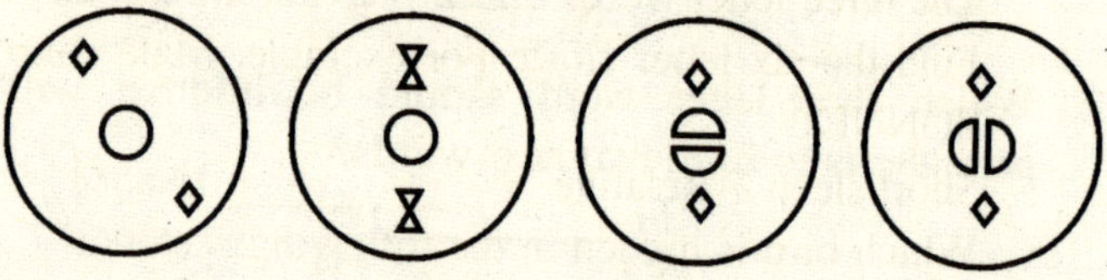

(1) (2) (3) (4)

9. Which three-letter word should be inserted within the parenthesis to form two new words?

Y (___ ___ ___) H

S (___ ___ ___) H

10. Which famous river is also the name of a country?

11. Which among the following group of letters is different from others?

(a) CD (b) HJ

(c) NP (d) TW

12. Which figure in the lower row should replace the question mark so that C and the chosen figure maintain the same relationship as A and B?

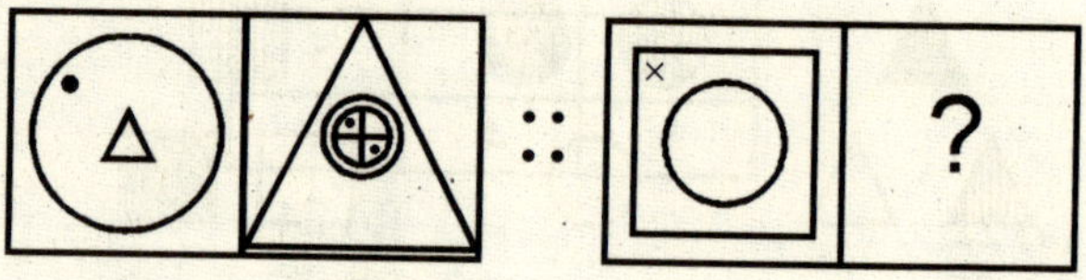

A B C D

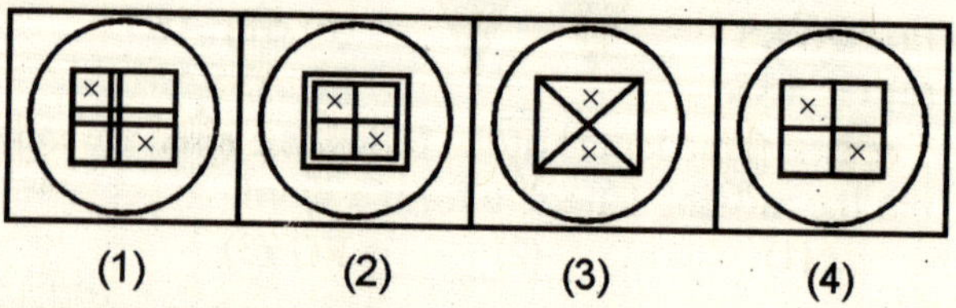

(1) (2) (3) (4)

13. A clue is preceded by the meaning of a word which has the same letters as the clue. Write its anagram, e.g. (Nakedness): UNTIDY = NUDITY

(Attract) : LAUREL =____________

14. NOTICE is composed of NOT and ICE, neither of which has any connection with NOTICE. Below are given two three-letter words which combine to form a six-letter word. The three-letter words are defined but not the six-letter word. Find the six-letter word. For example: Male child + Trap = SONNET

Short sleep + Relative = ___________ (Nappy)

15. Which bird is hidden in the following sentence?

Why do you regret?

16. Which mania describes "Obsession with a particular word which the person uses repeatedly or which intrudes into consciousness"?

(a) Phaneromania (b) Balletomania

(c) Onomatomania (d) Decalcomania

17. What number should replace the question mark?

18. Select a figure from the four options to complete the sequence above.

(1) (2) (3) (4)

19. Make a six-letter word to match the definition by putting letters in the blank spaces. Clue is given.

___ ___ ___ LET = Ticket

20. Select the correct figure among the four options to complete the first figure to make it symmetrical?

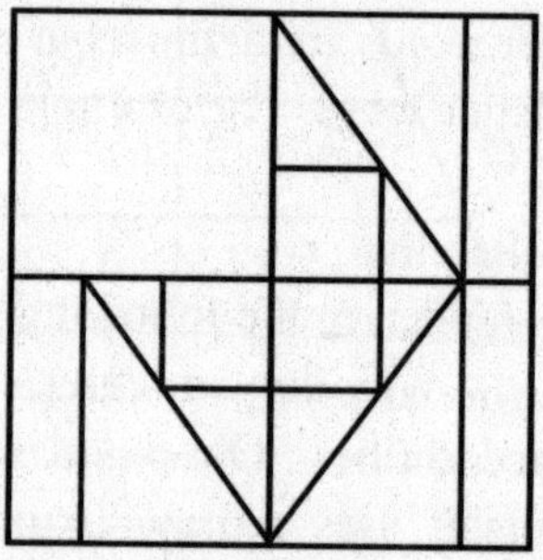

(1) (2) (3) (4)

21. If + means '=', – means '≠', × means '≤', and ÷ means '≥' then what will be the value of $6 = 2 \geq 3 \leq 6 \neq 3$?

22. Which among the four options should occupy the position indicated by the blank spaces so as to continue the sequence?

__y__ __yz __yx __y

(a) xxyyz (b) zxxyz

(c) zxxzx (d) xyxzx

23. Insert a three-letter word in the blank spaces which completes the first word and starts the second?

BACK(__ __ __)ICAL

24. How many triangles are there in this figure?

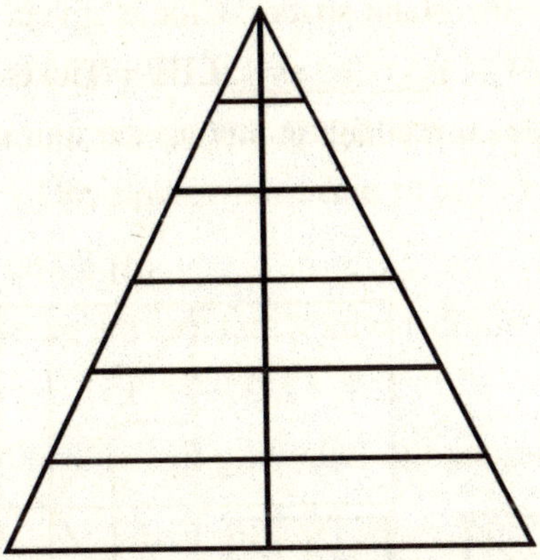

25. Which of the four alternatives is exactly the mirror image of the object placed in front of a plane mirror?

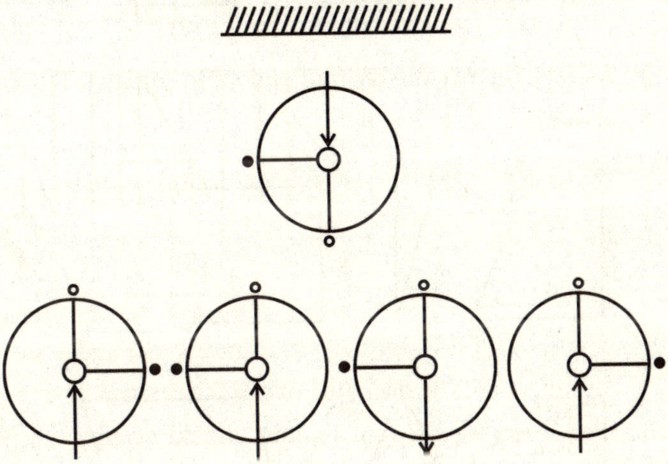

(1) (2) (3) (4)

❑

TEST-23

1. If BARACK is coded as 126 then how is coded OBAMA?
2. Find the group which is different from others?

   (a) ACE (b) CEG

   (c) GIL (d) KMO
3. Find the number which replaces the question mark?

   2, 7, 17, 37, 77, 157, ?
4. Which among the following figures is different from others?

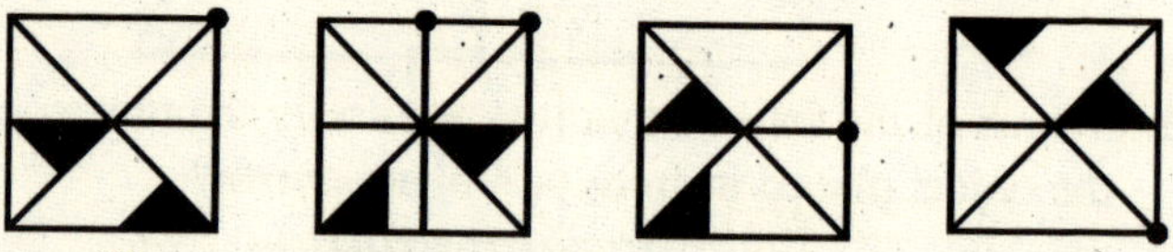

(1) (2) (3) (4)

5. Select a figure from the four options to complete the sequence above?

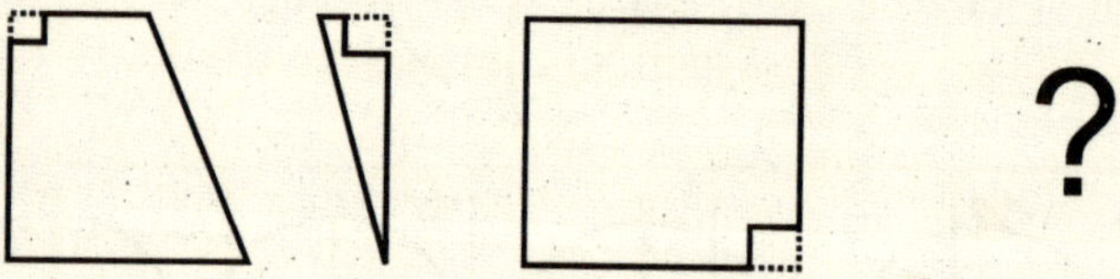

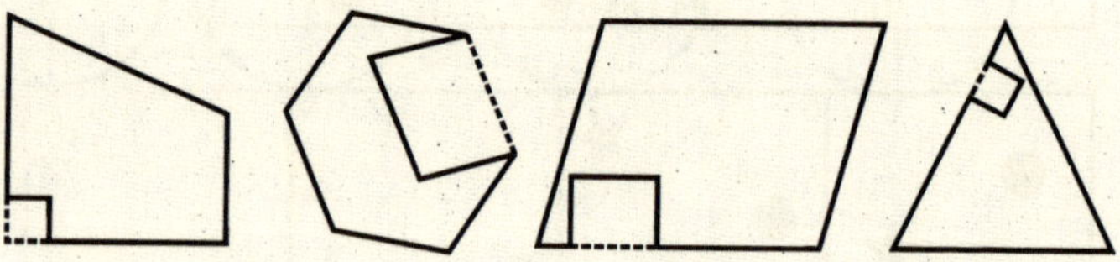

(1) (2) (3) (4)

6. A square sheet of paper is folded as shown by the dotted lines and then a hole is punched and cuts are made. Which option suggests its look when it is unfolded?

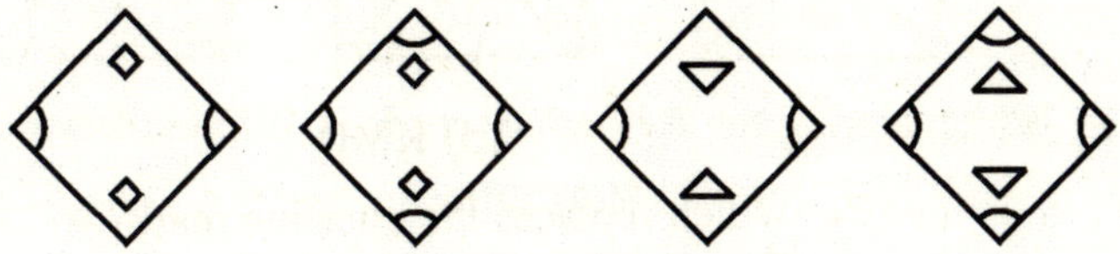

(1) (2) (3) (4)

7. What number should replace the question mark?

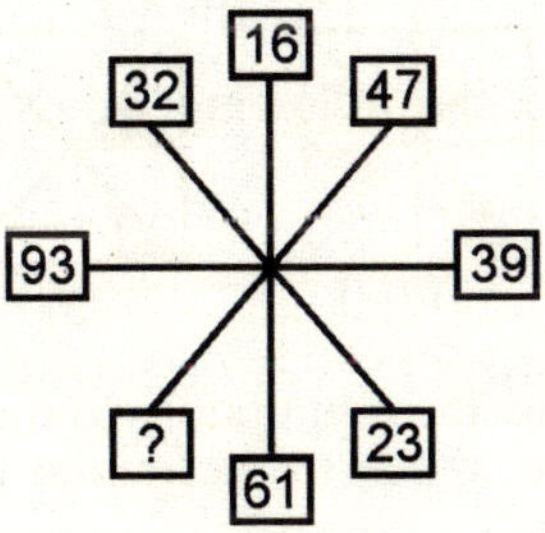

8. Which among the four options should occupy the position indicated by a question mark to continue the sequence?

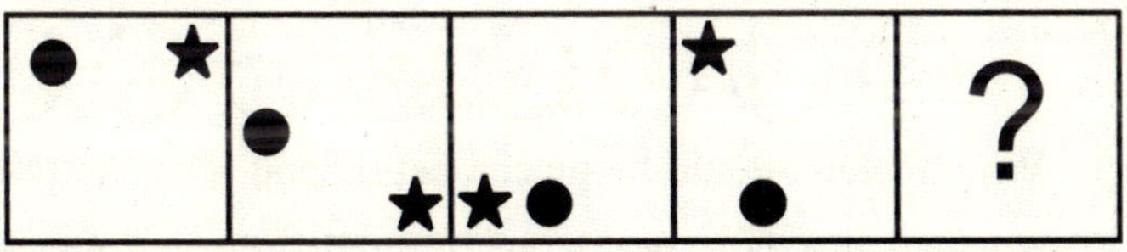

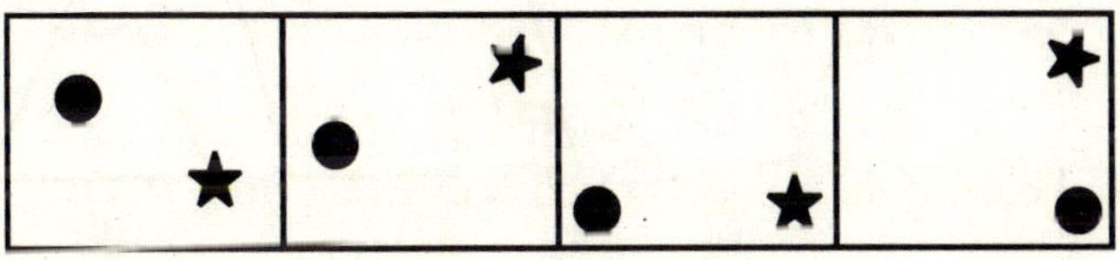

(1) (2) (3) (4)

9. Insert a three letter word in the blank spaces which complete the first word and starts the second?

HAND(_ _ _)SOME

10. What numbers should replace the question mark?

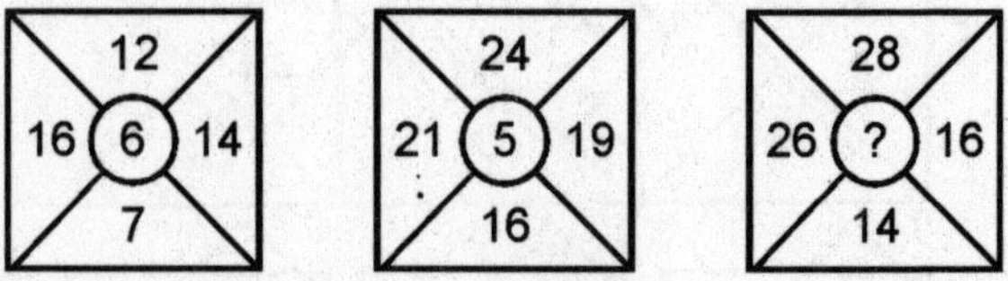

11. Which among the following words is different from others?

ROTTER

REPAID

REWARD

LAMINA

12. Which among the following words is different from other words?

(a) ABRACADABRA (b) DEFENCELESSNESS

(c) INDIVISIBILITY (d) BACALAUREATE

13. Make word to match the definition by putting letters in the blank spaces?

___ ___ ___ ___ MENT = Fundamental

14. What number should replace the question mark?

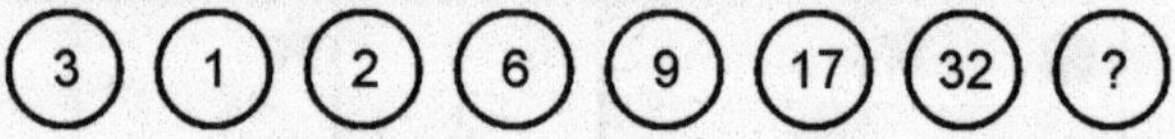

15. Which letter should be placed before and after the following word so that new words are formed that spell the some—forward and backward?

__ LIT __

16. Find out the number which is different from others?

(a) 11 (b) 24

(c) 39 (d) 48

17. Which among the four options should occupy the position indicated by a question mark to continue the sequence?

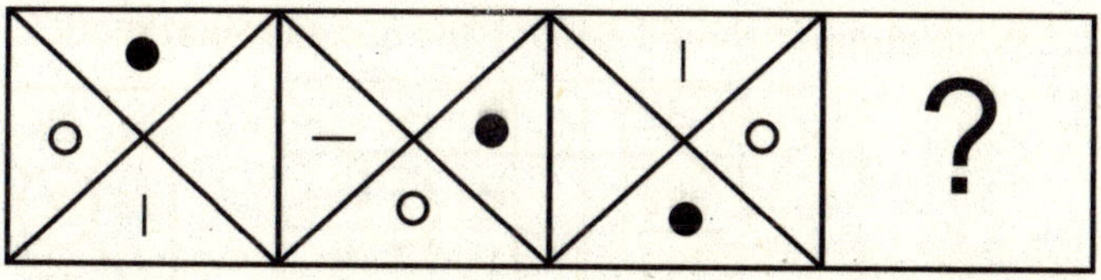

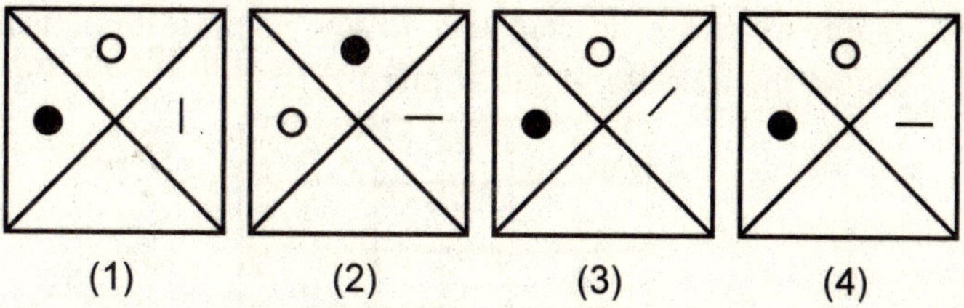

18. The following eleven-letter word contains MIT at its centre. Fill up the blanks to spell the name of an Indian actress and former Miss Universe?

___ ___ ___ ___ MIT ___ ___ ___ ___

19. Unscramble the following set of letters and spell the name of an animal?

ABEERV

20. Which of the four alternatives is exactly the mirror image of the object placed in front of a plane mirror AB?

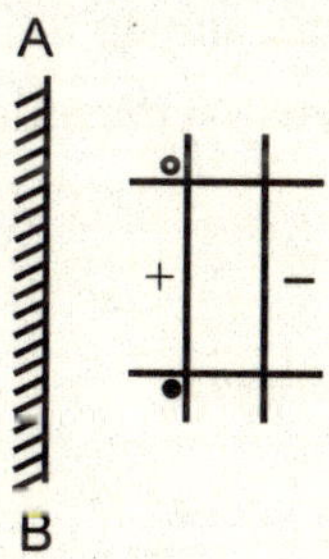

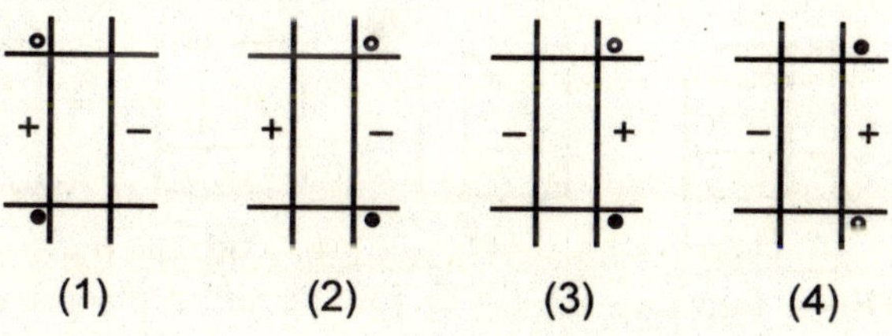

21. What number should replace the question mark?

31	4	8
63	9	18
93	12	?

22. Numbers given in each row follow some arithmetical rule. Select the number which is missing?

8	60	4
4	12	4
8	?	8

(a) 64 (b) 62

(c) 58 (d) 56

23. Select the correct alternative which when substituted for the question mark maintain the same relationship on both the sides of the sign "::"?

Govind Ballabh Pant: Politician:: Sumitranandan Pant: ?

(a) Actor (b) Poet

(c) Dancer (d) Yoga guru

24. Select the correct figure among the four options to complete the first figure to make it symmetrical?

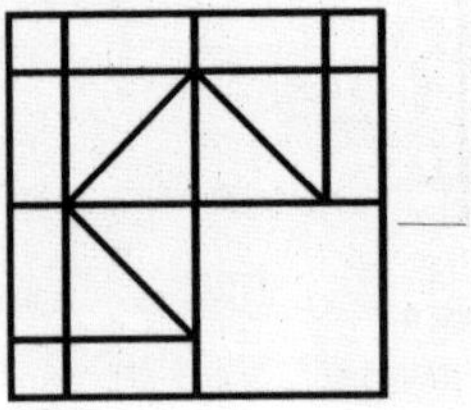

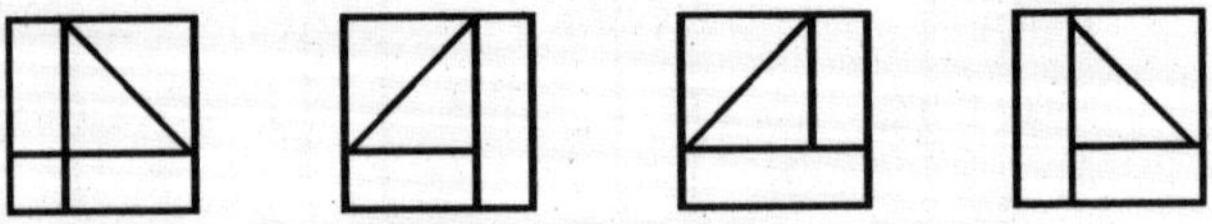

(1) (2) (3) (4)

25. Which figure in the lower row should replace the question

mark so that C and the chosen figure maintain the same relationship as A and B?

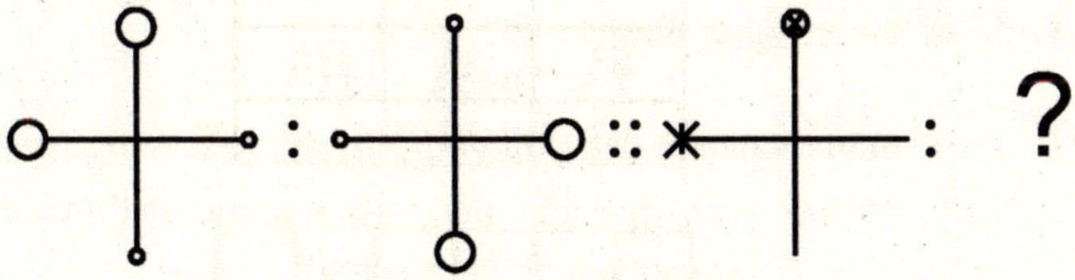

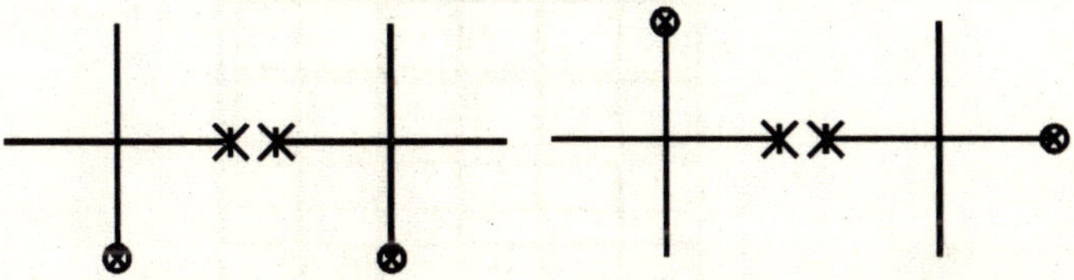

(1) (2) (3) (4)

❑

TEST-24

1. Find the missing number ("?").

   1, 3, 9, 19, 33, ?, 73

2. How many squares can you count in the following figure?

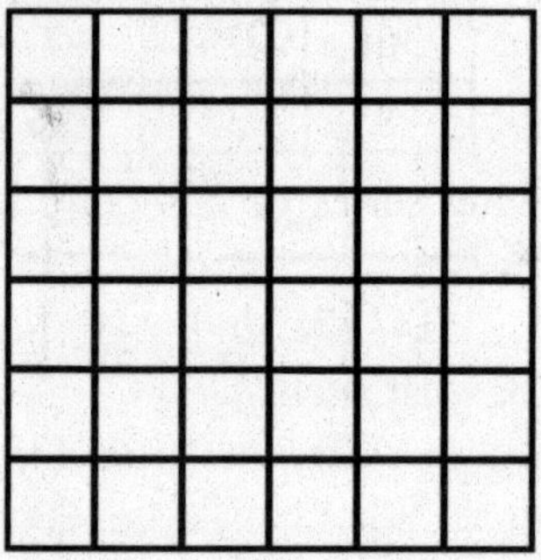

3. Put the key word in each box to make a two-word phrase from the list of words that precede. For example: BACK/REVOLVING/NEXT [DOOR]

   HIGH/GRASS/HARD [ ]

4. Which figure in the lower row should replace the question mark so that C and the chosen figure maintain the same relationship as A and B?

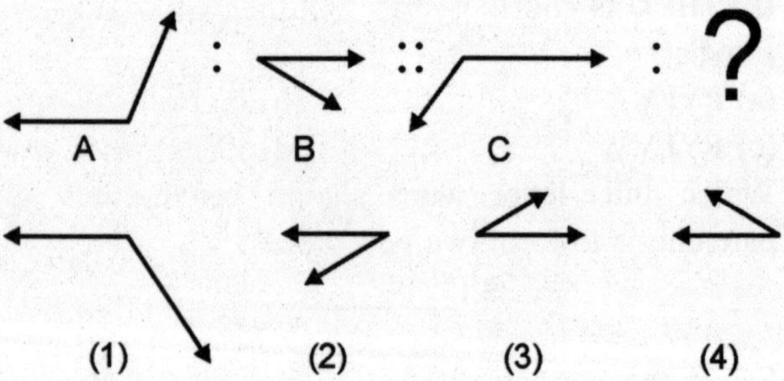

5. If 'X' stands for addition, 'Y' for subtraction, 'Z' for division, and 'W' for multiplication, then find the value of the following expression?

   18X9Y10Z7W14

6. The first two letters of the following five-letter word are missing. Find out the missing letters to form a word?

___ ___ AUD

7. What number should replace the question mark?

256	33	289
361	39	400
?	32	196

8. In the following series of numbers, which one is different from others?

114, 171, 209, 241, 247

9. If MAN is 28, what is DIM?
10. In a class, Saurav's position from the top is 11th and 29th from the bottom. What is the total number of students in the class?
11. Which among the following figures is different from others?

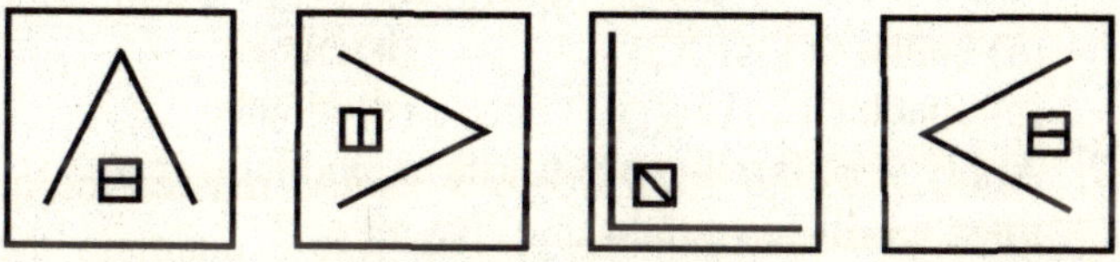

(1) (2) (3) (4)

12. If CHILD is coded as PUVYQ, then CLAIM will be coded as what?

(a) PYLVZ (b) PYNVZ
(c) PYLVW (d) PYMVW

13. Which three-letter word should be inserted within the parenthesis to form two new words?

A (___ ___ ___) D
D (___ ___ ___) F

14. Select the correct alternative that will maintain the same relationship on the two signs "::", if it is substituted for the question mark "?".

XZKM: ?:: VXIK: UWHJ

(a) WYJK (b) WYKI
(c) WYIK (d) WYJI

15. A square sheet of paper is folded as shown by the dotted lines and then a hole is punched on the corner. Which option suggests its look when it is unfolded?

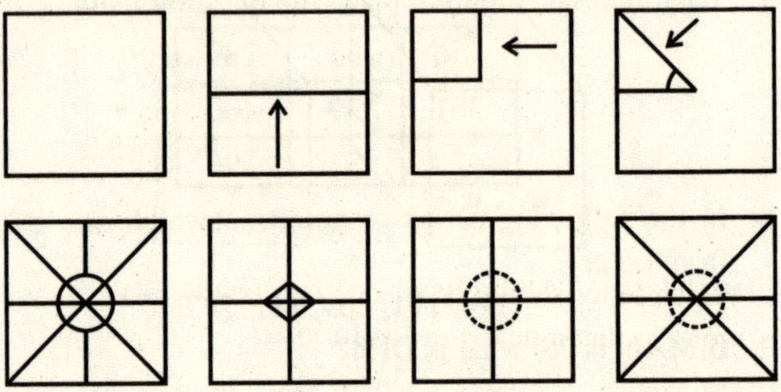

(1) (2) (3) (4)

16. Replace the dashes by letters so that the letter series is continued?

aba__ __ ba__aa__b__

(a) babba (b) bbbab
(c) ababb (d) bbabb

17. Apply your intelligence to fill in the blank spaces so that the three words have the same five letters?

___	___	L	___	S
___	T	___	___	___
___	E	A	___	___

18. Select a figure from the four options to complete the sequence above?

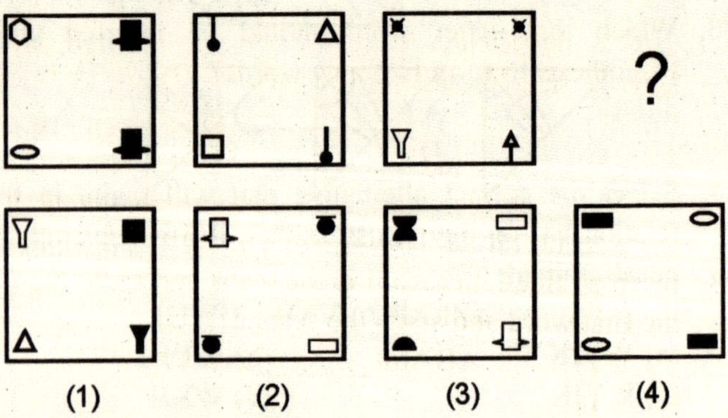

(1) (2) (3) (4)

19. Three positions of a dice are shown as follows when it is flipped. Which face appears opposite the one having four black dots?

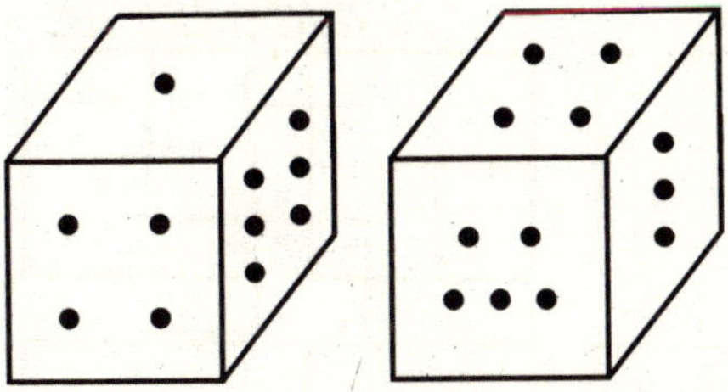

20. Which letter should be placed before and after the following word so that a new word is formed?

__ AUGH __

21. Select the correct alternative that will maintain the same relationship on the two signs "::", if it is substituted for the question mark "?".

Cattle: Herd:: ?: Pride

(a) Pig (b) Lion
(c) Snake (d) Goat

22. Select the correct figure among the four options to complete the first figure to make it symmetrical?

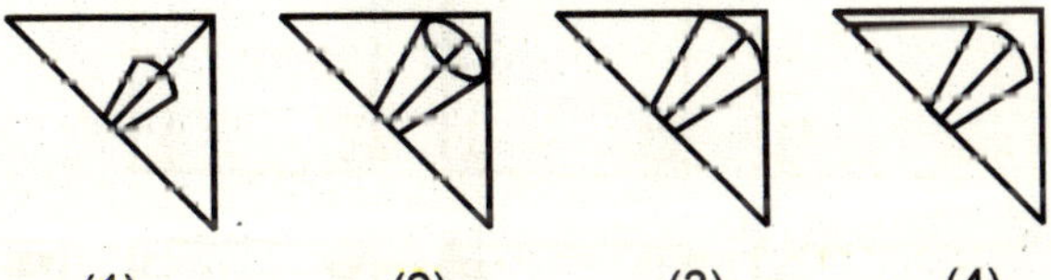

(1) (2) (3) (4)

23. Insert a three-letter word in the blank spaces which complete the first word and starts the second?

ADAM(__ __ __)ACID

24. If 3 = 0, 4 = 4, 5 = 10, then what is 6 equals to?

25. Which of the four alternatives is exactly the mirror image of the object placed in front of a plane mirror?

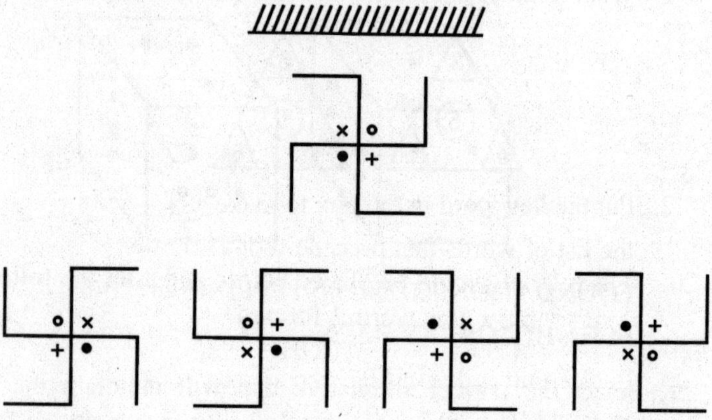

(1) (2) (3) (4)

TEST-25

1. What number should replace the question mark?

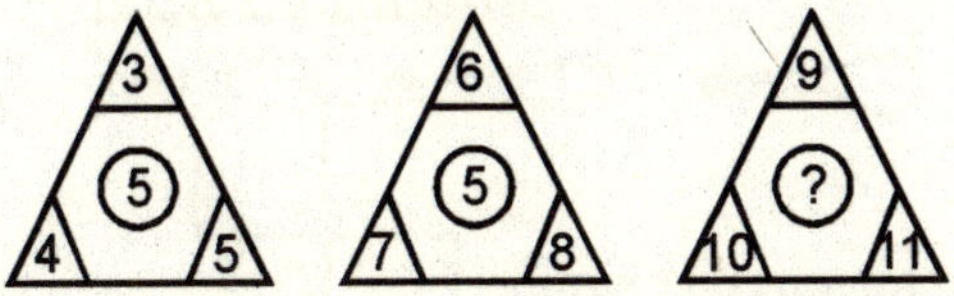

2. Put the key word in the box to make a two-word phrase from the list of words that precede. For example:
   FOUNDATION/KIDNEY/STEPPING [STONE]
   FLEA/BLACK/COMMON [ ]
3. In a certain code GLARE is coded as 12345. How is LARGE coded?
4. A circular sheet of paper is folded as shown by the dotted lines and then a cut is made. Which option suggests its look when it is unfolded?

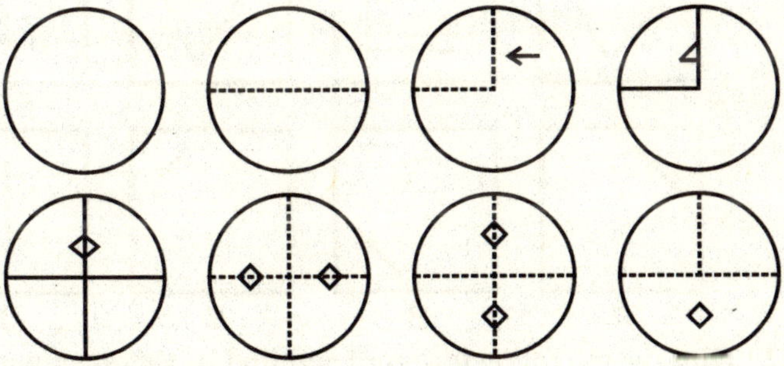

(1) (2) (3) (4)

5. Find the group of letters which is different from others?
   (a) NCT (b) QCV
   (c) SAU (d) PDX
6. Insert a three-letter word in the blank spaces which completes the first word and starts the second?

   PUP(__ __ __)ITE

7. Select a figure from the four options to complete the sequence above?

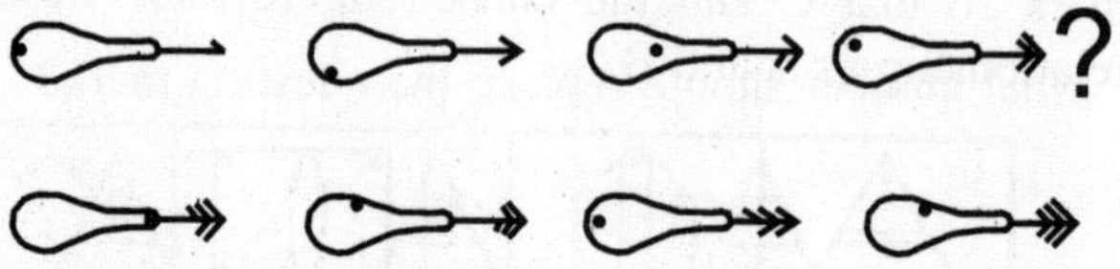

(1) (2) (3) (4)

8. Find the missing number?

0, 7, 26, ?, 124

9. The following word carries a shorter word within it in the normal sequence which conveys the same meaning as the longer word. Find the shorter synonym?

SEPARATE

10. Which among the following number is different from others?

61, 52, 63, 94, 46, 81, 121

11. Which among the four options should occupy the position indicated by a question mark to continue the sequence?

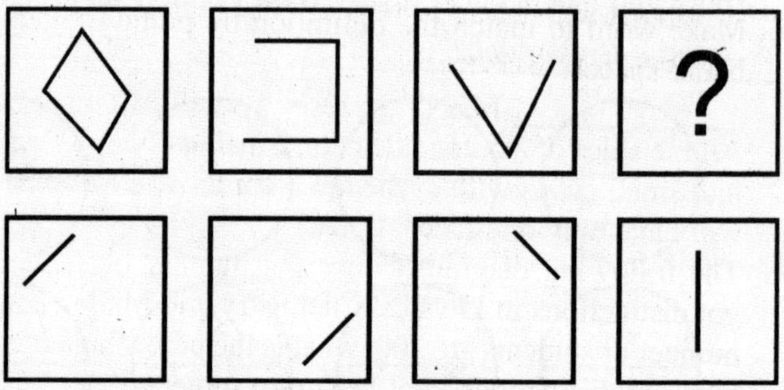

A B C D

12. Observe the following word and find its synonym within this word?

DESTRUCTION

13. Which key word should replace the question mark so as to make a two-word phrase from the list of words that follows, i.e. ____?____: BAG, MARSHAL, CONDITIONING (? is AIR) TAKE, PASS, MAIDEN [?]

14. Deciphet the following rebus?

G B O

Dull ____________

15. Which figure in the lower row should replace the question mark so that C and the chosen figure maintain the same relationship as A and B?

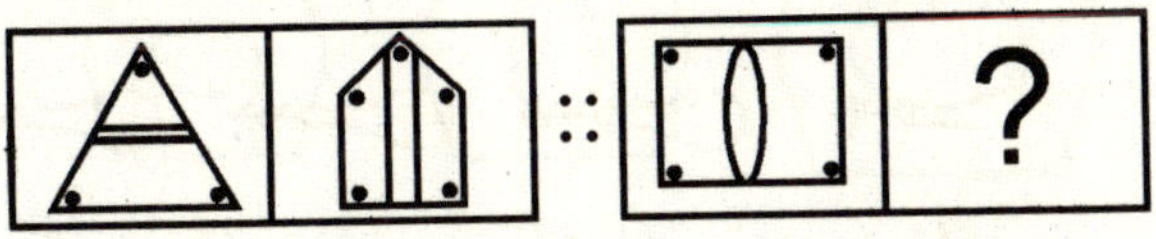

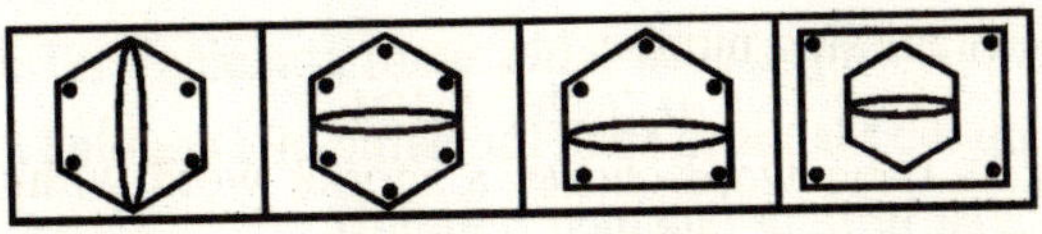

(1) (2) (3) (4)

16. Select the correct alternative that will maintain the same relationship on the two signs "::", if it is substituted for the question mark "?".

Ravi Shankar: Sitar:: Bismillah Khan: ?

(a) Tabla (b) Santoor
(c) Flute (d) Shehnai

17. Make word to match the definition by putting letters in the blank spaces.

___ ___ ___ ___ MENT = A small part

18. All the sides of a 5 cm side cube is painted red. Then it is cut into small cubes with each side 1 cm long. How many cubes will have only one face painted?

19. The following diagram shows the number of students who got distinctions in Physics, Chemistry and Maths. If the total number of students are 200, what is the percentage of students who got distinctions in at least two subjects?

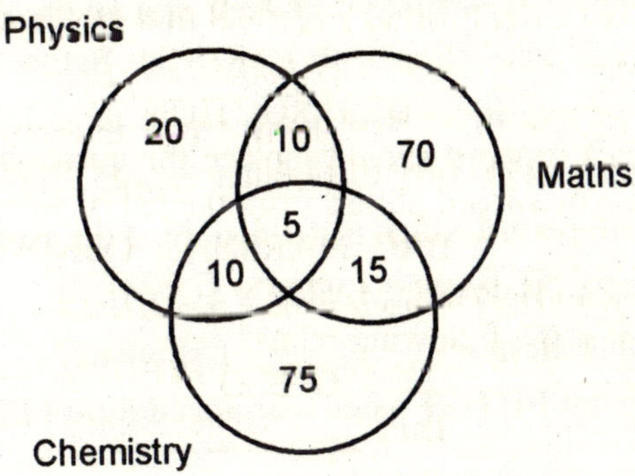

20. Which among the following figures is different from others?

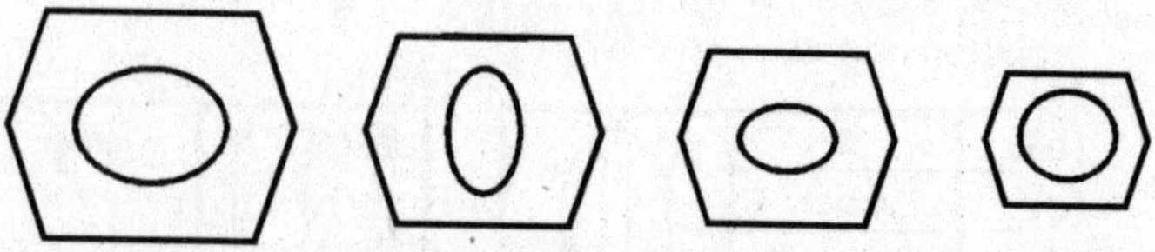

(1) (2) (3) (4)

21. The following eleven-letter word contains ZAT at its centre. Fill up the blanks to spell the name of a double Olympic gold medalist in long-distance running?

__ __ __ __ ZAT __ __ __ __

22. Select the correct alternative which when substituted for the question mark maintain the same relationship on both the sides of the sign "::".

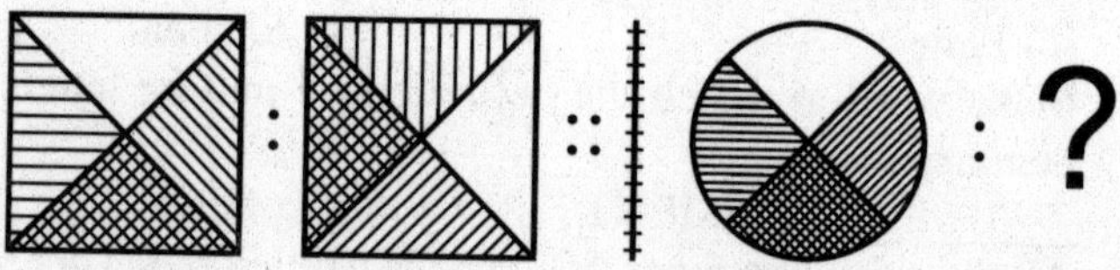

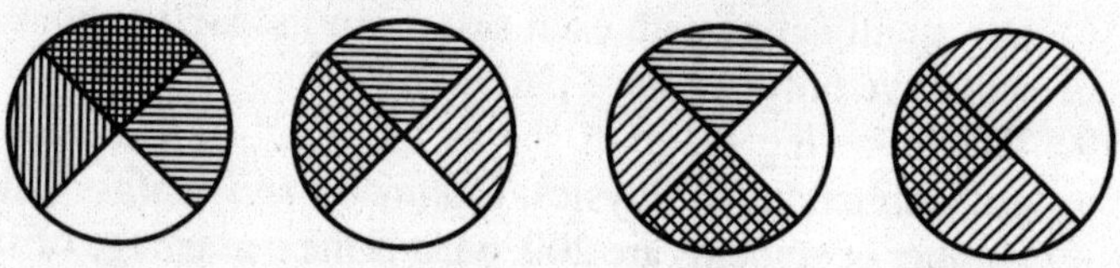

A B C D

23. PARDON is composed of PAR and DON, neither of which has any connection with PARDON. Below are listed some pair of words, each of them has a three-letter word as its meaning. The two three-letter words combine to form a six-letter word which is defined. Find the six-letter word. For example: Male child + Trap = SONNET

Watch + Seen = __________(Alternate)

24. The letter EILNST when rearranged form LISTEN, SILENT,

and TINSEL. In the following groups rearrange the letters to form anagrams. Clues are given.

ACEHRS

(a) ____________ Hunter

(b) ____________ Quest

(c) ____________ Burnt wounds

25. Select the correct figure among the four options to complete the first figure?

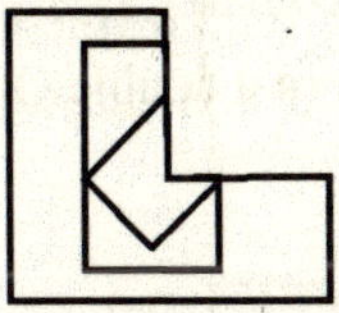

(1) (2) (3) (4)

❑

TEST-26

1. Find the missing number?

   3, 5, 9, 11, 15, 17, ?

2. A clue is preceded by the meaning of a word which has the same letters as the clue. Write its anagram, e.g.

   UNTIDY = NUDITY

   (Shoot) : STUPOR = ___________

3. Select the correct alternative that will maintain the same relationship on the two signs "::", if it is substituted for the question mark "?".

   Tagore: Poetry:: Picasso: ?

   (a) Art (b) Literature
   (c) Film (d) Painting

4. The surname of a famous Indian batsman, whose son was also a Test cricketer is revealed in the following group of words. Find out him?

   AN ARM JERK

5. Which among the following figures is different from others?

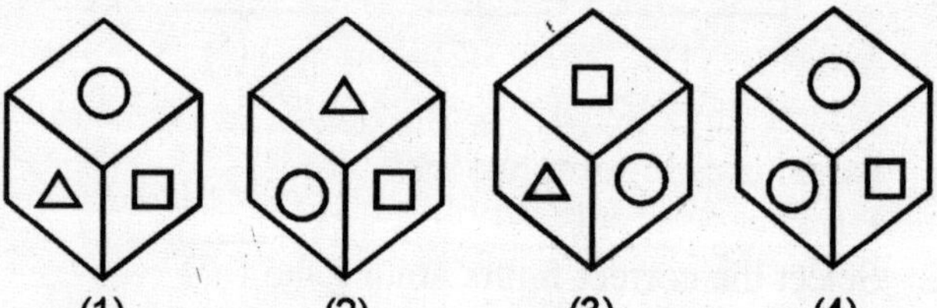

(1) (2) (3) (4)

6. The first three letters of the following word are missing. Find out the missing letters to form a word?

   ___ ___ ___ URB

7. What number should replace the question mark?

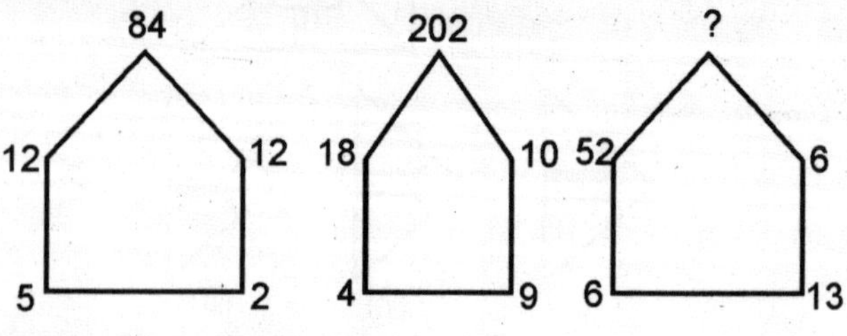

8. The following eleven-letter word contains ALU at its centre. Fill up the blanks to spell the name of a capital city of Asia?

___ ___ ___ ___ALU___ ___ ___ ___

9. Among the following numbers select three numbers that have the same answer when multiplied together as when added together?

1, 2, 3, 4, 5, 6, 7, 8, 9

10. A square sheet of paper is folded as shown by the dotted lines and then holes are punched and cuts is made. Which option suggests its look when it is unfolded?

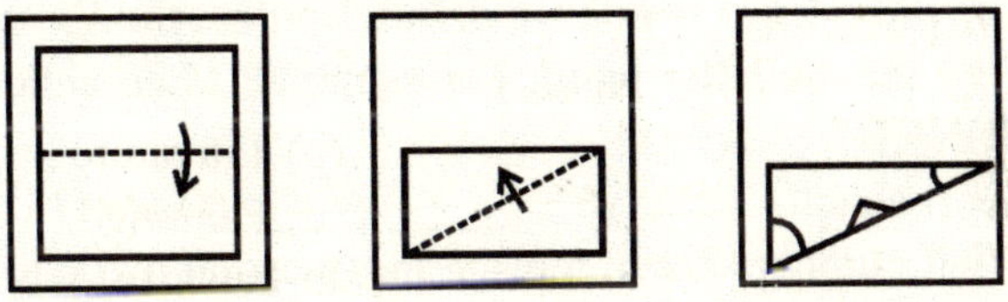

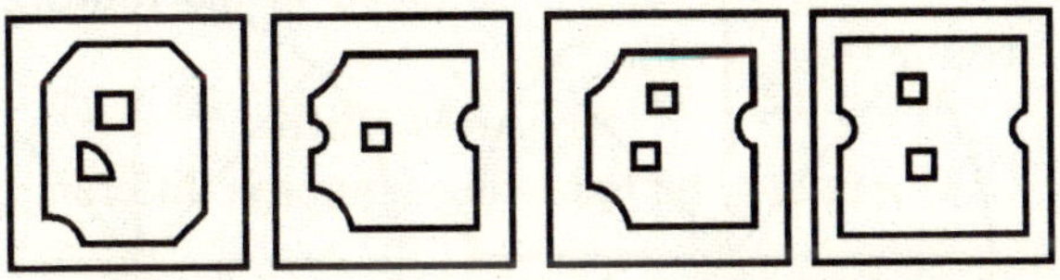

(1) (2) (3) (4)

11. Which three-letter word should be inserted within the parenthesis to form two new words?

P (___ ___ ___) E C (___ ___ ___) E

12. Select the correct figure among the four options to complete the first figure to make it symmetrical?

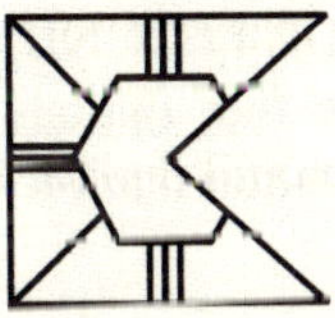

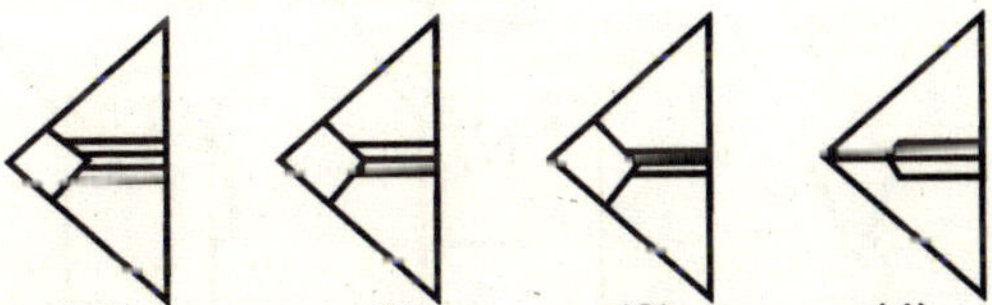

(1) (2) (3) (4)

13. Rearrange the letters on the left side to make a word that matches the clue?

AAABINR____________ (a sea)

14. In a certain code QUIZ is written as 106181 and GAME is written as 20261422. How PUZZLE is coded?

(a) 111611522 (b) 16212622
(c) 116111522 (d) 161111522

15. NOTICE is composed of NOT and ICE, neither of which has any connection with NOTICE. Below are given two three-letter words which combine to form a six-letter word. The three-letter words are defined but not the six-letter word. Find the six-letter word. For example: Male child + Trap = SONNET

Short sleep + Relative = __________ (Diaper)

16. What number should replace the question mark?

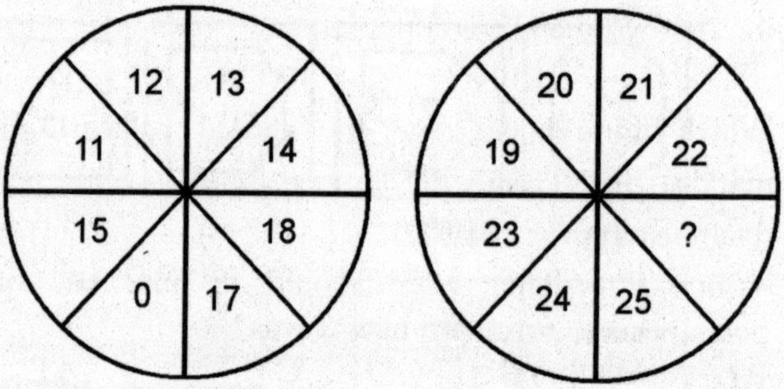

17. Which key word should replace the question mark so as to make a two-word phrase from the list of words that follows? i.e. ____?____: BAG, MARSHAL, CONDITIONING (? is AIR); [?] UP, SECOND, PERSONALITY

18. Which among the four options should occupy the position indicated by a question mark to continue the sequence?

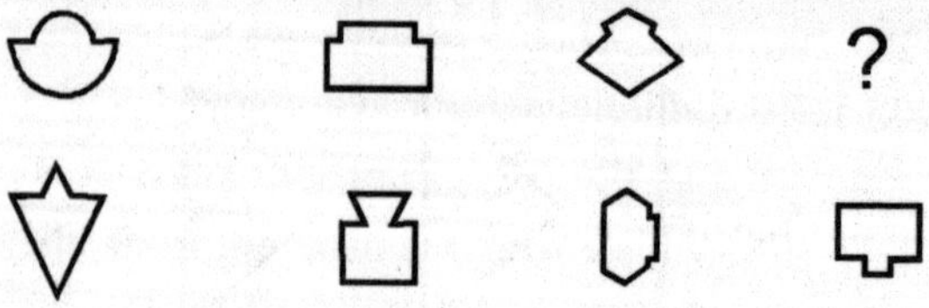

(1) (2) (3) (4)

19. Which of the four alternatives is exactly the mirror image of the object placed in front of a plane mirror AB?

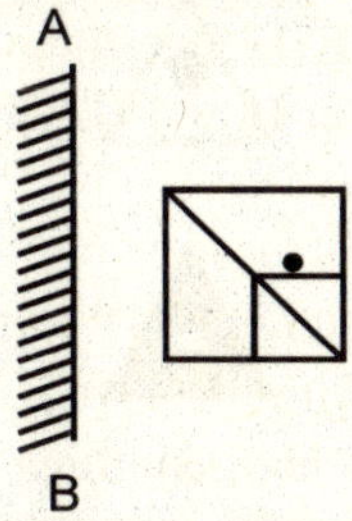

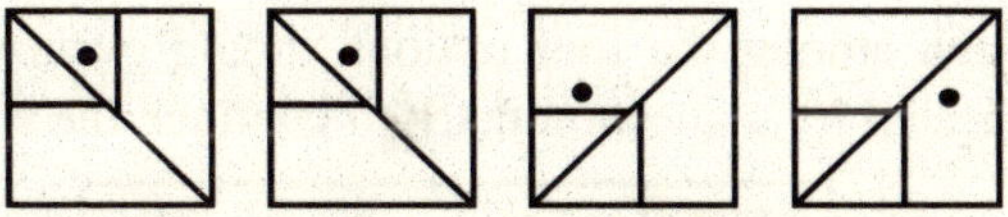

(1) (2) (3) (4)

20. Insert a three-letter word in the blank spaces which complete the first word and starts the second?

REST(__ __ __)WORK

21. Which figure in the lower row should replace the question mark so that C and the chosen figure maintain the same relationship as A and B?

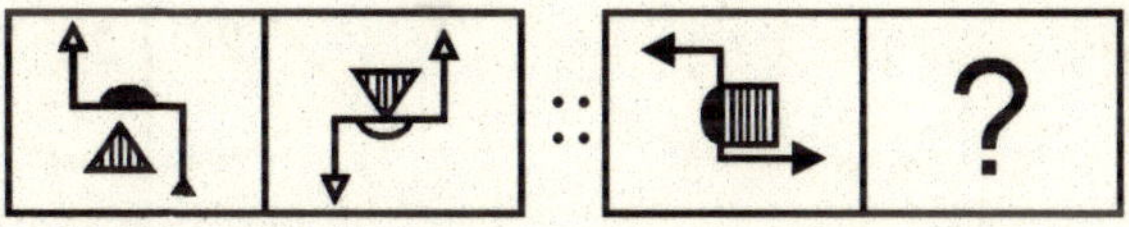

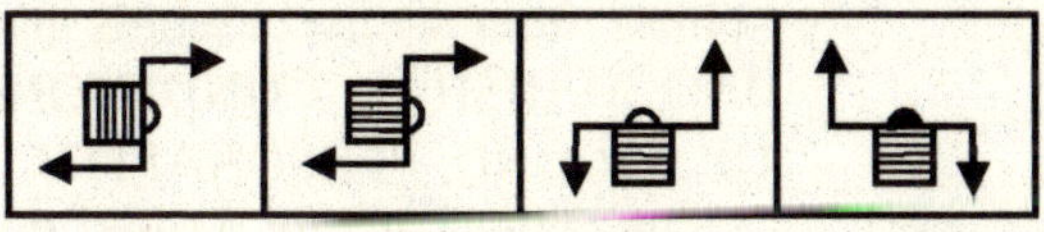

(1) (2) (3) (4)

22. The following word carries a shorter word within it in the normal sequence which conveys the same meaning as the longer word. Find the shorter synonym?

A D V A N C I N G Y E A R S

23. Find out the number which is different from others?

(a) 1/4 (b) 0.25

(c) 64/256 (d) 124/512

24. Select a figure from the four options to complete the sequence above?

(1) (2) (3) (4)

25. Which among the four options should occupy the position indicated by a question mark to continue the sequence?

(1) (2) (3) (4)

TEST-27

1. What fraction should replace the question mark?

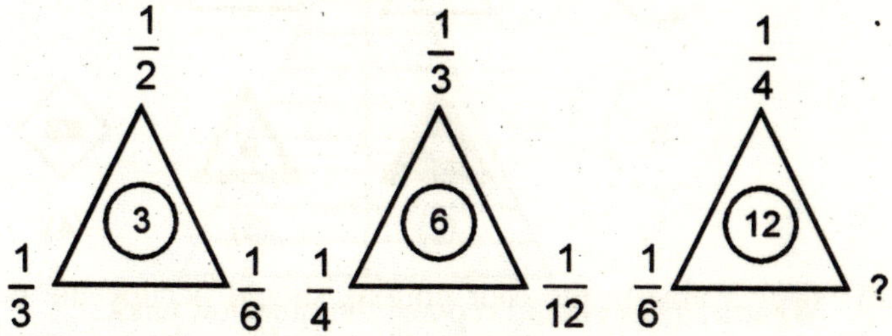

2. If V = 5, X = 10, and L = 50, what is C equal to?
3. Which figure in the lower row should replace the question mark so that C and the chosen figure maintain the same relationship as A and B?

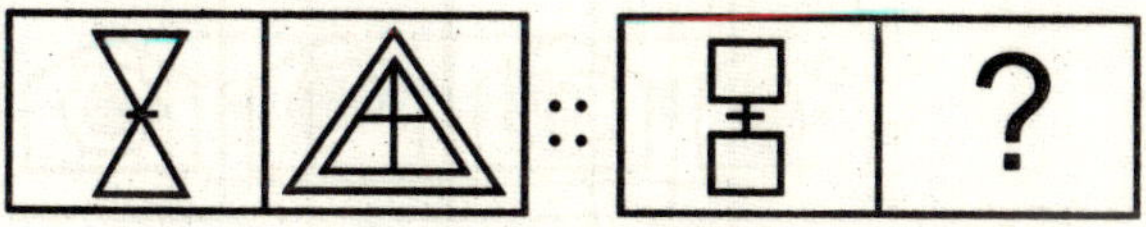

(1) (2) (3) (4)

4. Select the alternative whose numbers when placed at the missing spaces complete the following sequence?

__ 3 __ 1 __ 2 __ __ 112

(a) 23133 (b) 32113
(c) 33133 (d) 23123

5. Insert a three-letter word in the blank spaces which complete the first word and starts the second?

HOVE(__ __ __)WOOD

6. Find out the number which is different from others?
(a) 0/0
(b) 1/0
(c) 2/0
(d) 3/0

7. How many triangles are there in this figure?

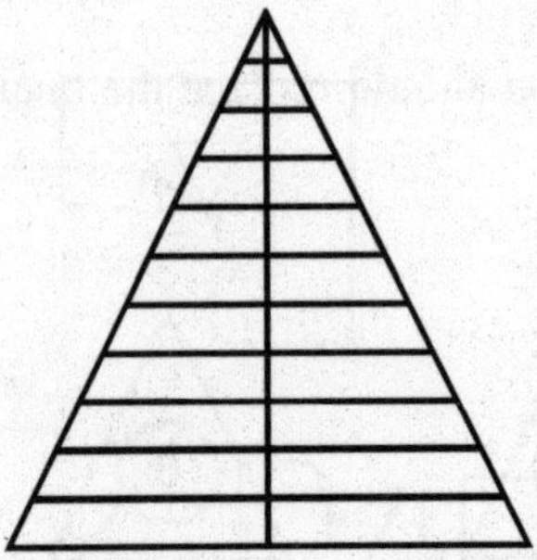

8. What number should replace the question mark?

2	5	7	14
6	3	9	18
8	8	16	32
16	16	32	?

9. Select the correct alternative that will maintain the same relationship on the two signs "::", if it is substituted for the question mark "?".

JKLM: LJMK:: TUVW: ?

(a) UTWV (b) VTWU
(c) VUTW (d) VTUW

10. Find a single word that defines both the words. For example: Quick bird would be Swift?
Throw assignment = ________

11. Which city is hidden in the following sentence?

Find or exit

12. Among the following, which number is different from others?

(a) 73826 (b) 84734
(c) 95642 (d) 16558

13. Select the correct figure among the four options to complete the first figure to make it symmetrical?

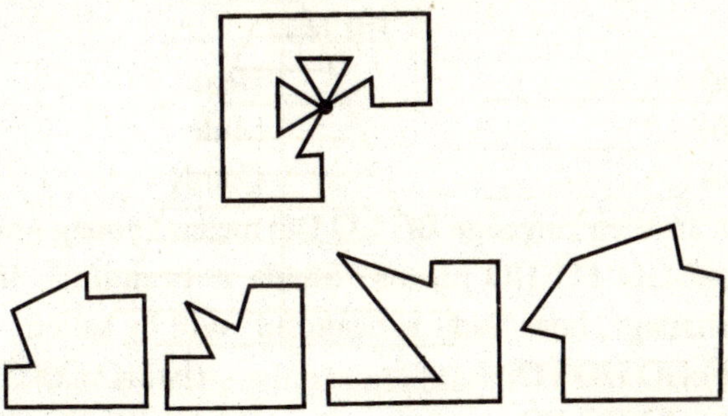

(1) (2) (3) (4)

14. A square sheet of paper is folded as shown by the dotted lines and then a hole is punched and a cut on the corner is made. Which option suggests its look when it is unfolded?

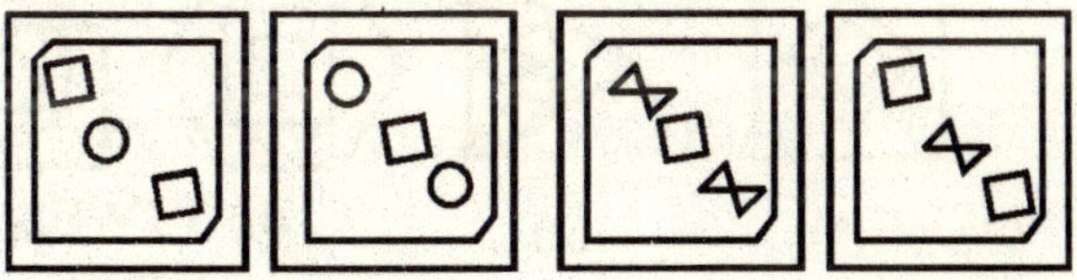

(1) (2) (3) (4)

15. Which among the four options should occupy the position indicated by a question mark to continue the same relationship?

Tendulkar: Cricket:: Sampras: ?

(a) Golf (b) Swimming

(c) Football (d) Tennis

16. The letter AACLRS when rearranged form LASCAR, RASCAL, and SACRAL. In the following group of letters rearrange the letters to form anagrams. Clues are given.

EILNST

(a) __________ Hear
(b) __________ Mute
(c) __________ Gaudy

17. In an alien language BO CO DO means "young graceful lady" and GO FO HO means "Sheila is beautiful". In the same language, how "lady is beautiful" will be called?
(a) GO HO FO (b) DO CO GO
(c) BO DO FO (d) BO FO HO

18. The following eleven-letter word contains EAG at its centre. Fill up the blanks to spell the name of former tennis champion from the USA?

__ __ __ __ EAG __ __ __ __

19. Which three-letter word should be inserted within the parenthesis to form two new words?

K (__ __ __) N
S (__ __ __) Y

20. Which among the following figures is different from others?

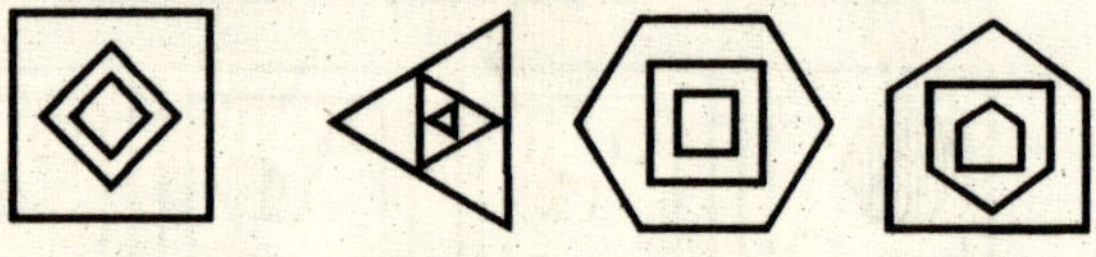

(1) (2) (3) (4)

21. The first three letters of the following word are missing. Find out the missing letters to form a word?

__ __ __ IOD

22. Put the key word in each box to make a two-word phrase from the list of words that precede. For example:
ZERO/LUNCH/ELEVENTH [HOUR]
GARDEN/LABOUR/TEA [ ]

23. Change the position of one of the digits in the equation 62 - 63 in such a way that the result is 1?

24. **Which of the four alternatives is exactly the mirror image of the object placed in front of a plane mirror?**

(1) (2) (3) (4)

25. **Select a figure from the four options to complete the sequence above?**

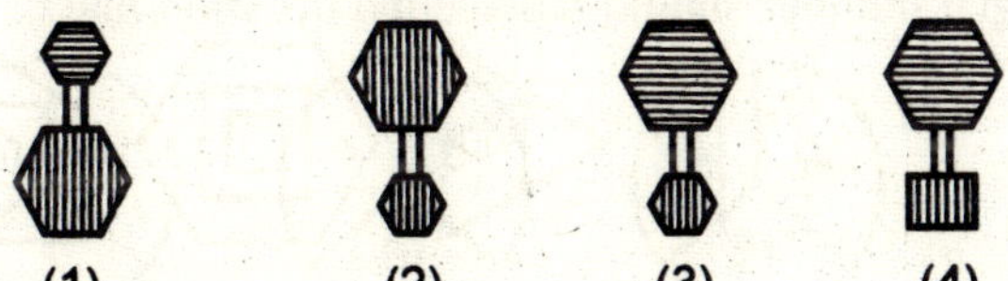

(1) (2) (3) (4)

TEST-28

1. Select the correct alternative that will maintain the same relationship on the two signs "::", if it is substituted for the question mark "?".

   Earth: Planet:: Pluto: ?

   (a) Satellite (b) Comet
   (c) Minor planet (d) Planet

2. A square sheet of paper is folded as shown by the dotted lines and then a hole is punched and cuts are made. Which option suggests its look when it is unfolded?

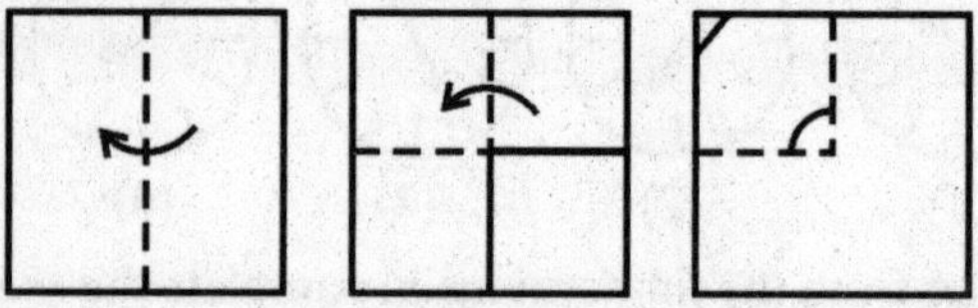

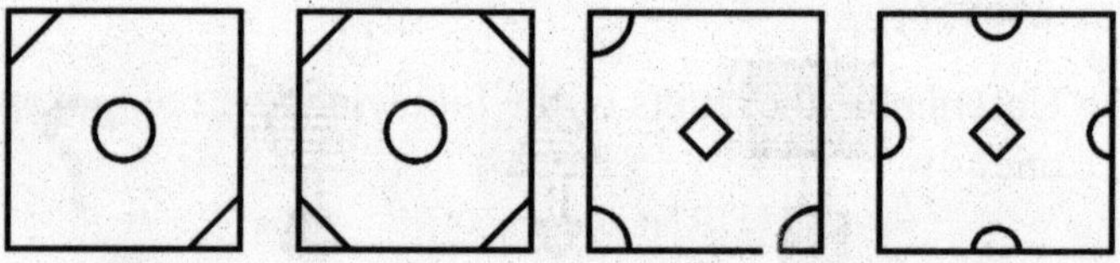

(1) (2) (3) (4)

3. What number should replace the question mark?

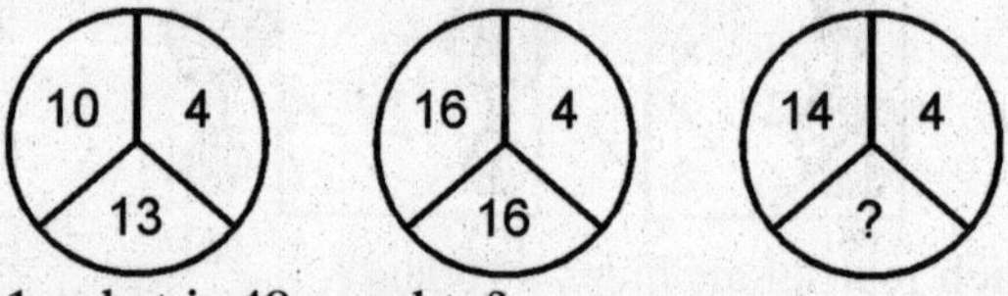

4. If 11 =11, what is 49 equal to?
5. Put the key word in each box to make a two-word phrase from the list of words that precede. For example:

   ZERO/LUNCH/ELEVENTH [HOUR]
   FLY/BETTER/CENTRE [ ]

6. Which word has the same property as PERCOLATION?

   (a) INCORPOREAL (b) CORRELATION
   (c) NEOTROPICAL (d) COOPERATION

7. Find out the missing number?

   0, 4, 18, 48, 100,?

8. If DRY = 29 (12.5), what is WET?

9. Select the alternative whose letters when placed at the missing spaces complete the following sequence?

__ l __ m __ k __ l __ n

(a) klnml (b) kllmn

(c) knlml (d) knllm

10. Expand the following word equation?

18C of M

11. Which three-letter word should be inserted within the parenthesis to form two new words?

R (___ ___ ___) E

S (___ ___ ___) H

12. Which among the following figures is different from others?

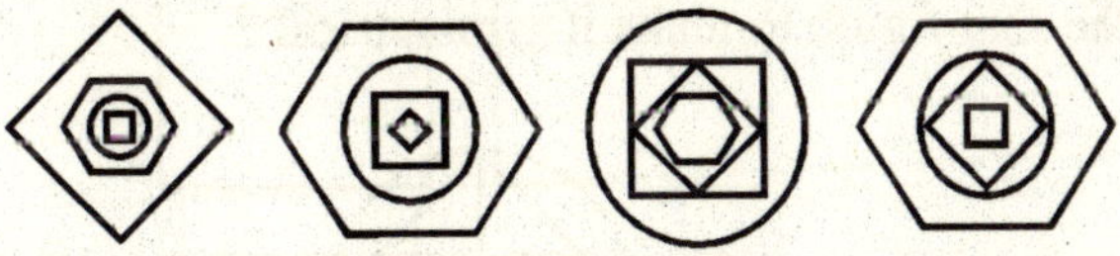

(1) (2) (3) (4)

13. Unscramble the letters of the following word to make a new one?

TURNER____________

14. What number should replace the question mark?

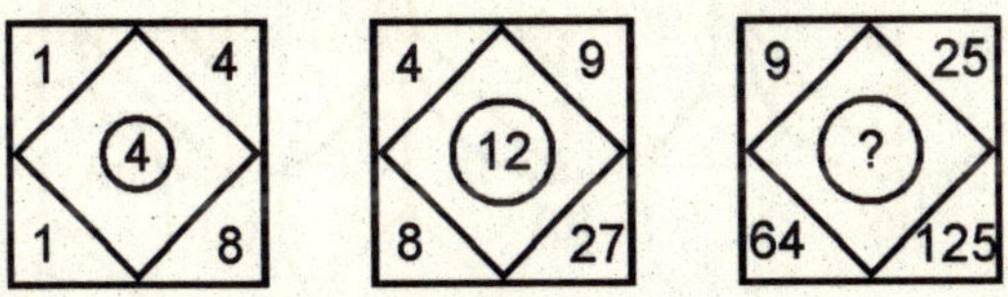

15. Which martial art hides a rodent?

16. Which among the four options should occupy the position indicated by a question mark to continue the sequence?

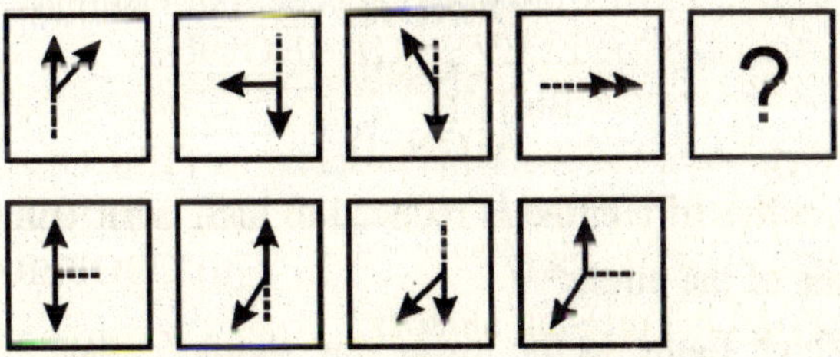

(1) (2) (3) (4)

17. Select the correct alternative that will maintain the same relationship on the two signs "::", if it is substituted for the question mark "?".

HLPT: CGKO:: ?: NRVZ

(a) BFJP (b) AEIN

(c) JNRW (d) MQUV

18. Find a single word that defines both the words. An example: Quick bird would be swift?

Stingy average = ________

19. Select the correct figure among the four options to complete the first figure to make it symmetrical ?

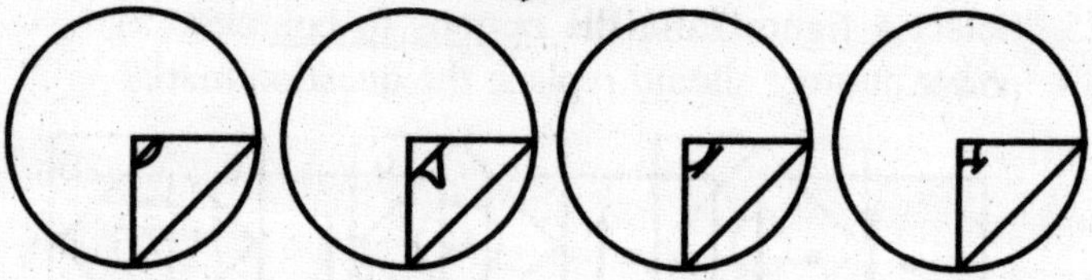

(a) (b) (c) (d)

20. Which among the following words is different from others?

FRIEGHT

DENOTE

CANINE

ATONED

21. If radius of a circle is reduced to half, what will be the new area of the circle?

22. Which figure in the lower row should replace the question

mark so that C and the chosen figure maintain the same relationship as A and B?

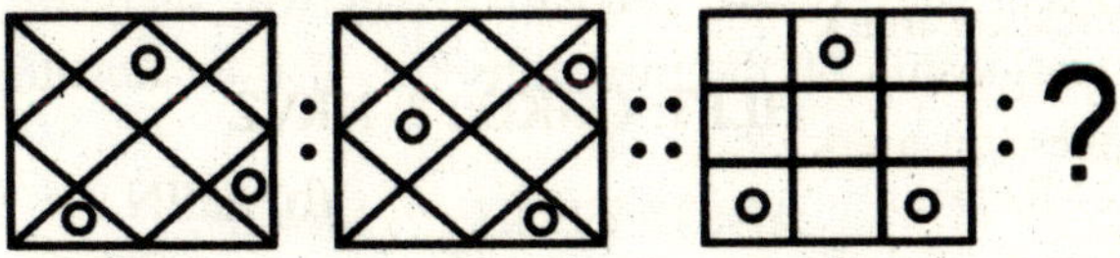

A B C

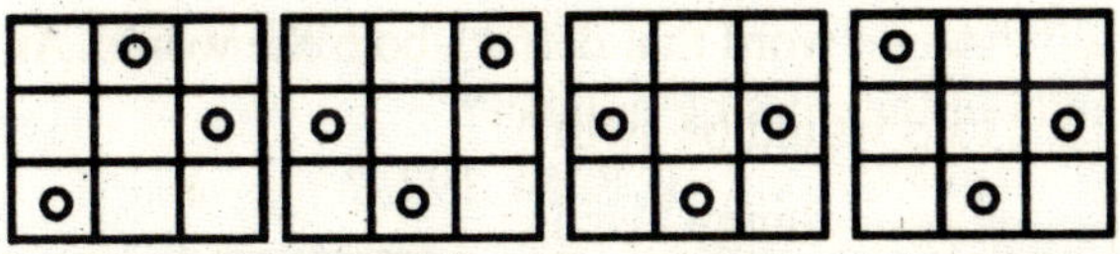

(1) (2) (3) (4)

23. Insert a three-letter word in the blank spaces which complete the first word and starts the second?

LIFT(__ __ __)HOOD

24. The following eleven-letter word contains RIM at its centre. Fill up the blanks to spell the name of an instrument that measures heat energy?

__ __ __ __ RIM __ __ __ __

25. Select a figure from the options to complete the sequence above.

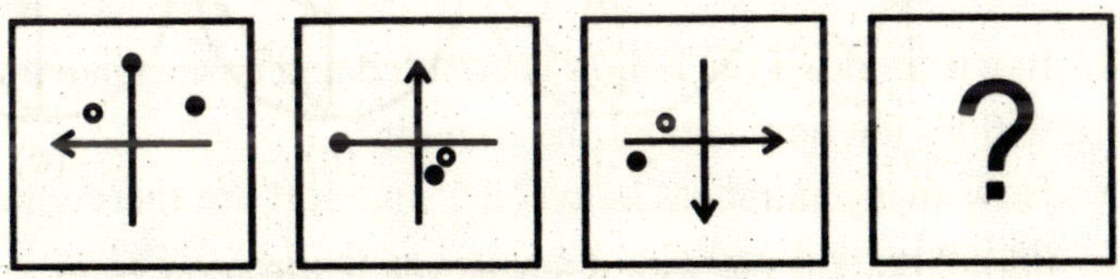

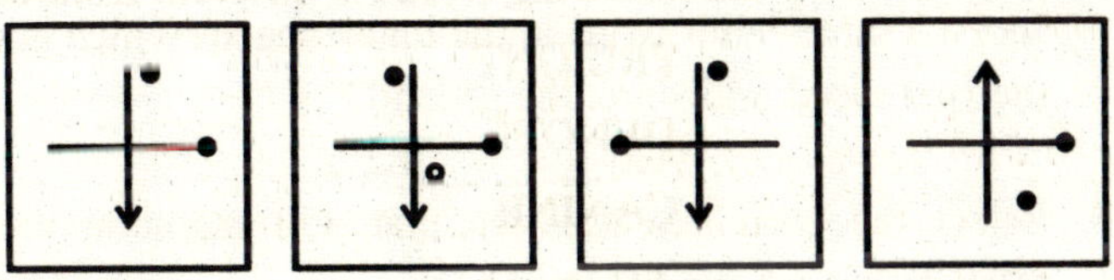

(a) (b) (c) (d)

TEST-29

1. Select the correct alternative that will maintain the same relationship on the two signs "::", if it is substituted for the question mark "?".

ABCD: EFGH:: ?: MNOP

(a) IJLM (b) IJLN
(c) IJKL (d) JKLN

2. Find out the missing number?

0, 8, 54, 192, ?

3. Which figure replaces the question mark to continue the sequence?

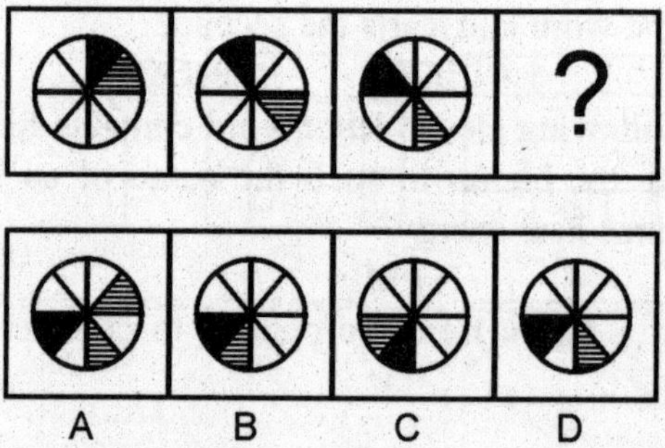

4. In a triangle, if the height is doubled and base is halved, what will be the new area of the triangle?
5. How many numbers between 1 and 100 are there which are divisible by 4 and also having 4 as the last digit?
6. Insert a three-letter word in the blank spaces which complete the first word and starts the second?

PAR(__ __ __)KEY

7. Select the correct alternative that will maintain the same relationship on the two signs "::", if it is substituted for the question mark "?".

Australia: Kangaroo:: ?: Panda

(a) Botswana (b) Spain
(c) China (d) Indonesia

8. What number should replace the question mark?

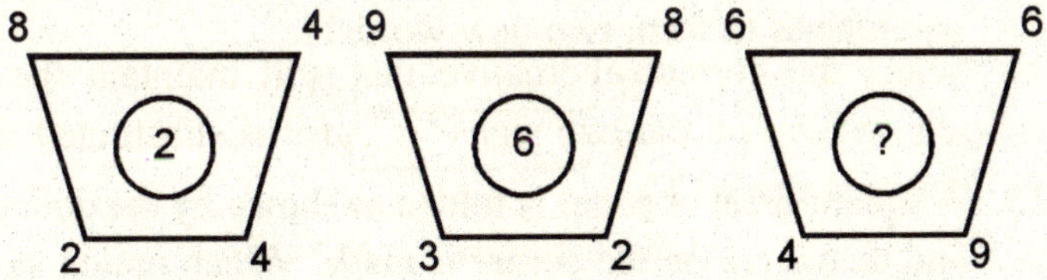

9. The following word carries a shorter word within it in the normal sequence which conveys the same meaning as the longer word. Find the shorter synonym?

INSTRUCTOR

10. Which figure in the lower row should replace the question mark so that C and the chosen figure maintain the same relationship as A and B?

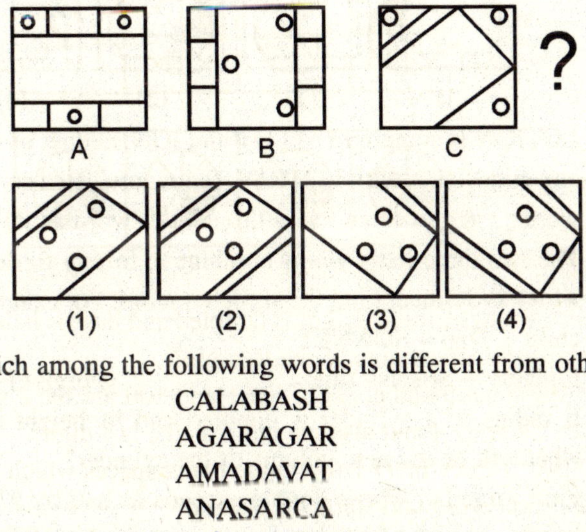

11. Which among the following words is different from others?

CALABASH
AGARAGAR
AMADAVAT
ANASARCA

12. The first three letters of the following word are missing. Find out the missing letters to form a word?

___ ___ ___ IFF

13. What are the values of "P" and "Q" in the following sum?

$$\begin{array}{r} 694P \\ 2Q93 \\ \hline 9541 \end{array}$$

14. Which three-letter word should be inserted within the parenthesis to form two new words?

R (___ ___ ___) D

W (___ ___ ___) R

15. A square sheet of paper is folded as shown by the dotted lines and then a cut on the corner is made. Which option suggests its look when it is unfolded?

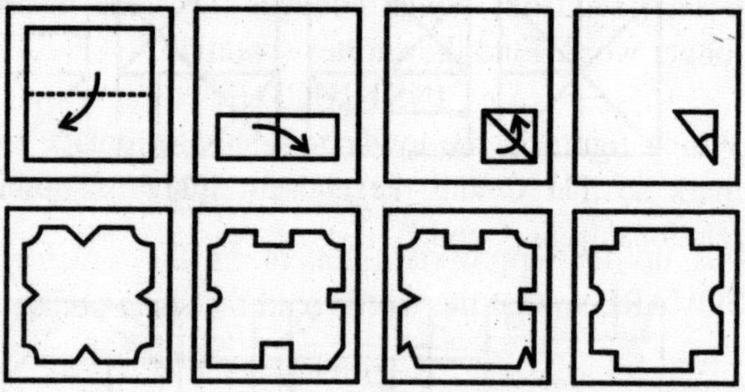

(1) (2) (3) (4)

16. LOTION is composed of LOT and ION, neither of which has any connection with LOTION. Below are listed some pair of words, each of them has a three-letter word as its meaning. The two three-letter words combine to form a six-letter word which is defined. Find the six-letter word. For example: Male child + Trap = SONNET

Equality + Spanish title = ___________ (Forgive)

17. If radius of a cylinder is doubled and its height is halved, what will be the new volume of the cylinder?

18. Find a number whose double exceeds its half by 9?

19. Put the key word in each box to make a Two-Word Phrase from the list of words that precede. For example:

FRENCH/INDUSTRIAL/GREEN | REVOLUTION |

CURRY/FACE/WASHING | |

20. Rearrange the letters of KAMPALA ROLE to reveal the name of a Bollywood actor who acted as the Defence Minister in the film *Aks*?

21. Which of the four alternatives is exactly the mirror image of the object placed in front of a plane mirror?

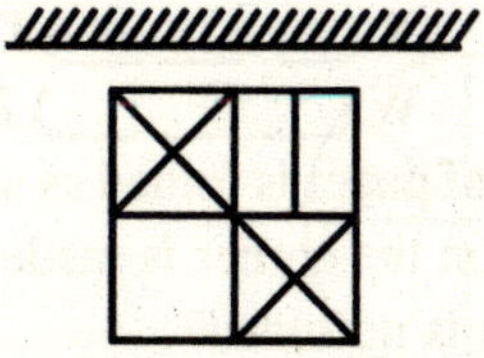

(1) (2) (3) (4)

22. Fill up the appropriate letters in the following WORD SQUARE so that the words read the same across and down?

	M	P	
M		L	
P			A
	T	A	

23. In a certain code ACE is written as 2610, how is FAB written in that code?

24. Select a figure from the options to complete the sequence above?

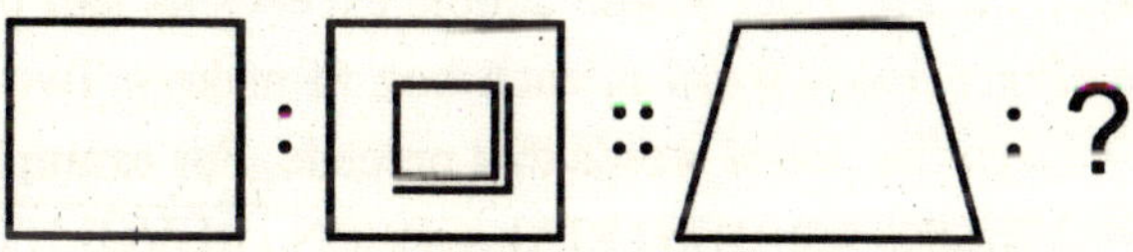

(a) (b) (c) (d) (e)

25. Select the correct figure among the four options to complete the first figure to make it symmetrical?

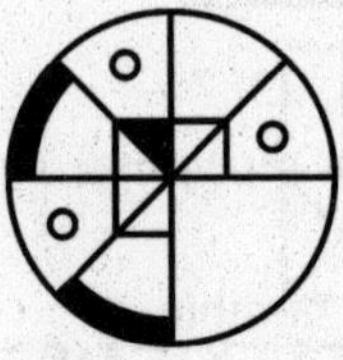

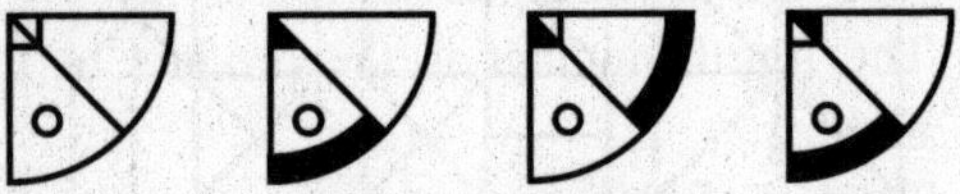

(1) (2) (3) (4)

TEST-30

1. Find the missing number?

   –1, 1, 4, 9, 14, 23, ?

2. Find a six-digit number, without repeating any digit with the following information:
   (a) Half of the digits are prime number.
   (b) One-half of the digits are even.
   (c) The fourth number is the product of the 2nd and 3rd number.
   (d) Total of all the six digits is a cubic number.
   (e) This six-digit number when multiplied by 2, 3, 4, 5, and 6 yields the numbers with same digits in cyclic order.

3. A sheet of rectangular paper when folded twice appears to be as in the Problem Figure. When one fold is removed, how it will look like among the four Answer Figures?

Problem Figure

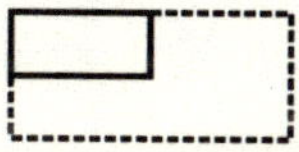

Answer Figures

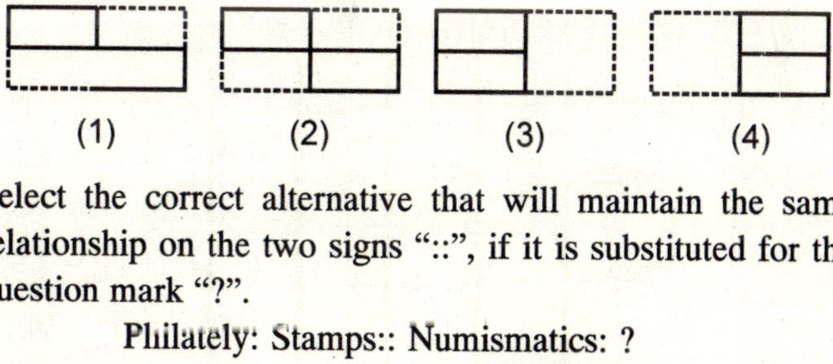

(1) (2) (3) (4)

4. Select the correct alternative that will maintain the same relationship on the two signs "::", if it is substituted for the question mark "?".

   Philately: Stamps:: Numismatics: ?

   (a) Maps (b) Pens
   (c) Posters (d) Coins

5. Which among the following groups of letters is different from others?

   (a) TRSQ (b) JHIK
   (c) KIJL (d) YWXZ

6. If π = x, ρ = +, ψ = –, and σ = ÷, then find the value of 7π4ρ16ψ4σ4?

7. What number should replace the question mark?

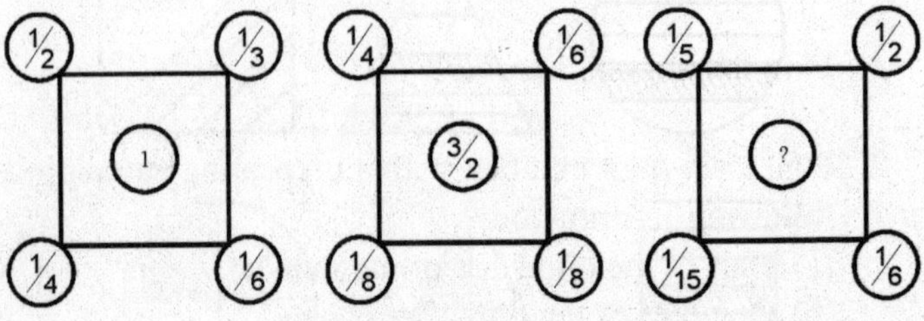

8. Which among the following cricketer is different from others?

AFRIDI

ANKOLA

ARJUNA

ARSHAD

9. Put the key word in each box to make a Two-Word Phrase from the list of words that precede. For example: ZERO/ LUNCH/ELEVENTH [HOUR]

FRENCH/INDUSTRIAL/GREEN [ ]

10. Which among the following figures is different from others?

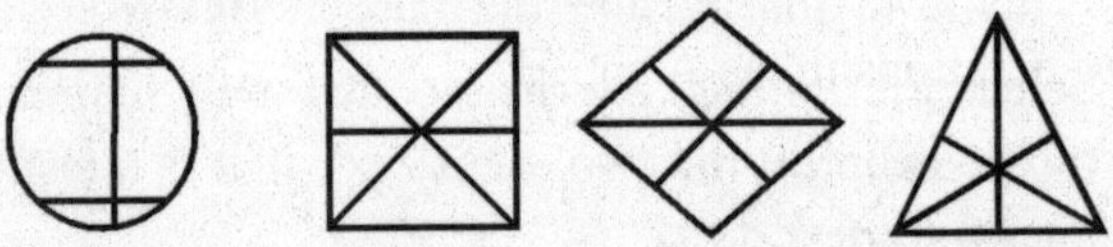

(1) (2) (3) (4)

11. Which among the following countries is different from others?

IRAN, PERU, LAOS, IRAQ

12. The first three letters of the following word are missing. Find out the missing letters to form a word?

___ ___ ___ HOR

13. Which figure comes next?

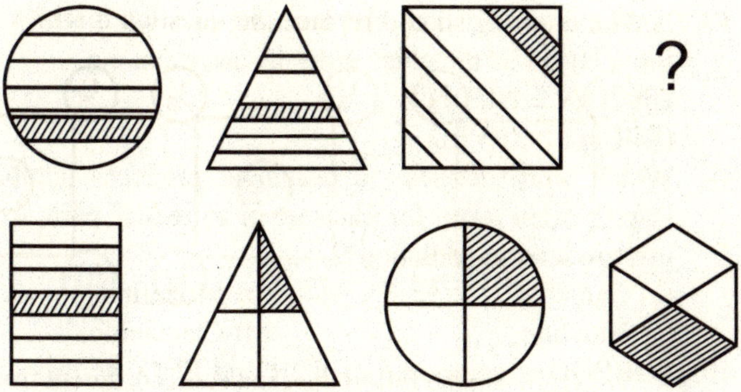

A B C D

14. What number should replace the question mark?

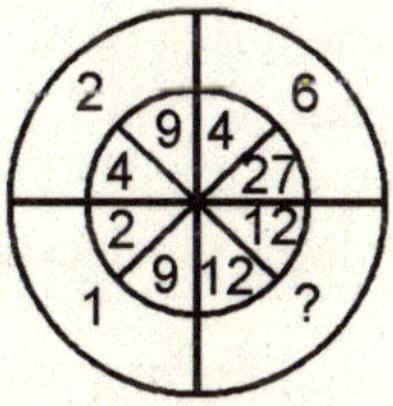

15. Which three-letter word should be inserted within the parenthesis to form two new words?

M (___ ___ ___) Y
L (___ ___ ___) R

16. Which figure in the lower row should replace the question mark so that C and the chosen figure maintain the same relationship as A and B?

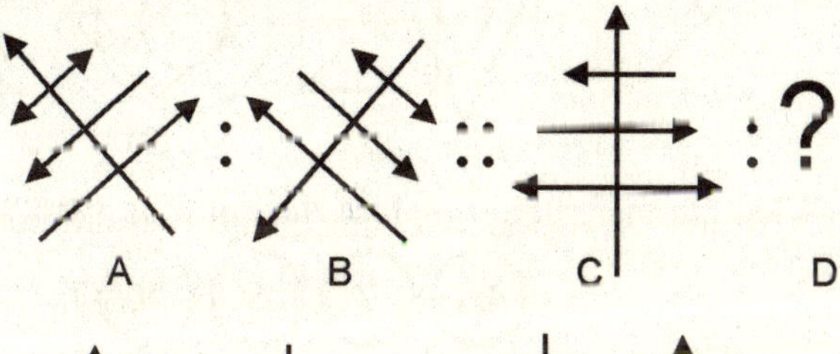

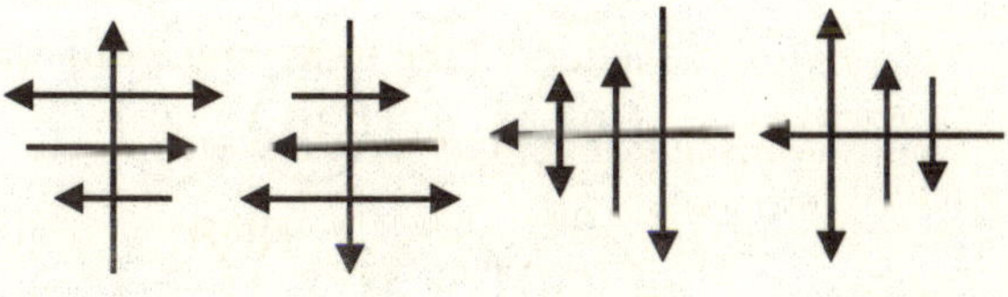

(1) (2) (3) (4)

17. A clue is preceded by the meaning of a word which has the same letters as the clue. Write its anagram, e.g.
UNTIDY = NUDITY
(Seller) : NERVED = __________

18. Which word defines, "a drug that produces numbness or stupor; often taken for pleasure or to reduce pain; extensive use can lead to addiction"?
(a) Cannibis (b) Modafinil
(c) Narcotic (d) Cannabinoids

19. FOREGO is composed of FOR and EGO, neither of which has any connection with FOREGO. Below are listed some pair of words, each of them has a three-letter word as its meaning.. The two three-letter words combine to form a six-letter word which is defined. Find the six-letter word. For example: Male child + Trap = SONNET
Join + Conducted = __________ (Deranged)

20. Which figure replaces the question mark?

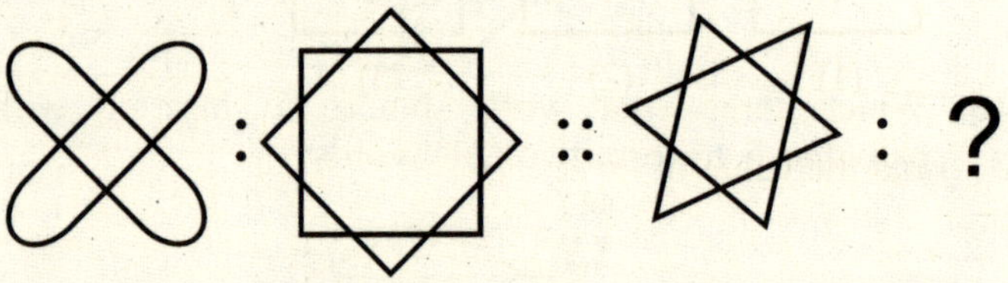

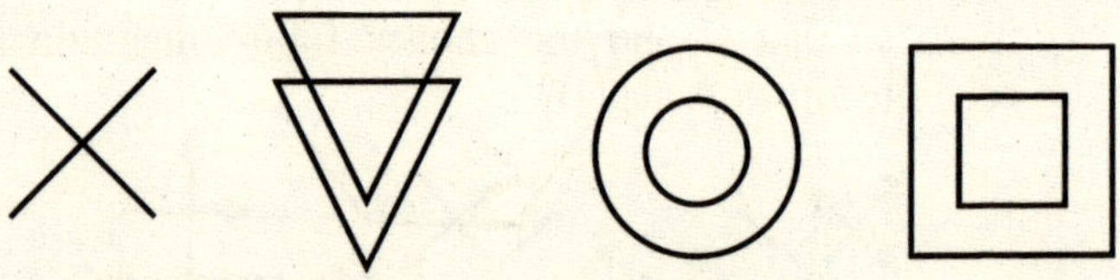

(a) (b) (c) (d)

21. What number should replace the question mark?

34	7	5	10
68	5	10	2
108	9	9	?

22. Find a single word that defines both the words. For example: Quick bird would be SWIFT.

Clear web ____________

23. The following 12-letter word contains ARD at its centre. Now the remaining nine blank spaces when rearrange forms two words: A REAL INCH. Fill up the blanks to spell the name of the first Indian hockey goalkeeper in the Olympics?

__ __ __ __ A R D __ __ __ __ __

24. Which among the four options should occupy the position indicated by a question mark to continue the sequence?

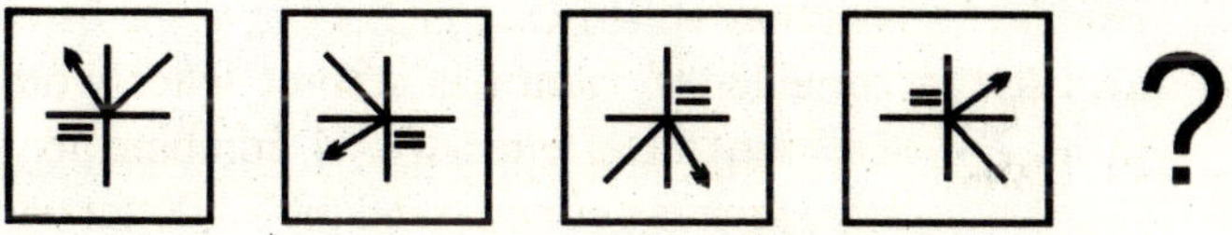

(1) (2) (3) (4)

25. Find the value of 'x'.

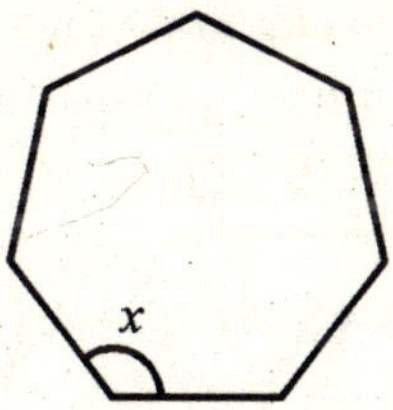

❑

TEST-31

1. Find the group which is different from others?

   (a) JE (b) OK

   (c) UQ (d) QM

2. Expand the following word equation?

   100S of D

3. Can you decipher an eight-letter word with the following clues?

   (a) The first three letters means 'alias'.

   (b) The 2nd, 3rd, 4th, and 5th letters form a goddess who was wife of Shiva.

   (c) The 3rd, 4th, and 5th letters form a person who was fourth caliph of Islam.

   (d) The 5th and 6th letters are short for an American state, Gem State.

   (e) the 7th letter is a blood group.

   (f) the last letter is one more than the square of 7.

   (g) The whole word is a political party of India.

4. What numbers should replace the question marks?

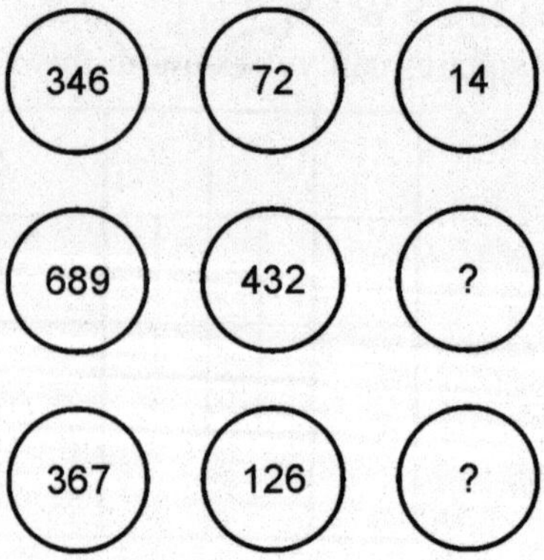

5. A sheet of paper when folded twice appears to be as in the Problem Figure. When one fold is removed, how it will look like among the four Answer Figures?

Problem Figure

Answer Figures

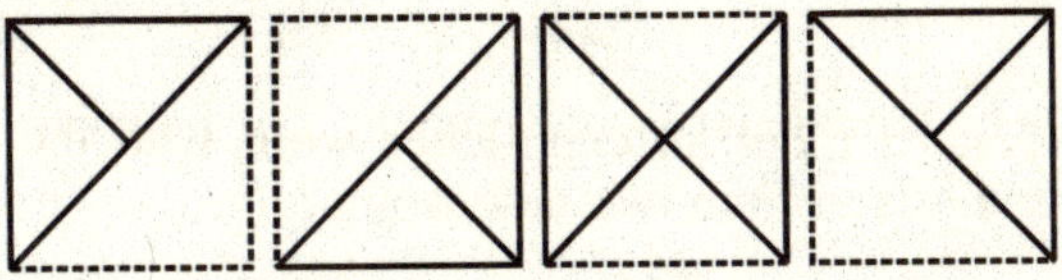

(1) (2) (3) (4)

6. What digit should be placed in front of a number 23076 so that it becomes four times than when the same digit is placed at the end of this number?
7. The first three letters of the following word are missing. Find out the missing letters to form a word.

___ ___ ___ OUP

8. Which among the following words is different from others?

AAACDN
AAAMNP
AABCIR
AABIMZ

9. Which letter should replace the question mark to continue the sequence?

Q U A Y Z I N C S W I M V E T ?

10. How many squares can you count in this figure?

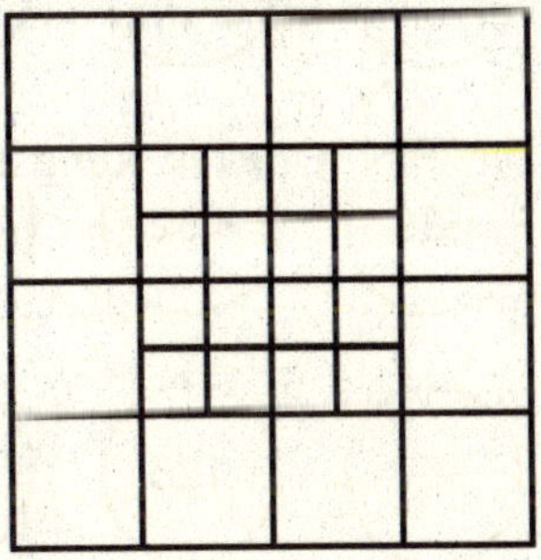

11. Find out the missing number?

100, 99, 95, 86, 70, 45, ?

12. Which among the following figures is different from others?

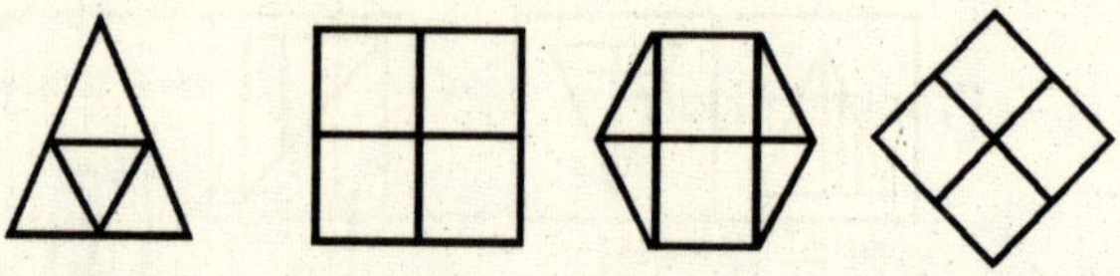

(1) (2) (3) (4)

13. Which three-letter word should be inserted within the parenthesis to form two new words?

B (___ ___ ___) N

C (___ ___ ___) D

14. If COBRA is GSFVE, then what is SNAKE?

(a) WREOI (b) WREOJ

(c) WREPI (d) WREPJ

15. What three digits should be placed at the question marks so that the following two conditions are satisfied?

167 + ??? = 495

(i) The equation should be true.

(ii) All the nine digits should be different.

16. Make three meaningful seven-letter words from the following set of letters?

ADEEGNR ________

________ ________

17. Select the correct alternative which when substituted for the question mark maintain the same relationship on both the sides of the sign "::".

Hockey: ? :: Cricket: Ranji Trophy

(a) Santosh Trophy (b) Charminar Trophy

(c) Rovers Cup (d) Aga Khan Cup

18. If CAT = 3/2 ½ 10 then what is FOX?

(a) 7/2 8 14 (b) 3. 7½ 12

(c) 3 8 11½ (d) 3. 6. 12½

19. Which figure in the lower row should replace the question mark so that C and the chosen figure maintain the same relationship as A and B?

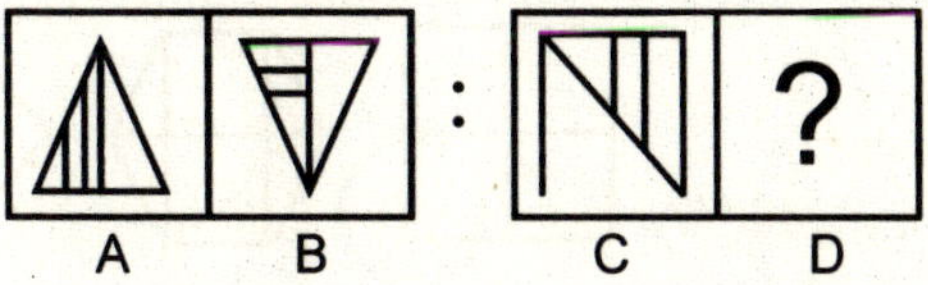

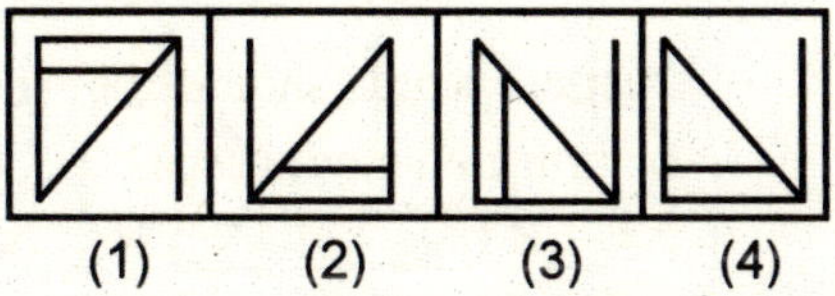

20. Find the number which replaces the qucstion mark.

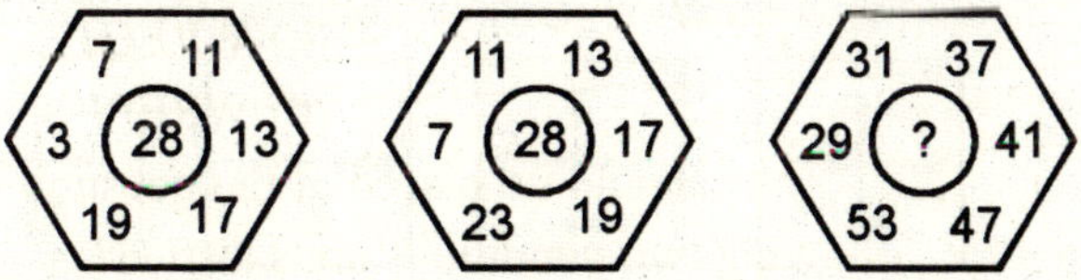

21. GALORE is composed of GAL and ORE, neither of which has any connection with GALORE. Below are listed some pair of words, each of them has a three-letter word as its meaning. The two three-letter words combine to form a six-letter word which is defined. Find the six-letter word. For example: Male child + Trap = SONNET

Fragment + Five times two = __________ (Corroded)

22. Which figure replace the question mark?

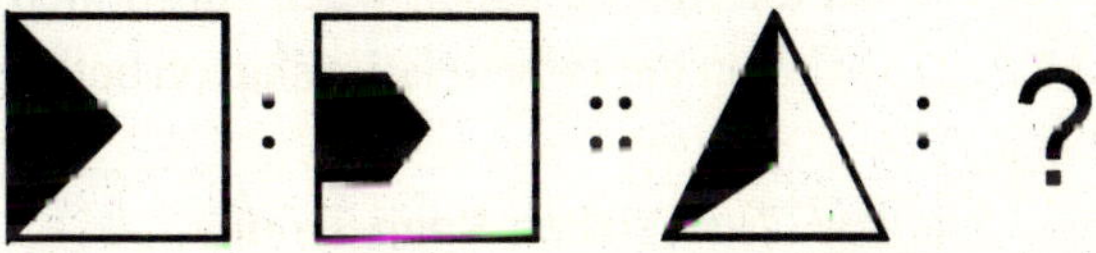

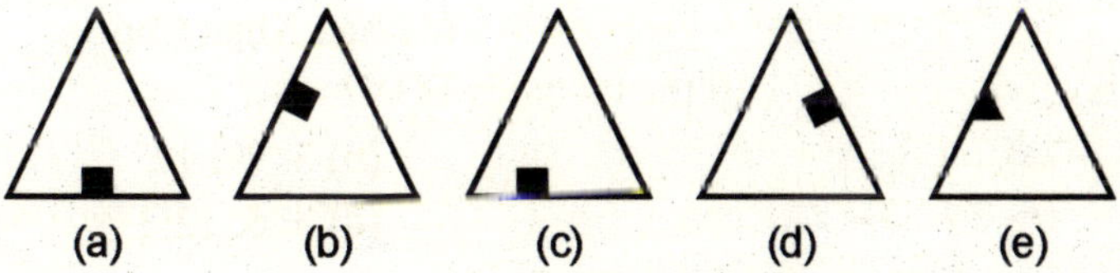

23. Which city is hidden in the following sentence?
Isaac crazy for chess.

24. Which of the four alternatives is exactly the mirror image of the object placed in front of a plane mirror?

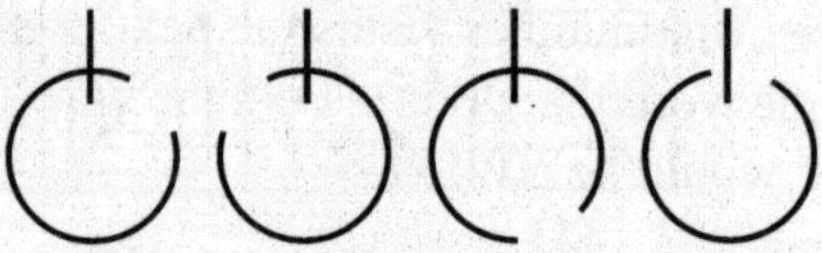

(1) (2) (3) (4)

25. Which among the four options should occupy the position indicated by a question mark to continue the sequence?

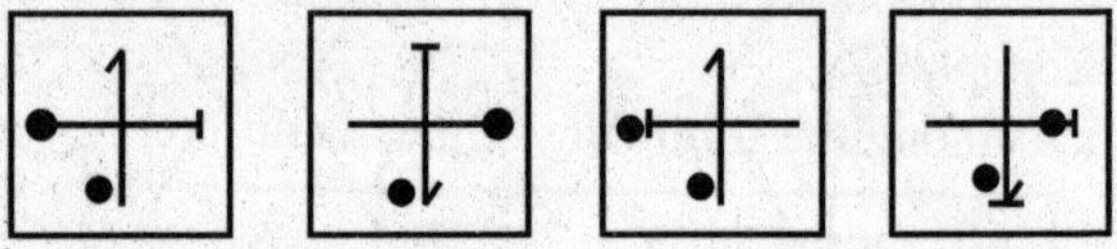

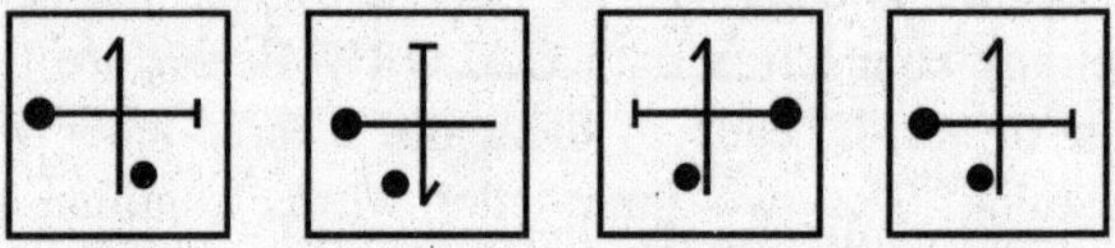

(1) (2) (3) (4)

❑

TEST-32

1. Make word to match the definition by putting letters in the blank spaces?

   ___ ___ ___ ___ ANT = Brave

2. What are two successive prime numbers in which the square of the first number when added to the second number yields a prime number, and the square of the second number when added to the first number yields the next prime number?
3. Find a single word that defines both the words. For example : Quick bird would be SWIFT.

   Dismiss bag ____________
4. Which psychological term indicates the fear of foreigners or strangers?

   (a) Cynophobia (b) Homophobia
   (c) Xenophobia (d) Gynophobia
5. Which among the following figures is different from others?

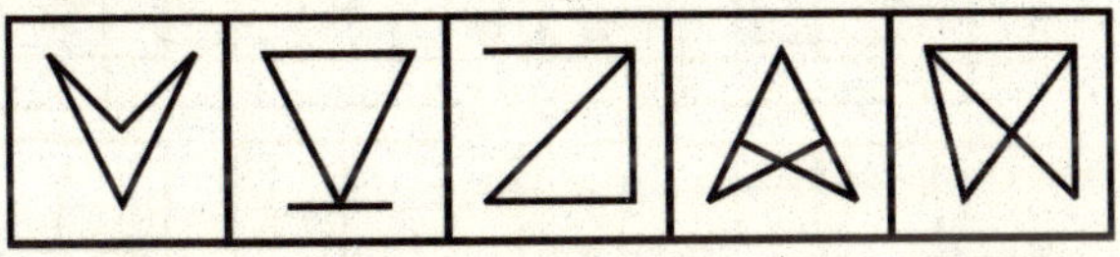

(a) (b) (c) (d) (e)

6. Find out the missing number?

   3, 15, 35, ?, 99, 143
7. Which among the following words is different from others?

   CUPRITE
   DEVISER
   REFOUND
   DEPRIVE
8. Which among the following letters is different from others?

   C H O P S

   (a) C (b) H
   (c) P (d) S
9. The following word carries a shorter word within it in the normal sequence which conveys the same meaning as the longer word. Find the shorter synonym?

   DESTRUCTION

10. Insert a three-letter word in the blank spaces which complete the first word and starts the second.

CURT(_ _ _)MENT

11. Which figure in the lower row should replace the question mark so that C and the chosen figure maintain the same relationship as A and B?

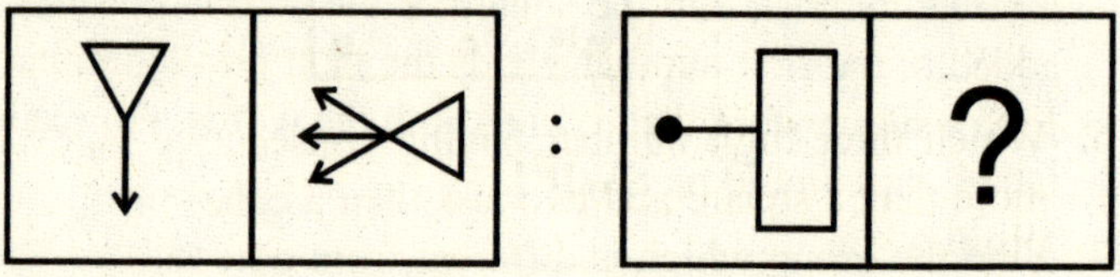

A B C D

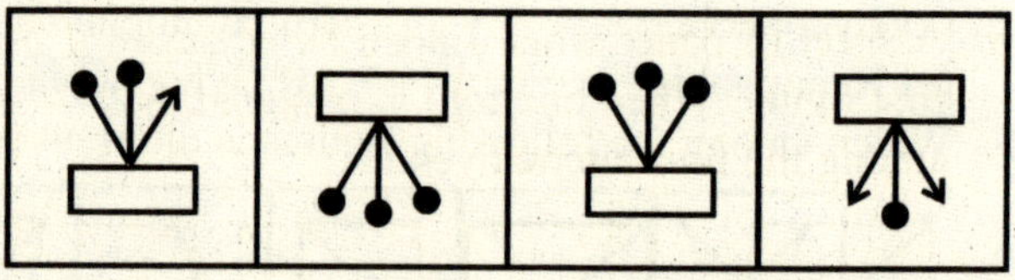

(1) (2) (3) (4)

12. A table fan is bought in ₹ 300 and the mechanic took ₹ 50 to fix it. At what price should it be sold to have a gain of ₹ 125?

13. Find out the number which is different from others?

(a) 0

(b) 4

(c) 18

(d) 49

14. Which among the following figures is different from others?

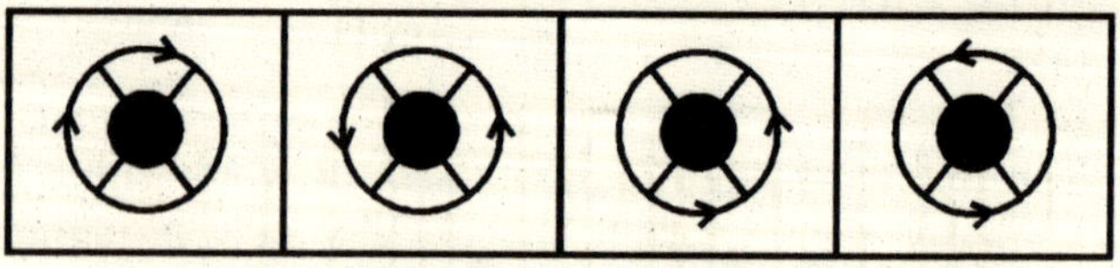

A B C D

15. How can you divide this figure into four parts so that each part contains three black dot and all the four parts are identical in shape and size?

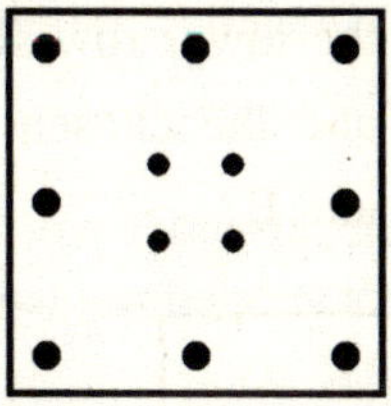

16. Which three-digit number having consecutive digits is two more than a square and two less than a cube?
17. Find the group which is different from others?

(a) FJ (b) DI
(c) OT (d) UZ

18. A sheet of paper when folded twice appears to be as in the first figure. When one fold is removed, how it will look like among the four alternatives?

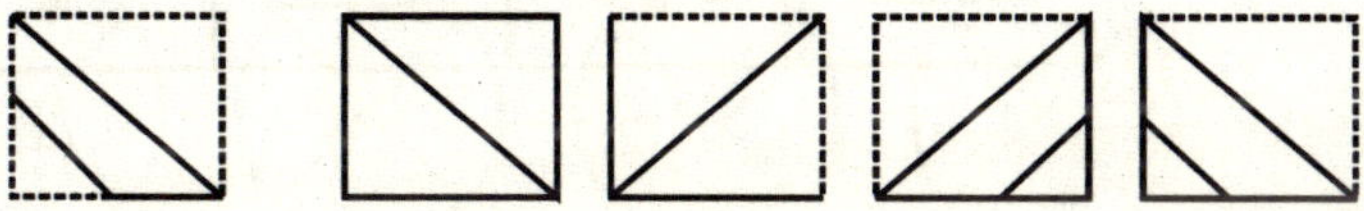

(1) (2) (3) (4)

19. Which letter should be placed before and after the following word so that a new word is formed?

___ EARL ___

20. Which among the four options should occupy the position indicated by a question mark to continue the sequence?

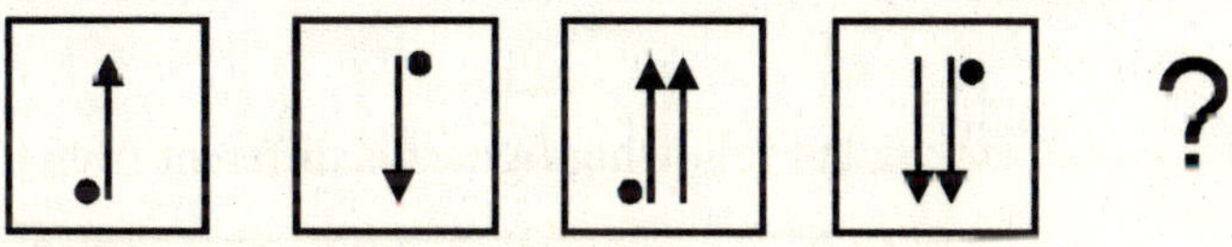

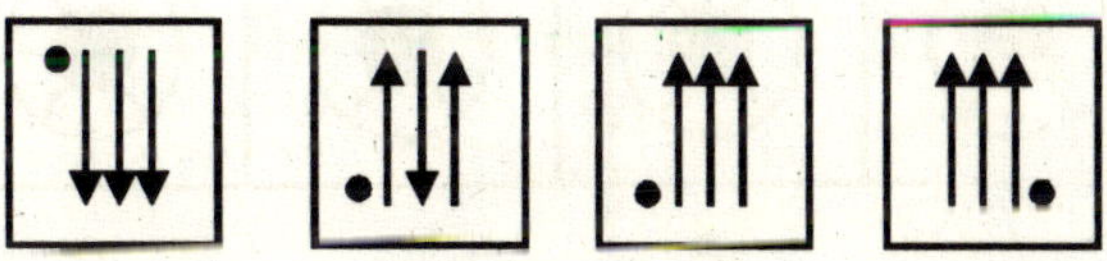

(1) (2) (3) (4)

21. Select the correct alternative which when substituted for the question mark maintain the same relationship on both the sides of the sign "::"?

Calligraphy: Graphically:: Incorporate: ?

(a) Co-operation (b) Provocative
(c) Callousness (d) Procreation

22. The following eleven-letter word contains AYK at its centre. Fill up the blanks to spell the name of one of the most loved Bollywood actors?

___ ___ ___ ___ AYK ___ ___ ___ ___

23. Which among the four options should occupy the position indicated by a question mark to continue the sequence?

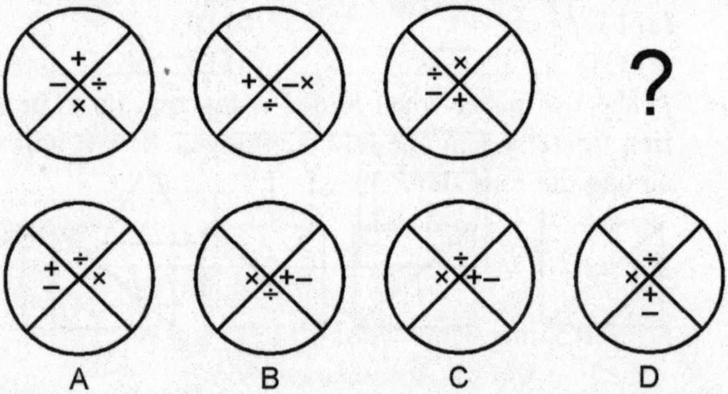

24. Insert a three-letter word in the blank spaces which complete the first word and starts the second?

INT(__ __ __)ION

25. Which among the four options should occupy the position indicated by a question mark to continue the sequence?

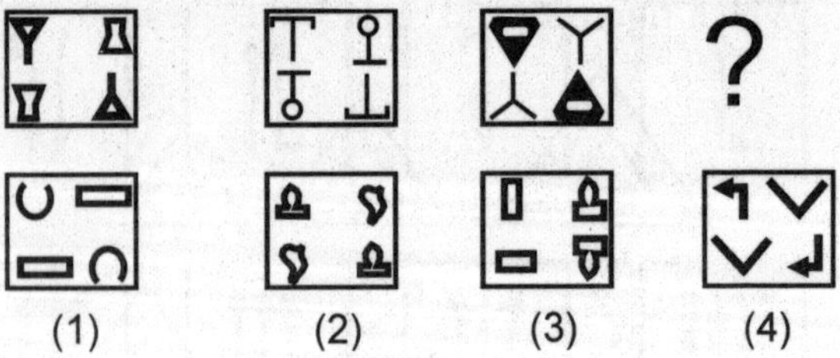

TEST-33

1. Which number is different from others?
   (a) 17
   (b) 35
   (c) 44
   (d) 65
2. Which figure in the lower row should replace the question mark so that C and the chosen figure maintain the same relationship as A and B?

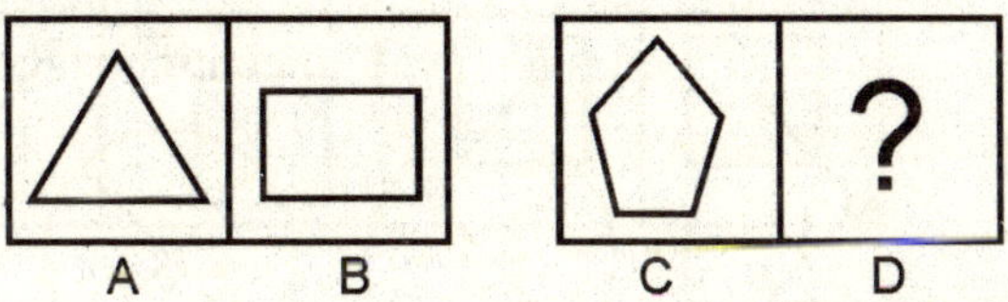

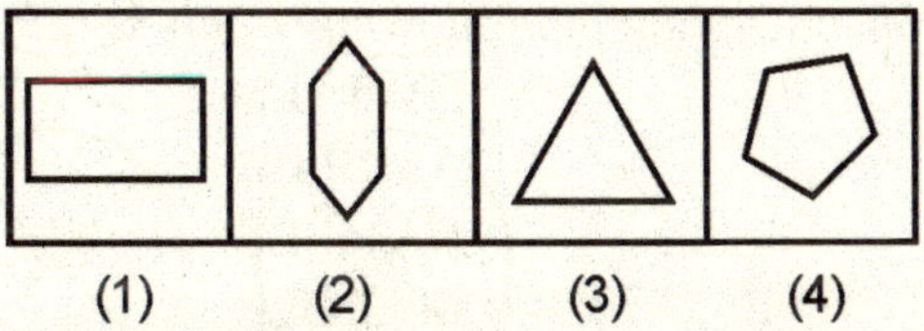

3. Insert a three-letter word in the vacant spaces which complete the first word and starts the second?

   CART(_ _ _)LESS
4. The following word carries a shorter word within it in the normal sequence which conveys the same meaning as the longer word. Find the shorter synonym.

   CURTAIL
5. Which figure should replace the question mark?

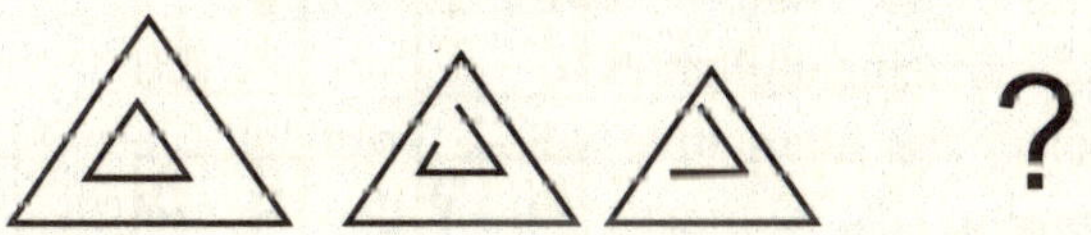

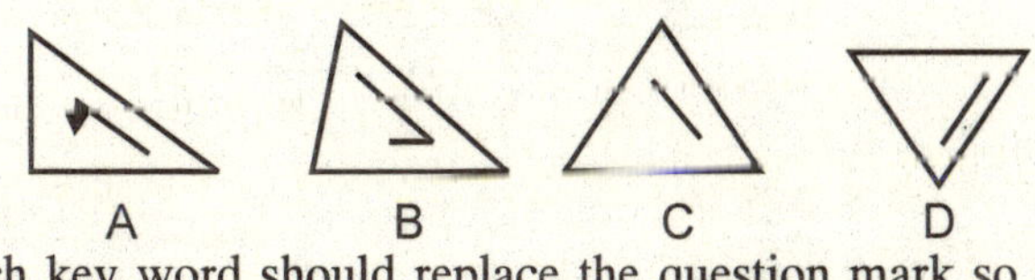

6. Which key word should replace the question mark so as to

make a two-word phrase from the list of words that follows, i.e. [?]: BAG, MARSHAL, CONDITIONING
(? is AIR)
RIGHT, BERMUDA, PASCAL [?]

7. Which among the following words is different from others?
OVERHAULING
ULTRAVIOLET
FACETIOUS
DISCOURAGE

8. Which among the following figures is different from others?

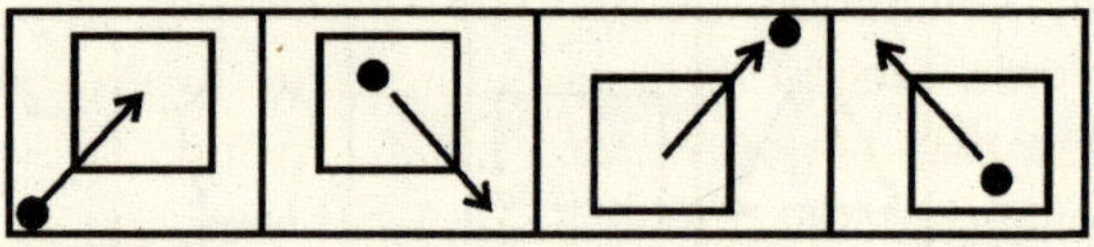

A B C D

9. Which among the following words is different from others?
EMBALM
AMBLER
RAMBLE
MARBLE

10. Select the correct alternative that will maintain the same relationship on the two signs "::", if it is substituted for the question mark "?".

?: MNO:: BCD: TUV

(a) CDE (b) GHJ
(c) EFH (d) BCE

11. Find a single word that defines both the words. For example: Quick bird would be Swift.
Advertisement charges = ________

12. Select the alternative whose fractions when placed at the missing spaces complete the following sequence?

$$\_\frac{5}{8}\_\frac{7}{8}\_\frac{7}{8}\_\frac{5}{8}\_\frac{3}{8}$$

(a) $\frac{5}{8}.\frac{5}{8}.\frac{3}{8}.\frac{5}{8}.\frac{7}{8}$ (b) $\frac{5}{8}.\frac{5}{8}.\frac{7}{8}.\frac{3}{8}.\frac{5}{8}$

(c) $\frac{7}{8}, \frac{5}{8}, \frac{3}{8}, \frac{5}{8}, \frac{7}{8}$ (d) $\frac{7}{8}, \frac{5}{8}, \frac{3}{8}, \frac{7}{8}, \frac{5}{8}$

13. How many small cubes of 2 cm size can be cut from a cube of side 6 cm?

14. Find the missing number?

    4, 7, 13, 22, 34, ?

15. Make a seven-letter word consisting of these letters only.

    CDEILMO?

16. BITTEN is composed of BIT and TEN, neither of which has any connection with BITTEN. Below are listed some pair of words, each of them has a three-letter word as its meaning. The two 3-letter words combine to form a six-letter word which is defined. Find the six-letter word. For example: Male child + Trap = SONNET

    Posses + a number = ___________ (Hurry)

17. Find the number which replaces the question mark?

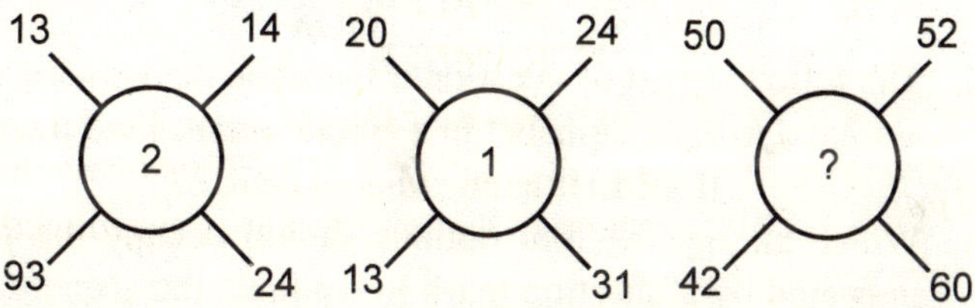

18. Unscramble the letters of the following word to make a new one?

    HORNET

    ____

19. Which among the following figures is different from others?

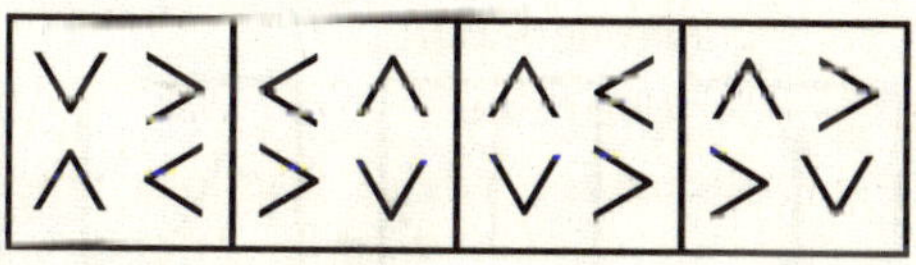

(a) (b) (c) (d)

20. Which three-letter word should be inserted within the parenthesis to form two new words?

    L (___ ___ ___) N

    P (___ ___ ___) L

21. Which alphabet is to be transplanted from the following pair of words so as to get mutual synonym? For example, in the pair AGE & RANGER, if 'R' from the second word is removed and add to the first word it becomes RAGE which is synonym of ANGER.

TINE and BID

22. Which among the four options should occupy the position indicated by a question mark to continue the sequence?

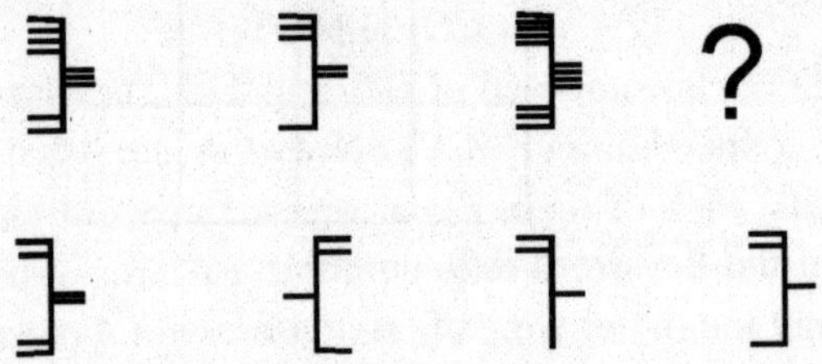

(1) (2) (3) (4)

23. The first three letters of the following six-letter word are missing. Find out the missing letters to form a word.

___ ___ ___ GUR

24. The following set of question is based on the numerical value assigned to each alphabet in a certain order. Find the answer.

If DELHI is 38, what is PARIS?

25. Which among the four options should occupy the position indicated by a question mark to continue the sequence?

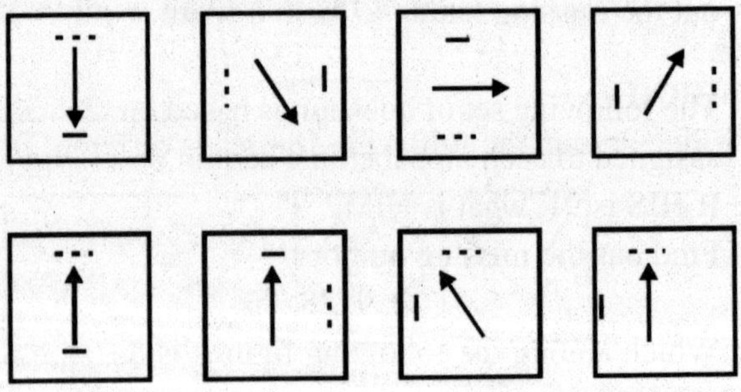

(1) (2) (3) (4)

❑

TEST-34

1. Find the number which replaces the question mark?

			14
21			
	32		
			?

2. Put the key word in each box to make a Two-Word Phrase from the list of words that precede. For example:

   FLEA/BLACK/COMMON [MARKET]

   SICK/MATERNITY/FRENCH [   ]

3. Which two figures are similar?

(1) (2) (3) (4) (5) (6) (7)

4. The first two letters of the following word are missing. Find out the missing letters to form a word.

   __ __ VOC

5. The following set of question is based on the numerical value assigned to each alphabet in a certain order. Find the answer? If HIS is 91, what is HIM?

6. Find out the missing number?

   2, 9, 28, 65, ?

7. Which among the following figures is different from others?

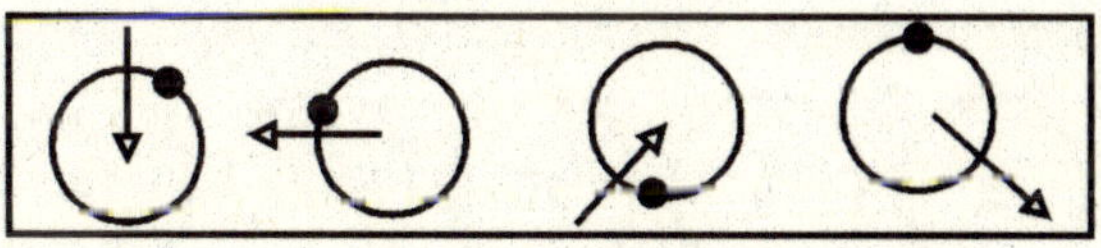

A B C D

8. Solve the following equation?
$8^2 \times 47^2 = abc376$
where a, b, and c are square numbers.
9. Select the alternative whose letters when placed at the missing spaces complete the following sequence?

__ b __ a __ b __ ab

(a) abba (b) abaa
(c) bbaa (d) abab

10. Rearrange the letters of the words WOMAN HITLER to make a new word to describe an important relation in a family?
11. Which figure in the lower row should replace the question mark so that C and the chosen figure maintain the same relationship as A and B?

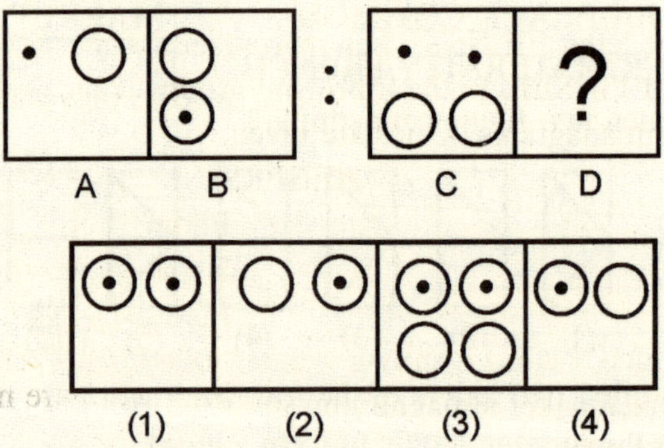

12. The first two letters of the following four-letter word are missing. Find out the missing letters to form a word?

__ __ RU

13. Make a nine-letter words by filling the blank spaces; the word describes a flaming torch which is used in processions at night?

__ __ __ __ __ EAUX

14. Find the number which replaces the question mark?

15. Which three-letter word should be inserted within the parenthesis to form two new words?

V (___ ___ ___) A

S (___ ___ ___) Y

16. Which among the four options should occupy the position indicated by a question mark to continue the sequence?

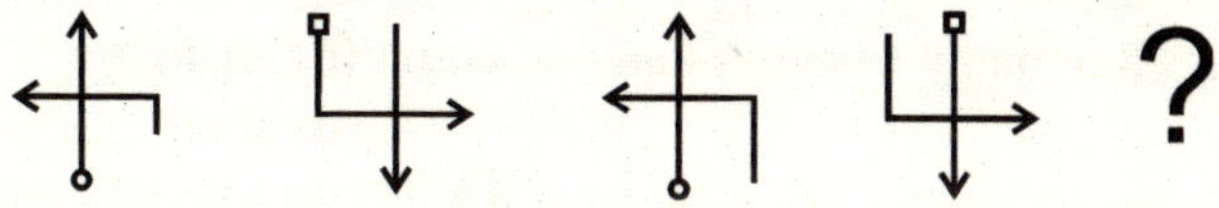

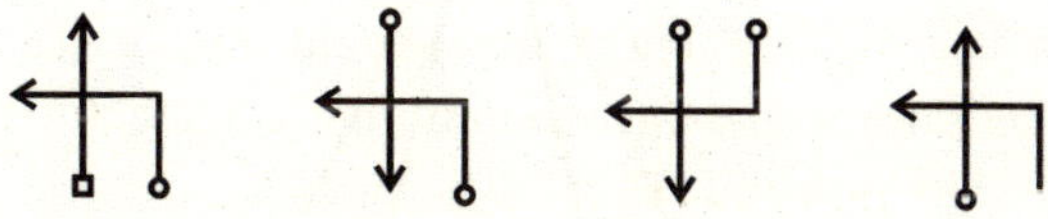

(1) (2) (3) (4)

17. The letter EILNST when rearranged form LISTEN, SILENT, and TINSEL. In the following groups rearrange the letters to form anagrams. Clues are given.

AEHPRS

(a) ____________ Idiom

(b) ____________ Nepalese mountaineer

(c) ____________ Metal-shaping machine

18. Which word among the following best describes 'watchmaker's magnifying glass?

(a) Loupe (b) Kerb

(c) Frit (d) Schooner

19. TATTOO is composed of TAT and TOO, neither of which has any connection with TATTOO. Below are listed some pair of words, each of them has a three-letter word as its meaning. The two three letter words combine to form a six-letter word which is defined. Find the six-letter word. For example: Male child + Trap= SONNET

Fate + Charged particle = ____________ (A wash)

20. Which among the following letter is different from others?

H	A	L	L	O

21. Choose the missing number ("?") from the given alternatives?

3, 6, 11, 18, ?

(a) 25
(b) 27
(c) 29
(d) 31

22. How many triangles can you count in this figure?

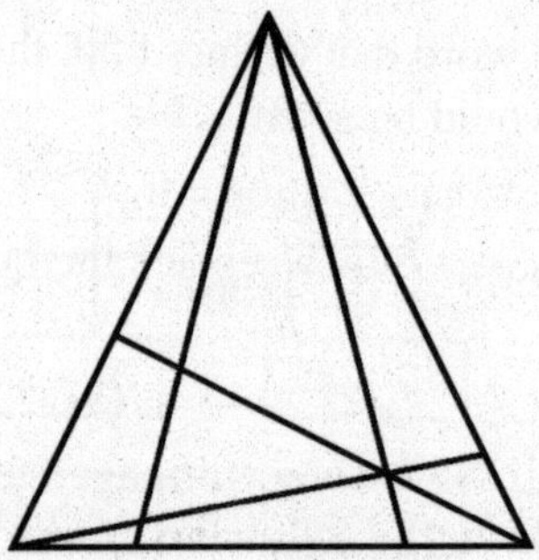

23. Which letter should be placed before and after the following word so that a new word is formed?

__IVI__

24. Which of the four alternatives is exactly the mirror image of the object placed in front of a plane mirror AB?

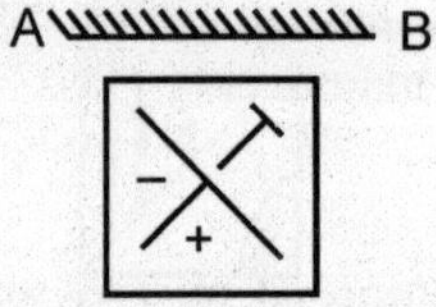

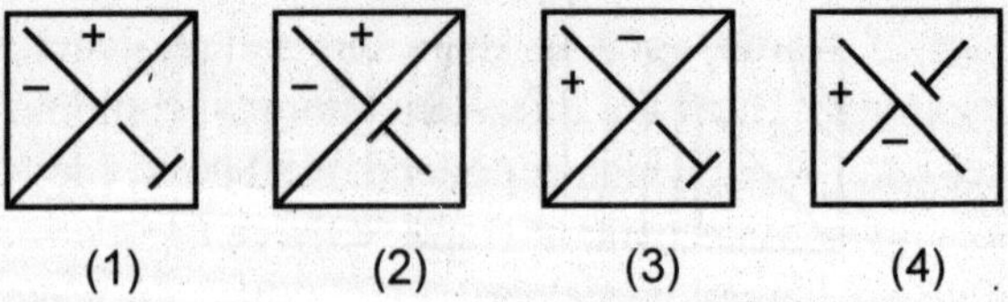

(1) (2) (3) (4)

25. What does glyptography deals with?

(a) Carving (b) Caving
(c) Stoning (d) Glazing

TEST-35

1. Find out the missing letters ("?")?

   a, o, b, p, c, q, ?, ?

   (a) d, n

   (b) p, d

   (c) d, r

   (d) d, q

2. Find a single word that defines both the words. For example: Quick bird would be swift.

   Costly darling = ______

3. Find the numbers which replace the question marks?

   12 × 42 ÷ 21 × 24 = 1

   23 × 64 ÷ 32 × 46 = 1

   46 × 96 ÷ ? × ? = 1

4. Which of the four alternatives is exactly the mirror image of the object placed in front of a plane mirror?

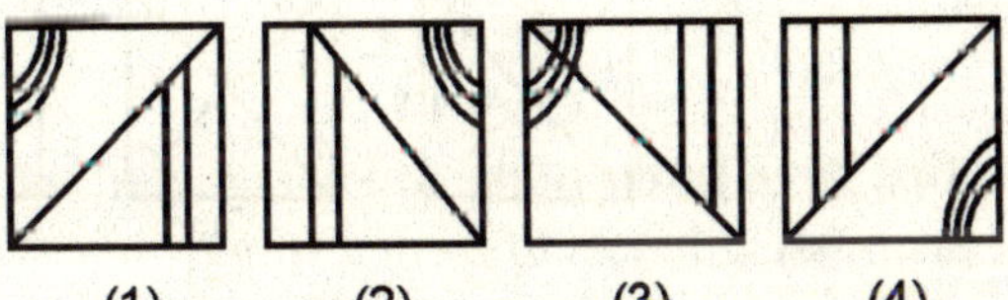

(1) (2) (3) (4)

5. The first three letters of the following word are missing. Find out the missing letters to form a word?

   ___ ___ ___ STE

6. What numbers should replace the question mark?

7. Select the correct alternative that will maintain the same relationship on the two **signs** "::", if it is substituted for the question mark "?".

GFJK: HGKL:: IHLM: ?

(a) JINM (b) JIMN

(c) JMIN (d) JMNI

8. Which among the following figures is different from others?

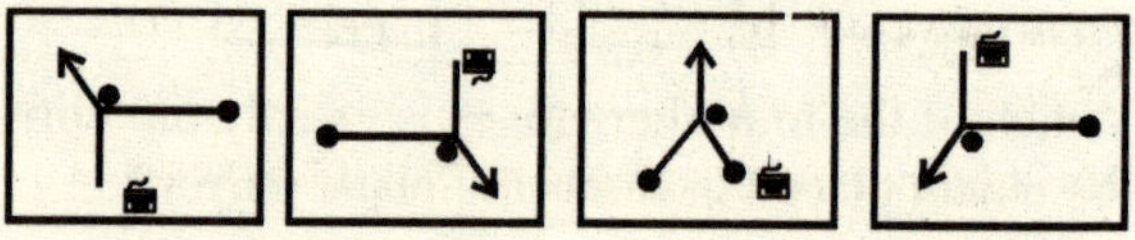

(1) (2) (3) (4)

9. What should be the next letter in this letter series?

R T Y U I ?

10. Which among the following words is different from others?

ANVIL

CAVIL

DEVIL

CIVIL

11. The first three letters of the following word are missing. Find out the missing letters to form a word?

__ ___ ___ BDA

12. Choose the missing number ("?") from the given alternatives?

9216, 4608, 2304, 1152, 576, ?

(a) 298

(b) 288
(c) 278
(d) 268

13. Which figure in the lower row should replace the question mark so that C and the chosen figure maintain the same relationship as A and B?

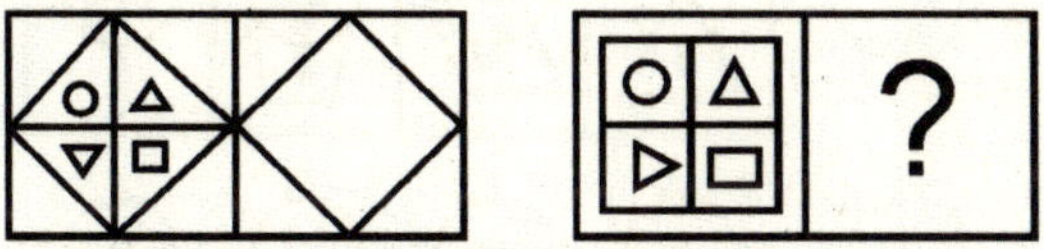

A B C D

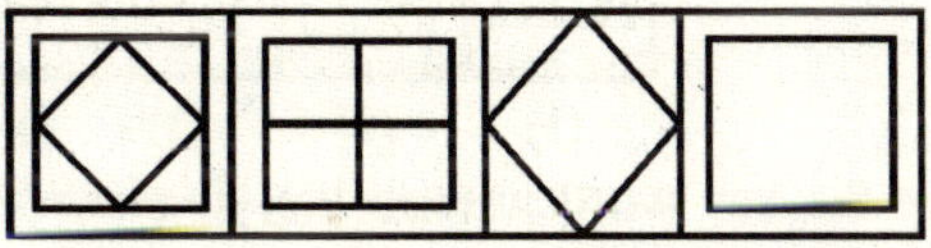

(1) (2) (3) (4)

14. Which three-letter word should be inserted within the parenthesis to form two new words?

W (___ ___ ___) N
L (___ ___ ___) S

15. What number with decimals should replace the question mark?

1.00	1.41	1.73	2.00	2.24	?

16. If x = +, y = –, z = ×, and w = ÷, then what is the value of

0.25w0.75x0.50y0.25z1?

(a) 0.36 (b) 0.46
(c) 0.56 (d) 0.66

17. If 10 × 2 = 10, 12 × 6 = 36, 15 × 8 = 60, then what is the value of 18 × 3?

18. Choose the missing number ("?") from the given alternatives?

122, 61, ?, 5, –2

(a) 36
(b) 32
(c) 28
(d) 24

19. Which Christian festival is revealed inside the following letters?

ABCDEFGHIJKMNOPQRSTUVWXYZ

20. Which figure replaces the question mark to continue the series?

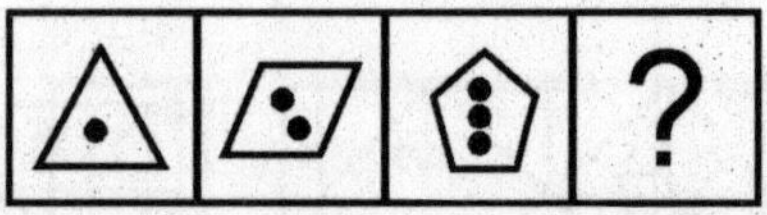

A B C

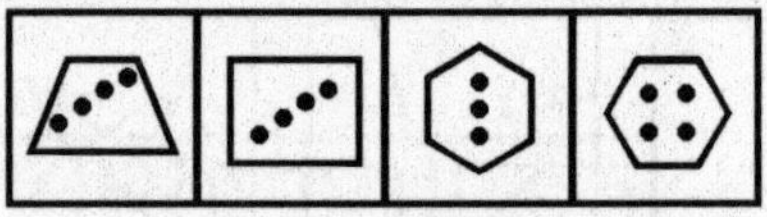

(1) (2) (3) (4)

21. Put the key word in each box to make a two-word phrase from the list of words that precede. For example: ZERO/LUNCH/ELEVENTH [HOUR]

BEAT/CANE/BROWN [ ]

22. Insert a three-letter word in the vacant spaces which complete the first word and starts the second?

FOR(__ __ __)ICE

23. Which among the four options should occupy the position indicated by a question mark to continue the sequence?

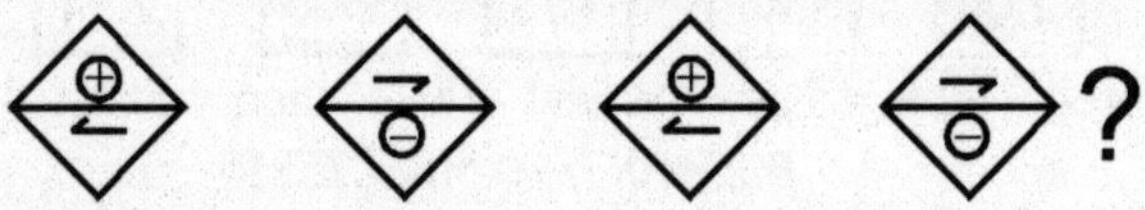

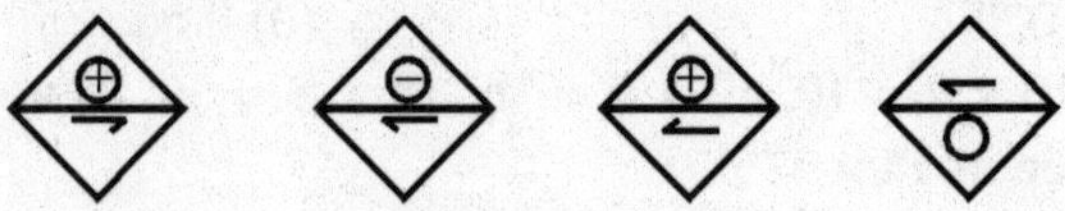

(1) (2) (3) (4)

24. Which among the following words is different from others?

FREEZE
DISTURB
THIRST
HIJACK

25. A square paper is being folded twice as shown by the dotted lines, then a cut is made. Which alternative suggests the appearance of the paper when it is unfolded?

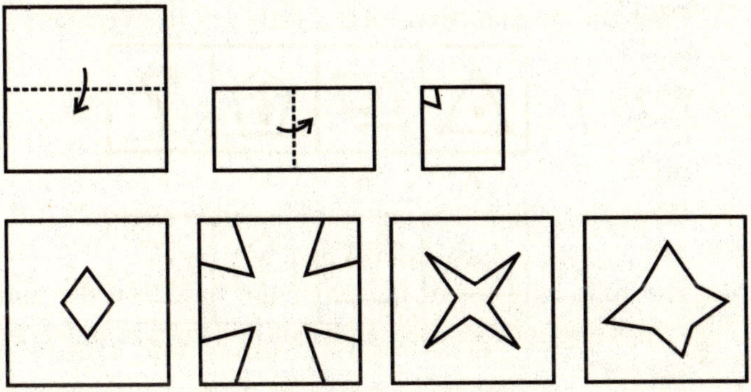

(1) (2) (3) (4)

❑

TEST-36

1. What are the two missing numbers in the following series?
   1, 1, 16, 4, 81, 9, ?, ?
2. Find out the number which is different from others?
   (a) –1
   (b) 1
   (c) 3
   (d) 7
3. What does the following word equation suggest?
   1000 Y in a M
4. The following set of questions are based on the numerical values assigned to each alphabet in a certain order. Find the answer?
   If CAT is 60, what is BAT?
5. Find out the group which is different from others?
   (a) ACE (b) CEG
   (c) GIL (d) KMO
6. In which eight-letter word the first seven letters are composed of the first six letters of the English language (the order of letters does not matter?
7. What four-digit number should replace the question mark?

8. Which among the following figures is different from others?

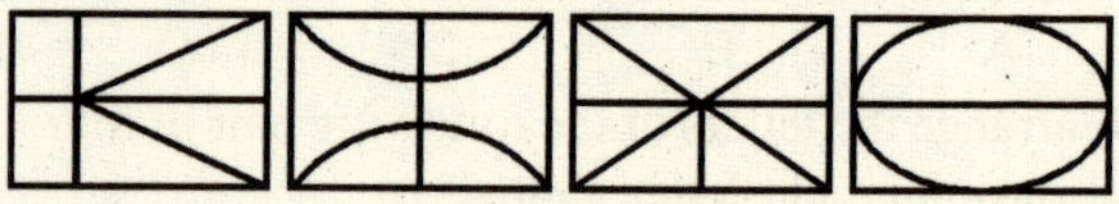

(1) (2) (3) (4)

9. The first three letters of the following word are missing? Find out the missing letters to form a word.
   ___ ___ ___ YME
10. Mrs Rosy has five daughters named: Doria, Rehana, Medina, Fatima, and Soniya. Now the sixth daughter is just born. What name she would like to have for her?

(a) Simona (b) Dora

(c) Laveena (d) Tiara

11. Which three-letter word should be inserted within the parenthesis to form two new words?

S (___ ___ ___) G

T (___ ___ ___) E

12. Select the correct option which has the same relationship to the third figure which is between the first two figures on the left.

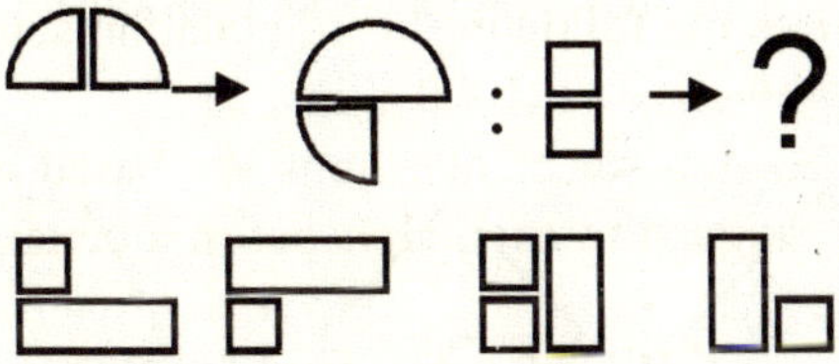

(1) (2) (3) (4)

13. Five girls are sitting in the first row of a music class. Pratima is on the right of Malini. Nalini is on the left of Malini but is on the right of Vinita. Pratima is on the left of Ankita. Which girl is on the extreme left?

14. Which letter comes next in the series?

S, M, H, D, W, M, ?

15. Which two figures are similar?

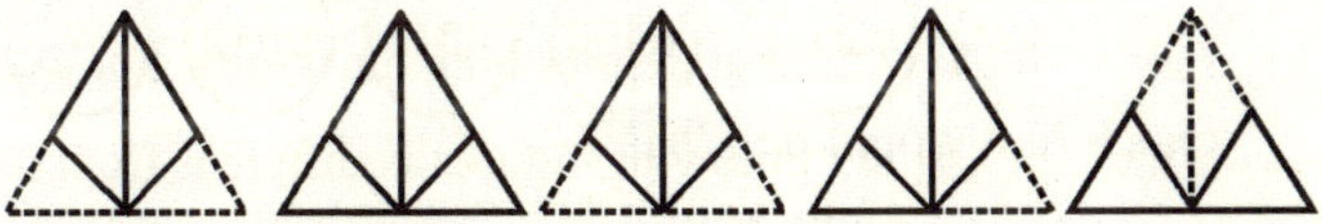

A B C D E

16. Rearrange the letters of the following pair of four-letter words to make an eight-letter animal?

MERE DUSK___ ___ ___ ___ ___ ___ ___ ___

17. What number should replace the question mark?

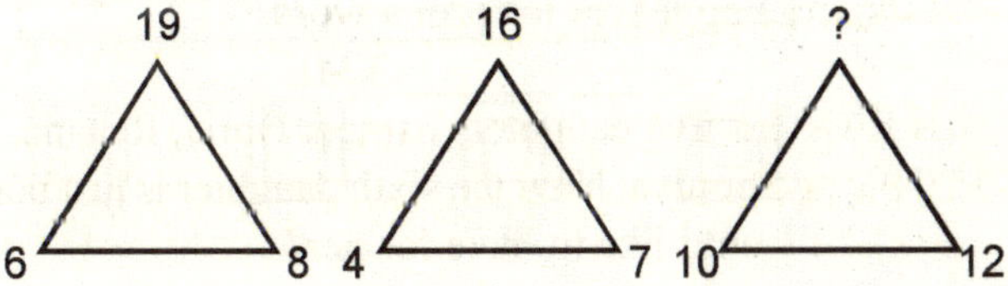

18. NAPKIN is composed of NAP and KIN, neither of which has any connection with NAPKIN. Below are given two three-letter words which combine to form a six-letter word. The three-letter words are defined but not the six-letter word. Find the six-letter word. For example: Male child + Trap = SONNET

Male adult + Your time of life = __________ (Deal)

19. Select the correct alternative which when substituted for the question mark maintain the same relationship on both the sides of the sign "::".

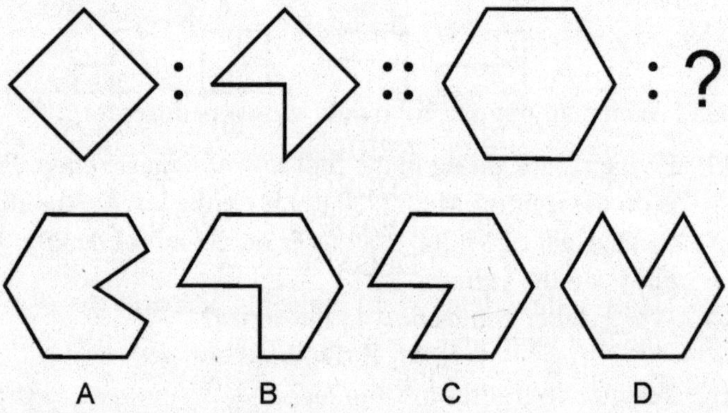

20. Find a single word that defines both the words. For example: Quick bird would be SWIFT.

Unite pair __________

21. Which figure in the lower row should replace the question mark?

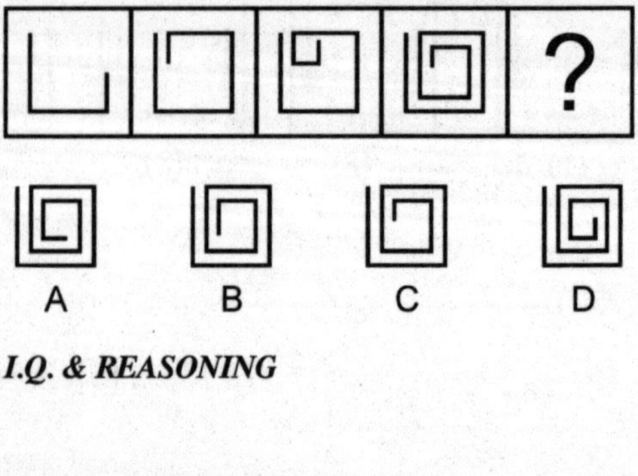

22. Which among the four options should occupy the position indicated by a question mark to continue the sequence?

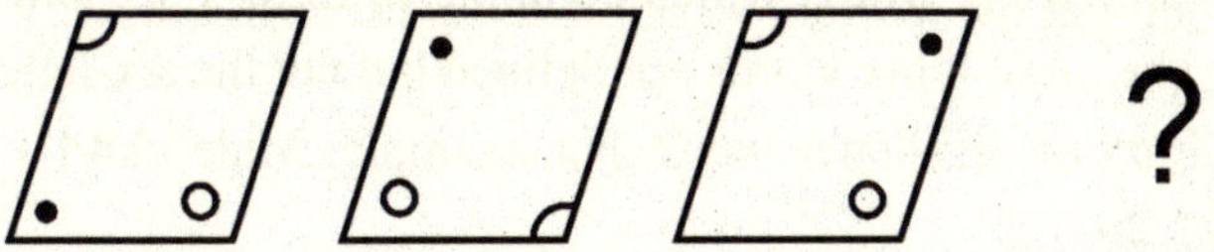

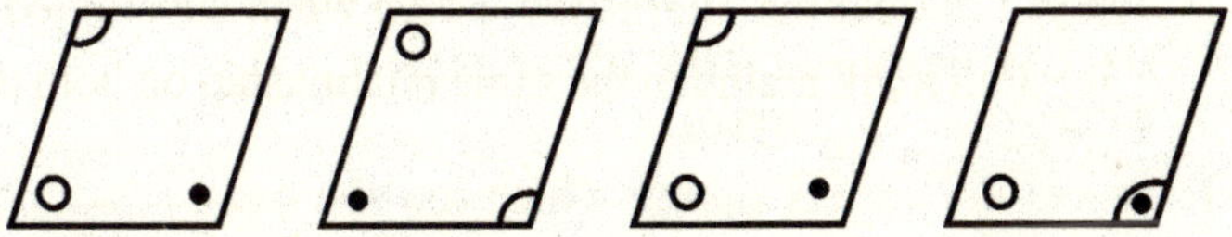

A B C D

23. Which among the following words is different from others?

ARREAR
CHURCH
READER
DECADE

24. Insert a three-letter word in the blank spaces which complete the first word and starts the second?

LINE(__ __ __)KIND

25. Which among the four options should occupy the position indicated by a question mark to continue the sequence?

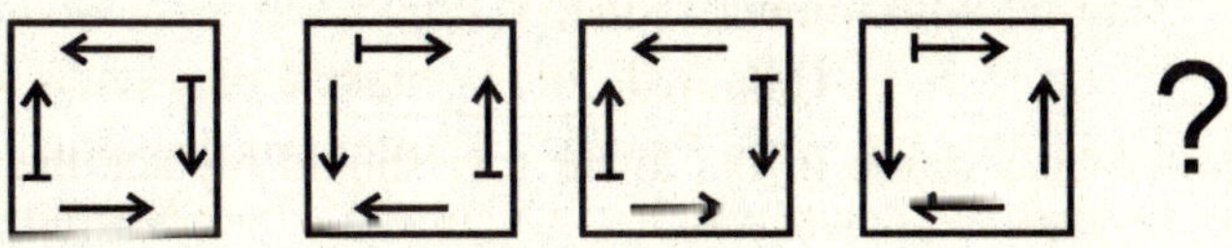

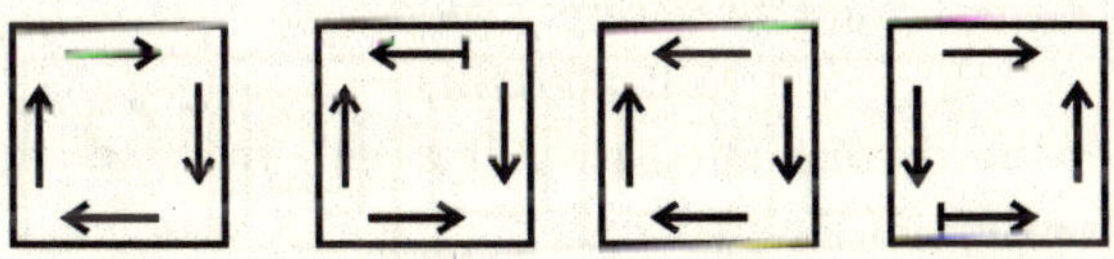

(1) (2) (3) (4)

❑

TEST-37

1. Find out the number which is different from others?
   (a) 9
   (b) 19
   (c) 29
   (d) 51
2. Insert a three-letter word in the blank spaces which complete the first word and starts the second?
   FORE(__ __ __)ITER
3. Select the correct option which has the same relationship to the third figure which is between the first two figures on the left.

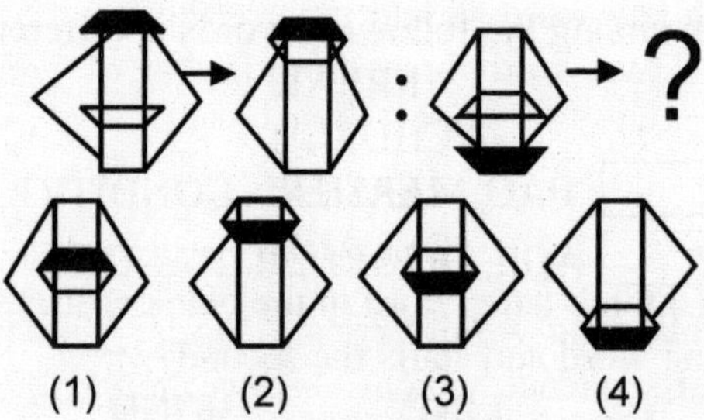

4. Find out the number which replaces the question mark?
   6, 30, 72, 132, 210, 306, ?
5. Starting with a letter I, and go on adding successively other letters N, S, G, T, R, A, T, and L, make a nine-letter word?
6. The following word carries a shorter word within it in the normal sequence which conveys the same meaning as the longer word. Find the shorter synonym?
   NOURISHED
7. Select the correct alternative that will maintain the same relationship on the two signs "::", if it is substituted for the question mark "?".
   adfh: jmoq:: jmoq: ?
   (a) adhf (b) quwy
   (c) quvx (d) svxz

8. Which among the following figures is different from others?

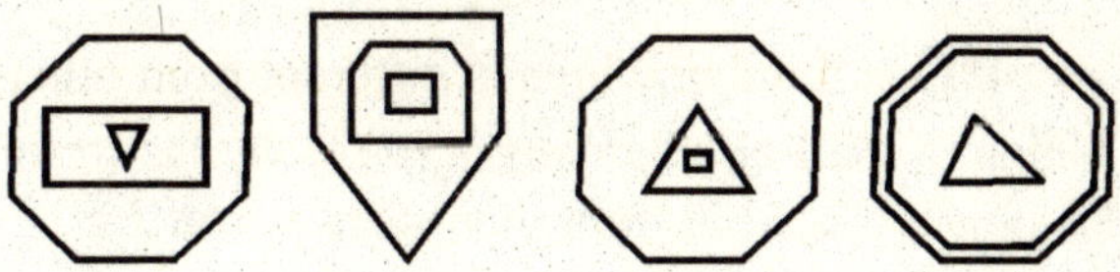

(1) (2) (3) (4)

9. What are the two missing numbers in the following series?

2, 3, 4, 5, 6, 7, 8, 11, ?, ?

10. Which among the following words is different from others?

TRITON
TRUSTY
PROMPT
STORMY

11. Which key word should replace the question mark so as to make a two-word phrase from the list of words that follows, i.e.

?	: BAG, MARSHAL, CONDITIONING (? is AIR)
?	AGE, DISORDER, HANDICAP

12. The following word carries a shorter word within it in the normal sequence which conveys the same meaning as the longer word. Find the shorter synonym?

AMICABLE

13. What is revealed in the following word equation?

64 S on a C B?

14. Find a single word that defines both the words. For example: Quick bird would be Swift.

Family row ____________

15. Select the most appropriate option to match the definition of 'juicy and fleshy'?

(a) Brawny (b) Pulpy
(c) Spicy (d) Succulent

16. Find the number which replaces the question mark?

(1) 3517
(2) 9305
(3) 8622

(4) 4717

(a) 3969 (b) 3970

(c) 3971 (d) 3972

17. Which of the four alternatives is exactly the mirror image of the object placed in front of a plane mirror AB?

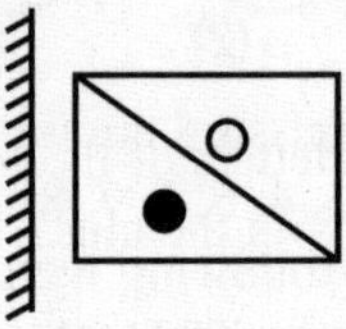

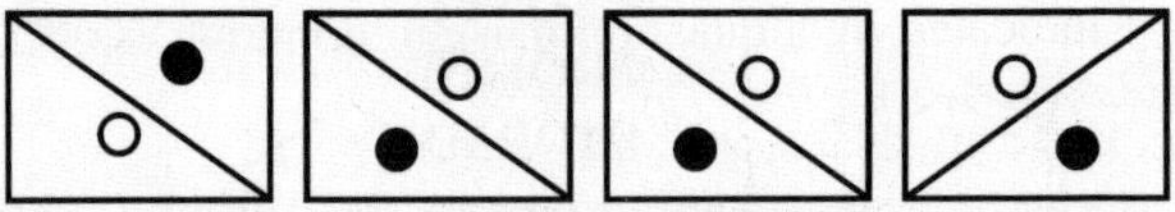

(1) (2) (3) (4)

18. Which bird is hidden in the following sentence?

Your collar knot is improper.

19. Which letter should be placed before and after the following word so that a new word is formed that is a palindrome?

__ OTATO__

20. ROTATE is composed of ROT and ATE, neither of which has any connection with ROTATE. Below are listed some pair of words, each of them has a three-letter word as its meaning. The two three-letter words combine to form a six-letter word which is defined. Find the six-letter word. For example: Male child + Trap = SONNET

Professional + By = ___________ (Correct)

21. The following eleven-letter word contains ROB at its centre. Fill up the blanks to spell the name of a famous Indian shehnai player.

_ _ _ _ _ HUL _ _ _ _ _

22. Which combination comes next?

Aα, Bβ, Cγ, Dδ, E?

(a) ξ (b) η

(c) θ (d) μ

23. Which two figures are similar?

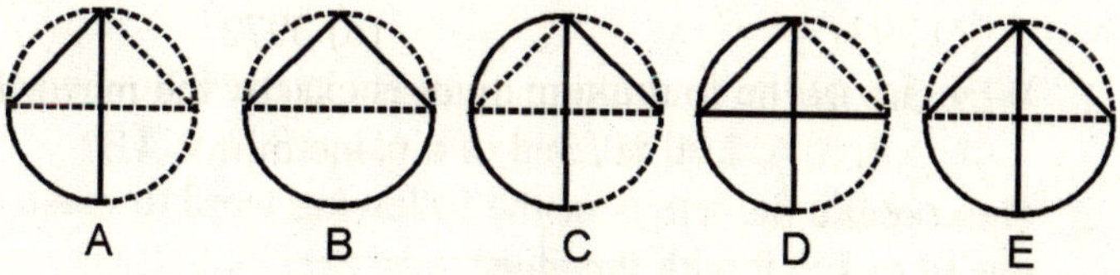

24. Unscramble the letters of the following word to make a new one to match it with the clue?
PRESUME______________ = Paramount

25. Which among the four options should occupy the position indicated by a question mark to continue the sequence?

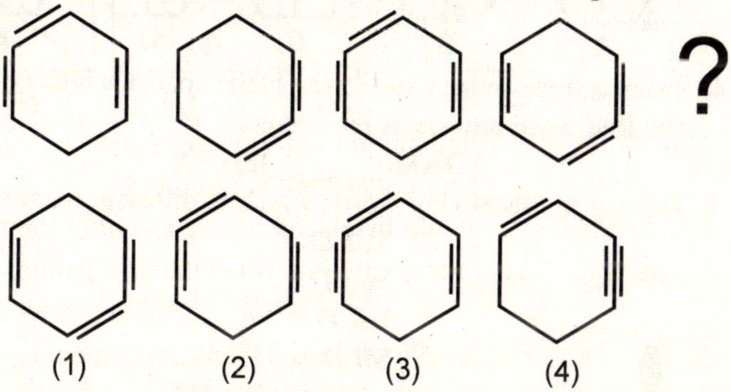

❑

TEST-38

1. What are the three missing numbers in the following series?

   1, 3, 6, 2, 4, 10, 3, 5, 14, 4, 6, 18, ?, ?, ?

2. Unscramble the letters of the following word to make a new one to match it with the clue?

   SERPENT________________= Existing

3. Which two figures are similar?

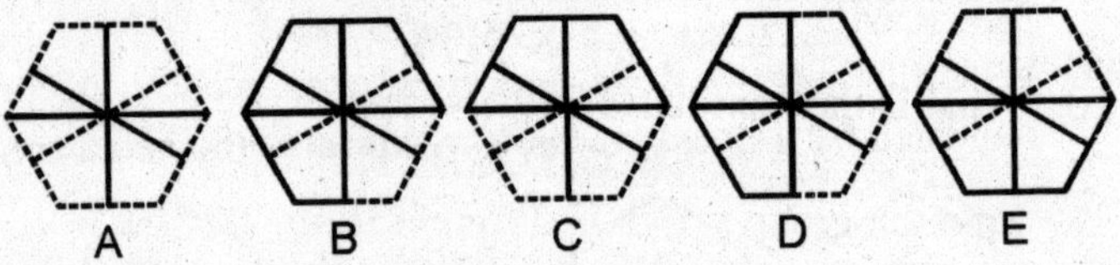

4. Insert a three-letter word in the blank spaces which complete the first word and starts the second?

   ADAM(_ _ _)ENNA

5. Among the following words which is different from others?

   MILD
   WILD
   GILD
   SILD

6. Which fraction should come against H?

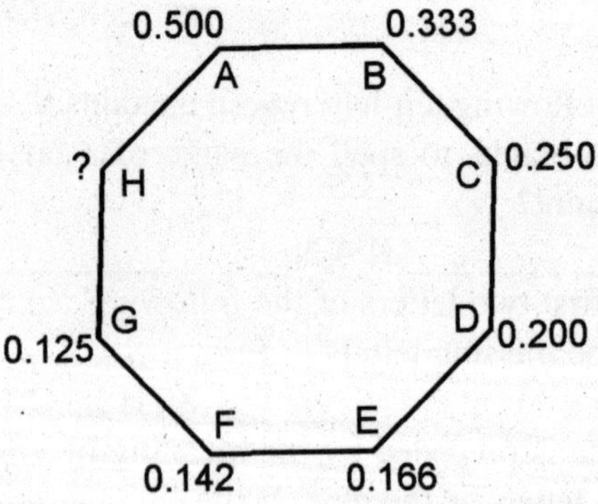

7. The following set of questions are based on the numerical values assigned to each alphabet in a certain order. Find the answer.

   If DO is 60, what is BY eual to?

8. Which among the following figures is different from others?

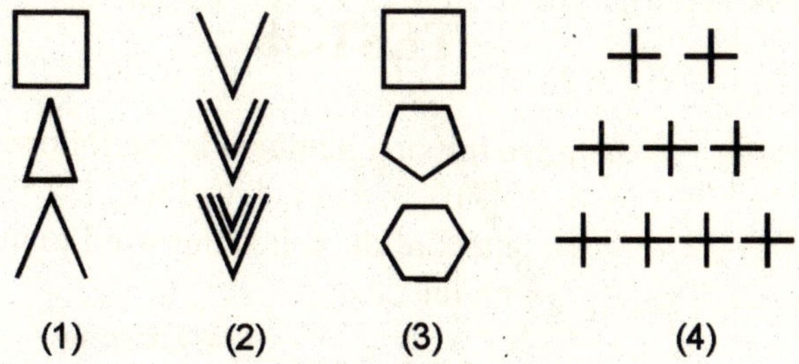

9. What number replace the question marks?

81, 4, ?, 8, 9, 16, 3, ?, ?

10. What is the next letter in the sequence?

B, C, D, E, G, P, ?

11. Find the group which is different from others?

(a) JVL (b) AND

(c) CPF (d) FSI

12. Select the correct option which has the same relationship to the third figure which is between the first two figures on the left?

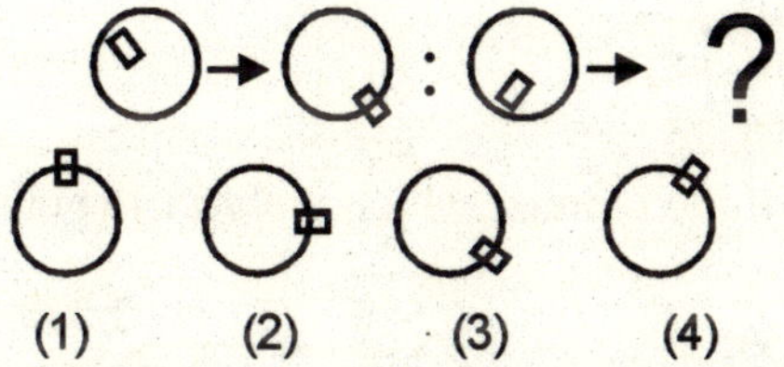

13. The following ten-letter word contains KAN at its centre. Fill in the blanks to spell the name of a famous Indian scholar and saint?

___ ___ ___ ___ KAN ___ ___ ___

14. The first two letters of the following word are missing. Find out the missing letters to form a word?

___ ___ XTH

15. A clue is preceded by the meaning of a word which has the same letters as the clue. Write its anagram, e.g.

UNTIDY = NUDITY

(Risk) : GARDEN = ___________

16. Which of the four alternatives is exactly the mirror image of the object placed in front of a plane mirror AB?

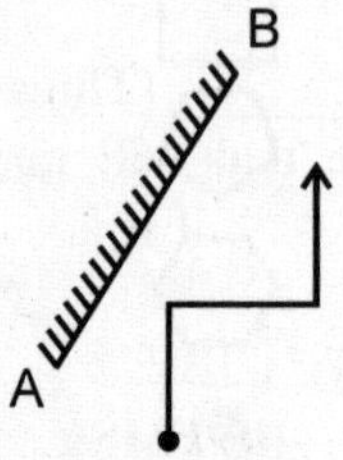

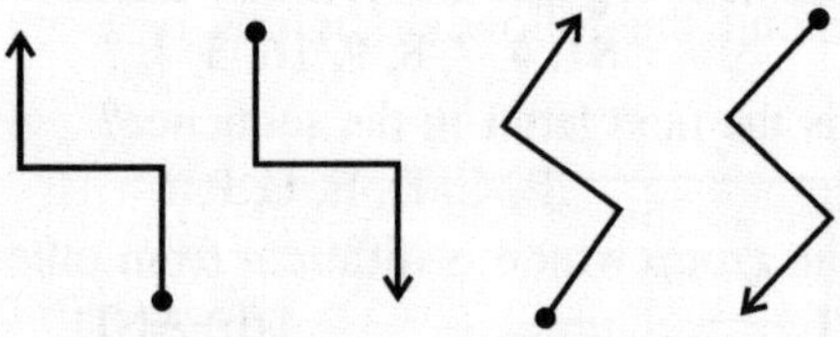

1 2 3 4

17. Choose the missing number ("?") from the given alternatives?

1, 2, 1, 2, 4, 4, 3, 6, 9, 4, 8, 16, ?, ?, ?

(a) 5, 12, 25
(b) 5, 10, 25
(c) 5, 10, 36
(d) 6, 10, 25

18. Find out the number which replaces the question mark?

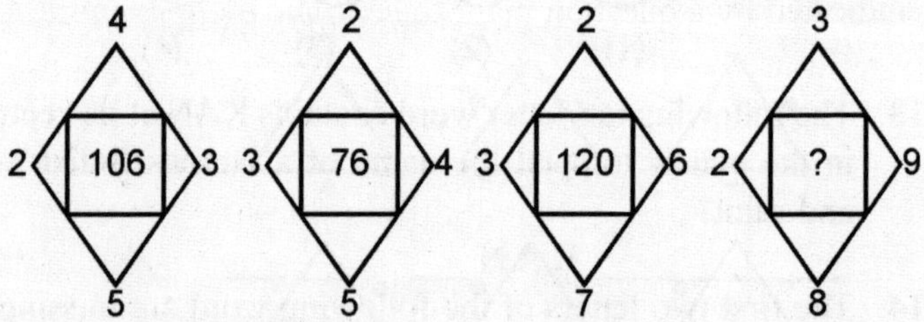

19. Apply your intelligence to fill in the blank spaces so that the three words have the same five letters?

___A___T___; ___ ___ ___ ___ P; ___R___ ___S

20. OUTSET is composed of OUT and SET, neither of which has any connection with OUTSET. Below are listed some pair of words, each of them has a three-letter word as its meaning.

The two three-letter words combine to form a six-letter word which is defined. Find the six-letter word. For example: Male child + Trap = SONNET

Demon + Terminate = __________ (Threaten)

21. Select the correct alternative that will maintain the same relationship on the two signs "::", if it is substituted for the question mark "?".

BIOU: DKQW:: CJPV: ?

(a) EKQW (b) FMSY

(c) ELRX (d) EKRX

22. Which among the following figures replaces the question mark?

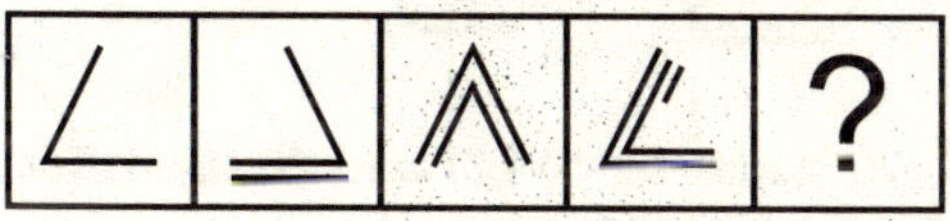

A B C D E

23. Find a single word that defines both the words. For example: Quick bird would be Swift.

Permit aid = _______

24. Which among the four options should occupy the position indicated by a question mark to continue the sequence?

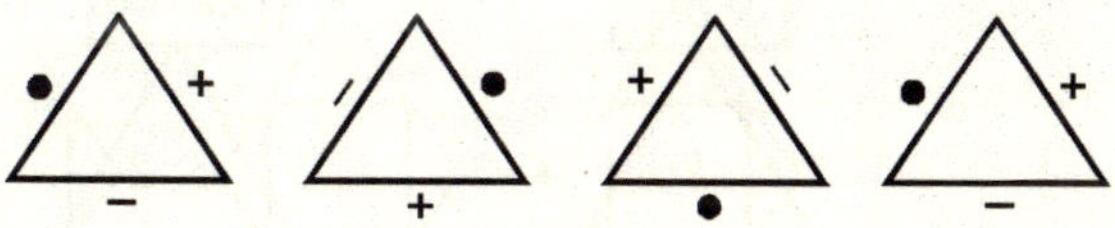

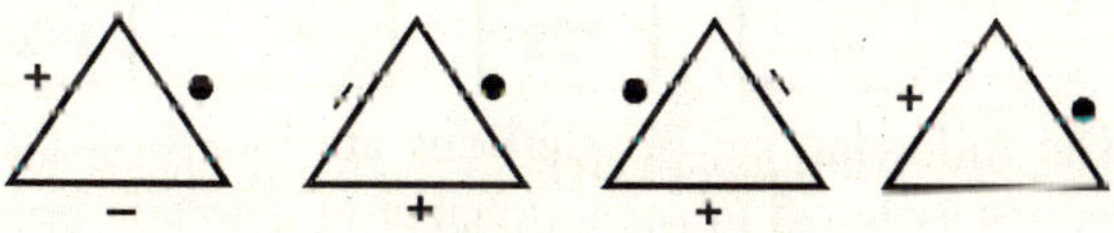

(1) (2) (3) (4)

25. Insert a three-letter word in the blank spaces which complete the first word and starts the second?

GALL (_ _ _) HILL

❑

TEST-39

1. What are the two missing numbers in the following series?

   9, 3, 17, 15, 25, 27, 33, 39, ?, ?

2. Select the correct option which replaces the question mark to continue the figure series?

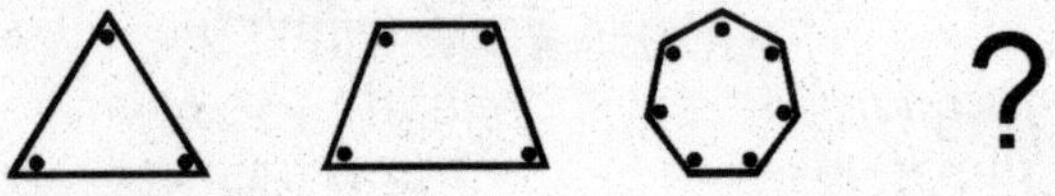

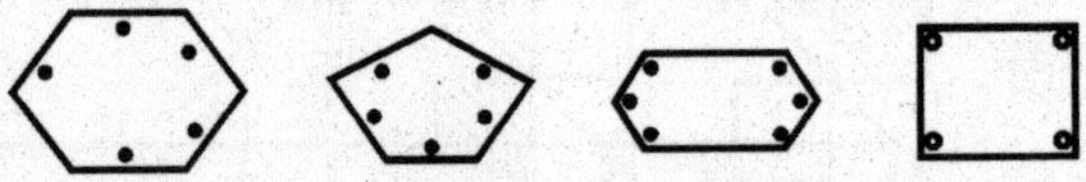

(1) (2) (3) (4)

3. If 59370 stands for SPLIT and 26 stands for AN, for which word does 932602765 stand?

4. In the following letter sequence five letters have been left out which are given as on of the four alternatives under each blank space. Find the correct alternative?

   mal__ __ lal __ ama __ lala __ la

   (a) allal (b) lalal
   (c) allal (d) lalll

5. Find the number which replaces the question mark?

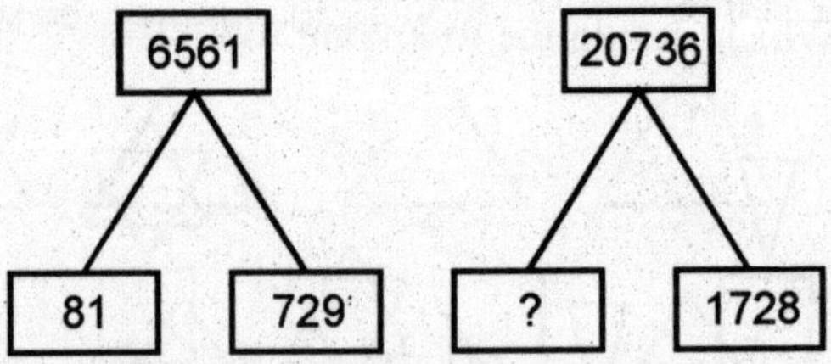

6. The following set of questions are based on the numerical values assigned to each alphabet in a certain order. Find the answer?

   If HIS is 91, what is HIM?

7. Which single vowel should be placed in blank spaces so as to form a nine-letter word which has Indian origin?

   M__H__R__J__H

8. Which of the four alternatives is exactly the mirror image of the object placed in front of a plane mirror AB?

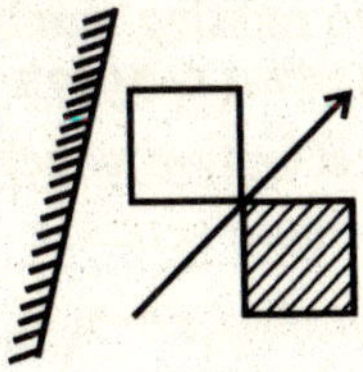

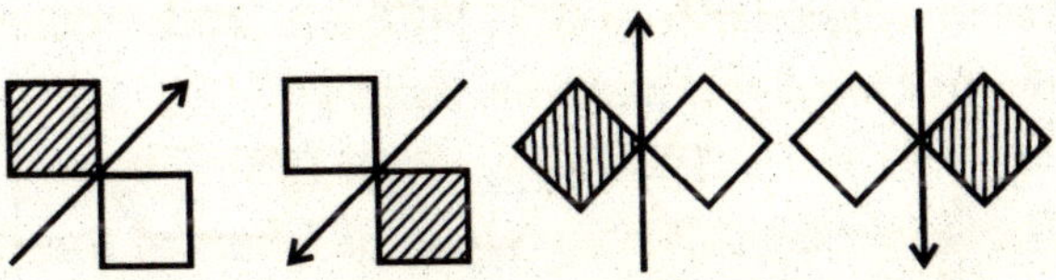

(1) (2) (3) (4)

9. Find out the missing number?

47, 53, 59, ?, 67, 71

10. Which among the following letters is different from others?

L F N H Z

(a) L (b) F

(c) N (d) Z

11. The first three letters of the following word are missing. Find out the missing letters to form a word?

___ ___ ___ AXY

12. Which among the following figures is different from others?

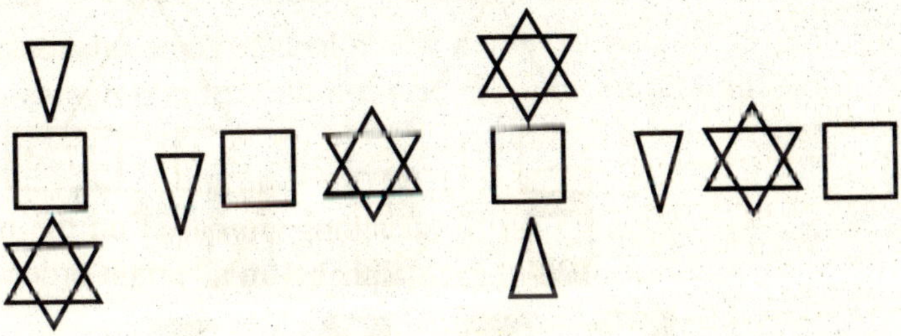

(1) (2) (3) (4)

13. Which key word should replace the question mark so as to make a two-word phrase from the list of words that follows?

i.e. [?] : BAG, MARSHAL, CONDITIONING is AIR
WOODEN, SEA, DARK [?]

14. Which three-letter word should be inserted within the parenthesis to form two new words?

P (__ __ __) A

H (__ __ __) Y

15. What does the following word equation suggest?

12 S of Z

16. Insert a three-letter word in the blank spaces which complete the first word and starts the second?

DEMI(__ __ __)LIKE

17. Rearrange the following group of letters to form anagrams. Clues are given?

ELRSTU

(a) __________ Gloss

(b) __________ Outcome

(c) __________ Whisper

18. What number should replace the question mark?

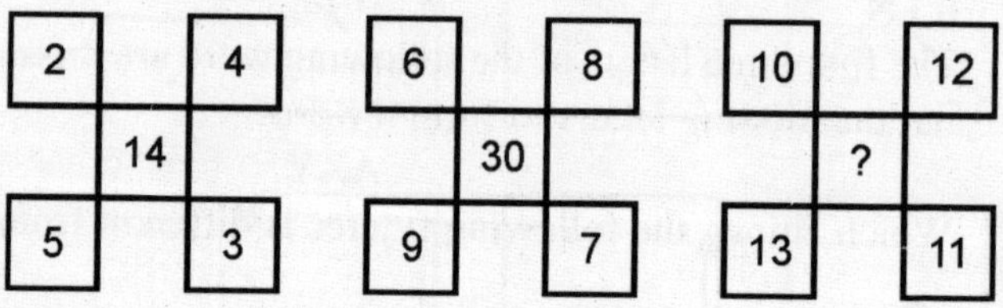

19. Select the correct option which has the same relationship to the third figure which is between the first two figures on the left?

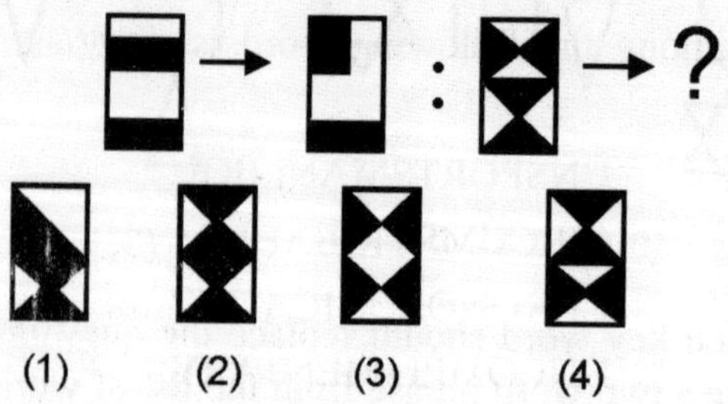

(1) (2) (3) (4)

20. PERSON is composed of PER and SON, neither of which has any connection with PERSON. Below are listed some pair of words, each of them has a three-letter word as its meaning. The two three-letter words combine to form a six-letter word which is defined. Find the 6-letter word. For example: Male child + Trap = SONNET

Central+ Obtain = ___________ (Dwarf)

21. What number replaces the question mark?

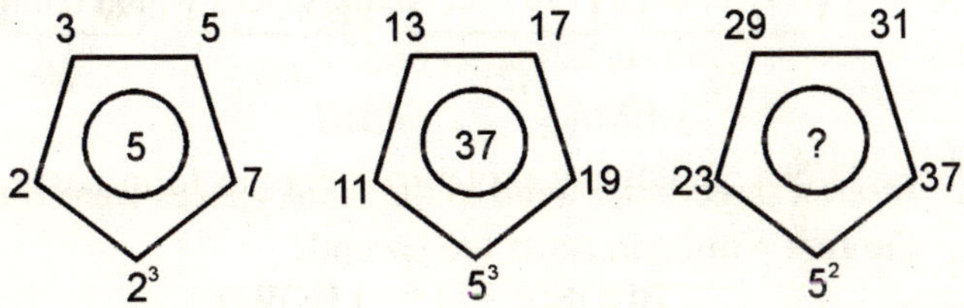

22. Which among the four options should occupy the position indicated by a question mark to continue the sequence?

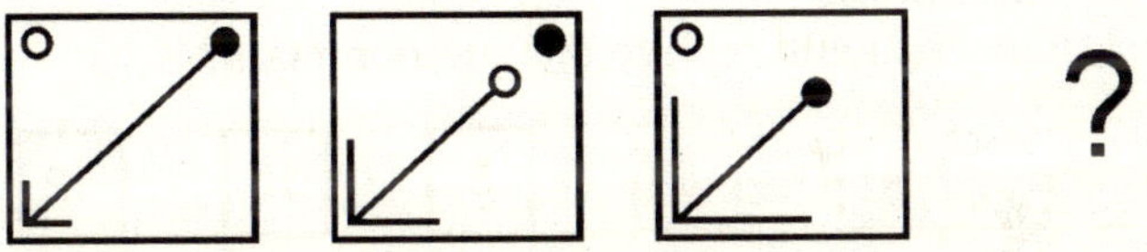

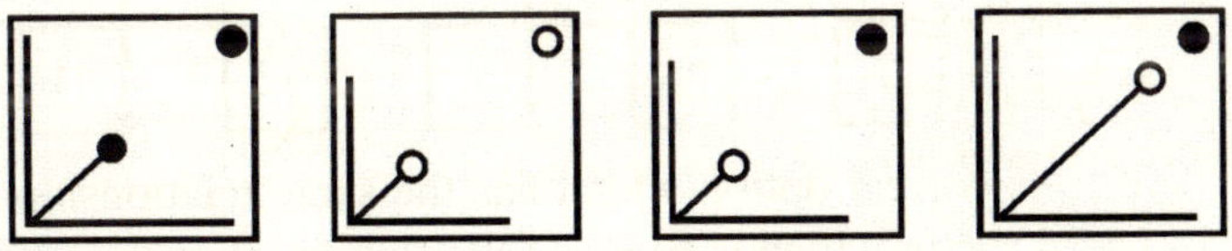

A B C D

23. Which among the following word is different from other words?

UNSPORTSMANLIKE
CIRCUMSCRIBABLE
CHRONOLOGICALLY
UNCOMPLIMENTARY

24. Which among the four options should occupy the position indicated by a question mark to continue the sequence?

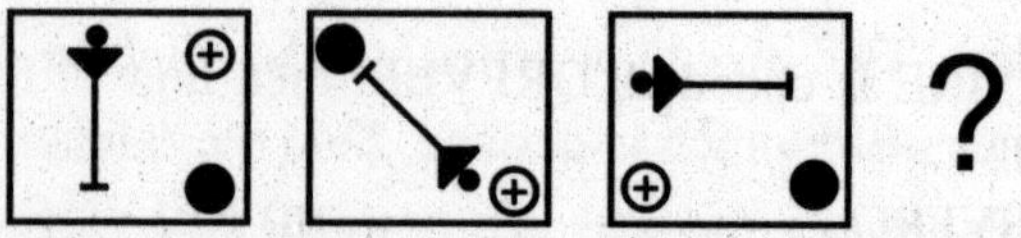

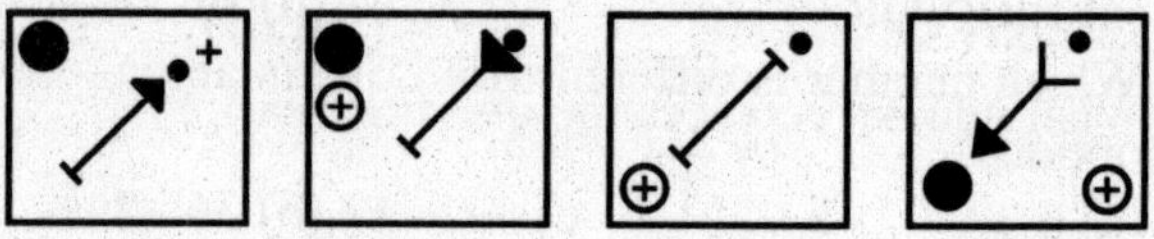

(1) (2) (3) (4)

25. Insert a three-letter word in the blank spaces which complete the first word and starts the second?

BOOK (_ _ _) DOWN

TEST-40

1. If DESIRE is coded as QRFVER, then how is RESIDE be coded?
   (a) ERVFRQ (b) REFVQR
   (c) ERFVQR (d) ERVFQR
2. Which number is different from others among the following options?
   (a) 6 (b) 36
   (c) 226 (d) 1296
3. What numbers should replace the question mark?
   3, 7, 14, 23, 36, ?
4. Which of the four alternatives is exactly the mirror image of the object placed in front of a plane mirror AB?

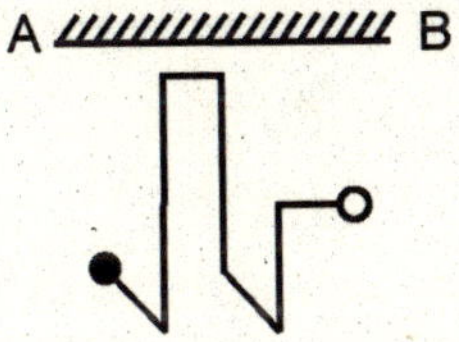

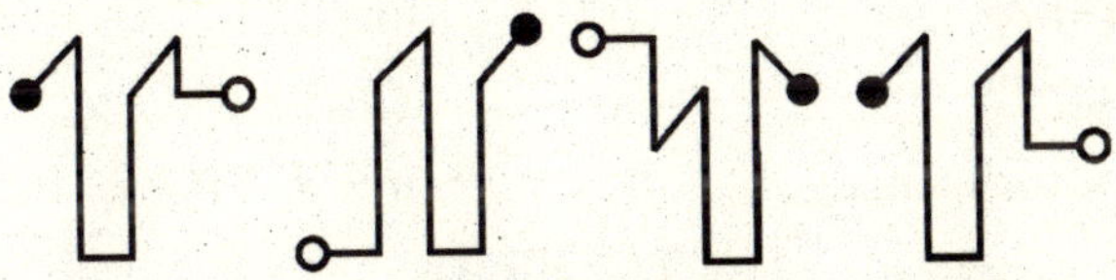

(a) (b) (c) (d)

5. If A = Addition; B = Division; C = Multiplication; D = Subtraction, then find the value of the following expression?
   (½)C2B(1/2) A(1/2)D(1/4)
   (a) ¼ (b) ¾
   (c) 6/4 (d) 9/4
6. Insert a three-letter word in the blank spaces which complete the first word and starts the second?
   PATH(__ __ __)SIDE
7. If XYZ = 25 and NOP = 15, then what is the value of ACE?
   (a) 1 (b) 2
   (c) 3 (d) 4

8. Which among the following figures is different from others?

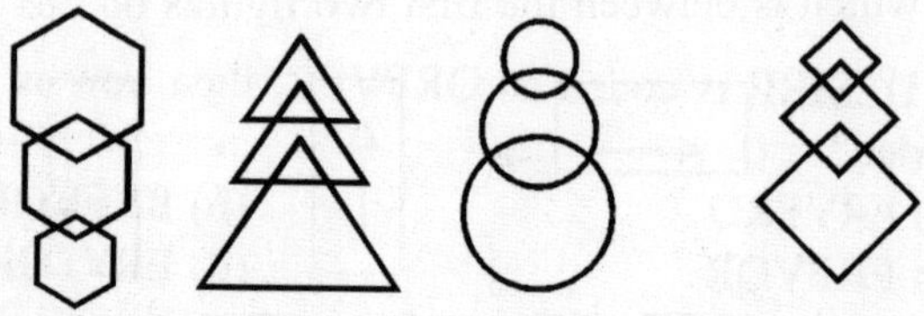

(a) (b) (c) (d)

9. The following word carries a shorter word within it in the normal sequence which conveys the same meaning as the longer word. Find the shorter synonym.

MASCULINE

10. Shobha's rank is 15th from the top and 21st from the bottom in her class. How many students are there in her class?
(a) 35 (b) 36
(c) 37 (d) 38

11. A couple has five married sons and each one of them have four children. How many members are there in the family?
(a) 25 (b) 27
(c) 32 (d) 34

12. Which among the following words is different from others?

BOLERO
BONITO
BEZOAR
BOTONE

13. Choose the missing number ("?") from the given alternatives?

1, 1, 3, 4, 5, 9, 7, 9, 12, ?, ?, ?

(a) 12, 10, 15
(b) 10, 13, 12
(c) 10, 13, 15
(d) 15, 13, 10

14. Which figure has the same relationship to the third figure which is between the first two figures on the left?

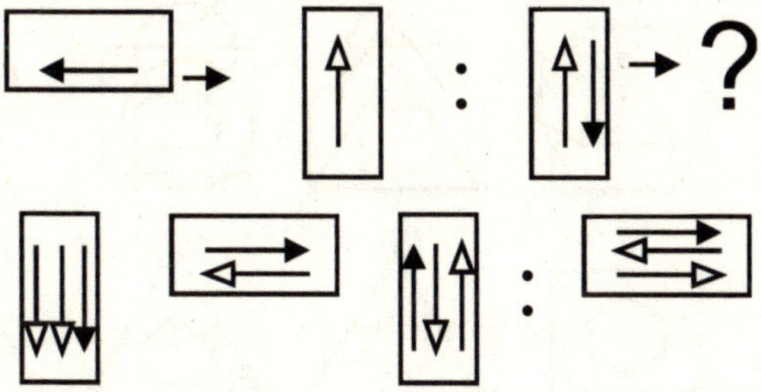

(1) (2) (3) (4)

15. What does the following word equation suggest?

366 D in a LY

16. Select the correct alternative that will maintain the same relationship on the two signs "::", if it is substituted for the question mark "?".

___? ___ : Distance:: Farad: Capacity

(a) Dyne (b) Henry

(c) Parsec (d) Lumen

17. Find a single word that defines both the words. For example: Quick bird would be swift.

Doubt booking ____________

18. Which two figures are similar?

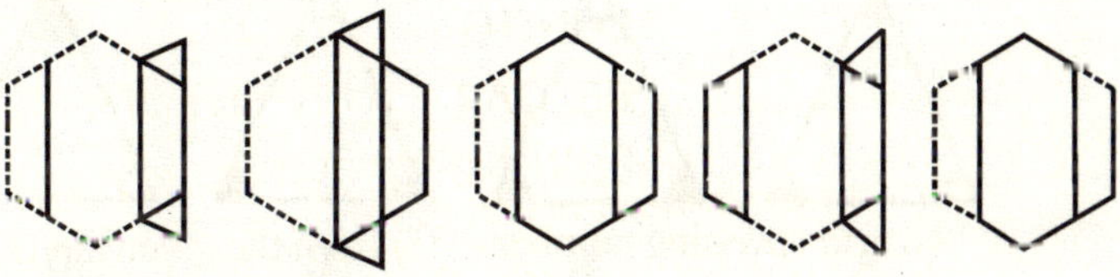

A B C D E

19. The following 7-letter word contains ART at its centre. Fill up the blanks according to the clue which is given in the parenthesis?

___ ___ A R T ___ ___ (Surprise)

20. Which among the four options should occupy the position indicated by a question mark to continue the sequence?

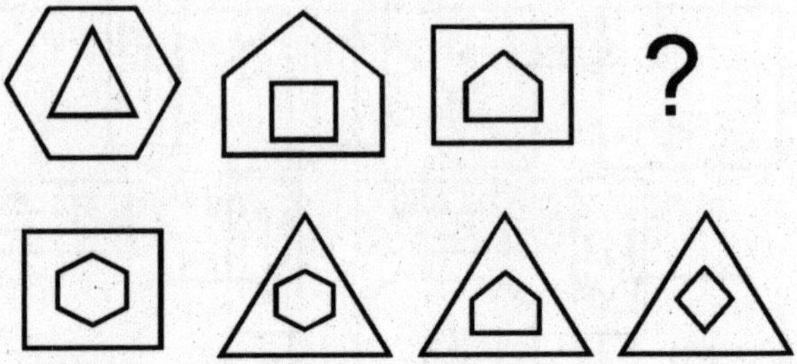

(a) (b) (c) (d)

21. Make word to match the definition by putting letters in the blank spaces.

___ ___ ___ ___ MENT = Anything that adorns

22. Sushma already have four daughters: Sadhna, Reshma, Gayatri, and Madhuri. Just few days back she had another girl. On the *namkaran sanskar*, Punditji suggestrd some names. Can you guess what name finally Sushma chose?

(a) Nisha (b) Surekha

(c) Padmini (d) Dharana

23. Which figure is different from others?

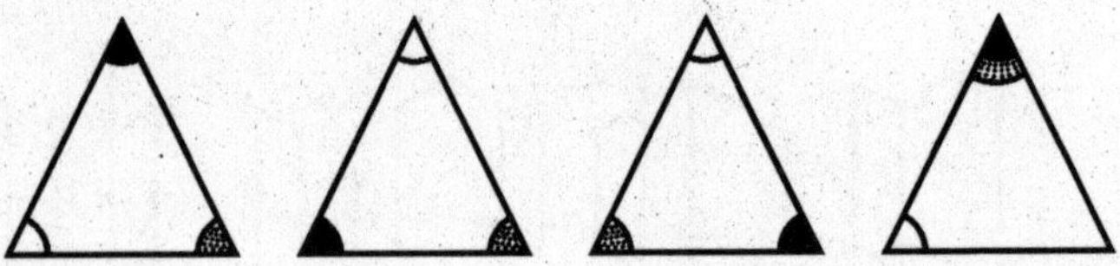

A B C D

24. What will be the next number in the following series?

6, 10, 13, 3, 12, ?

25. A square paper is folded twice as shown in the figure. Then the corners of the twice-folded triangle are cut straight. How

the square paper will look when it is brought to the original position?

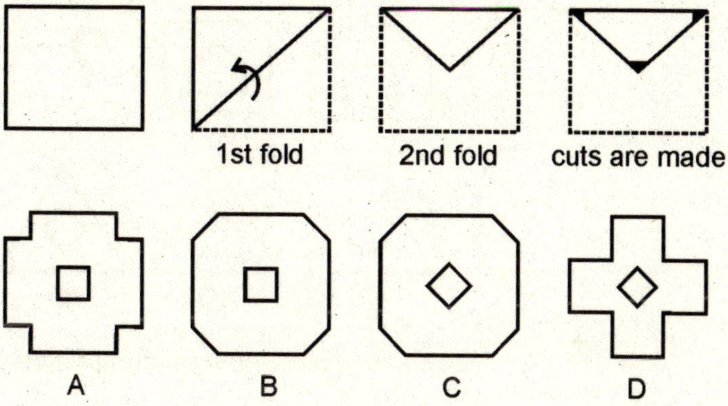

ANSWERS

TEST-1

1. MILK
2. ARC
3. [a; these are prime numbers in reverse order.]
4. [4; $(7 \times 9) - (5 \times 7) = 63 - 35 = 28$]
5. LUCID
6. [a; initial letter of each month.]
7. [4]
8. Firm
9. [c; in others one letter is skipped backward in each group.]
10. [CALORIE; other units are named after scientists.]
11. [3]
12. [LIE]
13. [a; B and A are of the same age and twice the age of C who is twice older than D. E is twice the age of B and A. Thus, E is the oldest and D is the youngest.]
14. [ELEPHANT]
15. [MIDGET]
16. [Shoot]
17. [3; when two plane mirrors are inclined at angle of 90º, the number of images n is given by the formula

    $n = \frac{360^\circ}{90^\circ} - 1$]
18. [a; in others the sequence of letters is: – 2 + 1 + 2.]
19. [D; in others, the internal figures are almost half of the outer figures.]
20. [b; double the first digit and add the second digit to get the result.]
21. [2]
22. [HER]
23. [1; the number of circles are decreasing by one.]
24. [BROKER]
25. [2; outer figure is removed.]

❑

TEST-2

1. [b; sequence of prime numbers + 1]
2. [c; others are multiple of 13.]
3. [c]
4. [1; divide 'left' number by 'right' number and 'upper' number by 'lower' number; then the difference of these two gives the number at the centre.]
5. [ONE]
6. [GARBAGE]
7. [CRY]
8. (3)
9. [DESSERT]
10. [c; the sequence is: 3rd letter = 2nd letter + 17; 2nd letter = 1st letter – 13.]
11. [30; Individual units = 16
    Four units together = 9
    Nine units together = 4
    Sixteen units together = 1
    TOTAL NUMBER OF FIGURES = 30
    Alternately: In case of a square figure, the formula is $N = n^2 + (n - 1)^2 + (n - 2)^2 + (n - 3)^2 + \ldots$ where N is total number of squares and 'n' is the number of small squares in a row.]
12. [MALARIA]
13. [1]
14. [CACTI]
15. [1; the cut on edge moves clockwise through one unit of length and the dot is moving ½ length in anti-clockwise direction.]
16. [a; series becomes: pQppQ pQppQ pQppQ
17. [b; as per statement
    Kailash Naresh Mohan Prakash Akash
18. [ADVANCE]
19. [PEA]
20. [4]
21. [GARAGE; others start and end up in same two letter.]

22. [4; when three holes are made diagonally, three more holes appear diagonally but on opposite side.]
23. [BONNET; other words have letters in alphabetic order.]
24. [SECTION]
25. [2; the number of side decreases by 1.]

❑

TEST-3

1. [d sequence is: –2 –3 +1.]
2. [3; in others, the shaded portions are placed alternately.]
3. [ELEGANT]
4. [STER]
5. [4; R moves diagonally. The other sign moves half unit of length.]
6. [c; n^2 + subsequent Prime Numbers]
7. [24]
8. [EARLY; RELAY; LAYER]
9. [c]
10. [b; A=2, B=4; C=6;…Z=52.]
11. [16; each line of the five circles equals 88.]
12. [4; black dot moves anti-clockwise and the white one moves clockwise.]
13. [IMP + ART = IMPART]
14. [1; the rectangle contains shaded triangle diagonally in the same direction.]
15. [M, N, P, T]
16. [Upright]
17. [3]
18. [INFORMALITY, other words have different letters.]
19. [Walsh]
20. [3; when two holes are punched near the centre of the edge, two more holes appear.]
21. [0; the numbers are in alphabetical order: Eight, Five, Four, Nine, One, Seven, Six, Ten, Three, Two, Zero.]
22. [d]
23. [ARMS]
24. [b; 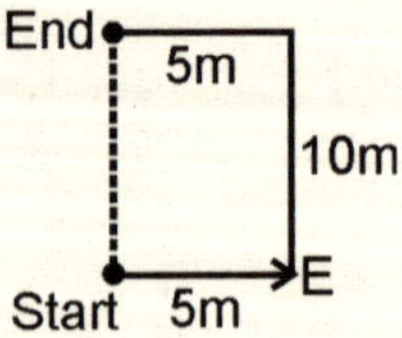

25. [c]

❑

TEST-4

1. [3; in others, the inside lines are placed after a gap.]
2. [30]
3. [c; series is: xyz   xxyyzz   xxxyyyyzzz]
4. [ROCK]
5. [2; the small circles are mirror images.]
6. [L; Letters formed by solid lines.]
7. [TRO: TROPHY]
8. [1]
9. [RAP]
10. [12; add up the three numbers placed at the vertex of a triangle and reverse the digits; e.g. 10 + 11 + 12 = 33.]
11. [1; the hole is made near one corner and a hole is punched. On unfolding the paper there will be two holes very near to each other.]
12. [b; let the present age of Anushka be x and that of Mona be y. After four years Anushka will be 20 years; as such 20 = 2 (y – 1); so y = 11.]
13. [SWARTHY]
14. [1; the number of side of figure intersecting the circle is increasing by one.]
15. [BON]
16. [COCOA]
17. [d]
18. [POISON; others form two separate words when split.]
19. [SAFETY]
20. [b]
21. [Bore]
22. [Monkey]
23. [D]
24. [3; the whole of plus sign is shaded.]
25. [AMMONIA]

❑

TEST-5

1. [AGE]
2. [DIAGNOSTIC; others words contain different letters.]
3. [GOLDEN]
4. [b; successive number is twice the previous number, add 2 to it.]
5. [4]
6. [Flat]
7. [Zero; add the numbers of top and bottom rows that equals the sum of numbers of the middle row, e.g. (1+4+2+6+5) + (3+6+8+1+0) = 36; 36 – (9+ 9 +9 +9) = 0]
8. [4; others have four sides.]
9. [d; 1810; Z=1, Y=2,…A=26]
10. [6+12+24=42]
11. [HAMLET]
12. [2]
13. [c; the sequence is: ♣♦♣♣♣♦♣♦♣♣♣♦]
14. [c; letter series skipping three letters in reverse direction.]
15. [4; the figure is moving anticlockwise w˙th 90º alternately.]
16. [b; subsequent letters are advanced by si ⸢ places.]
17. [3; the number of small lines inside the figure is increasing by one and the figure itself is moving 45 degrees in clockwise direction.]
18. [CAPITOL; OPTICAL; TOPICAL]
19. [RAW]
20. [4]
21. [3]
22. [BLURB]
23. [72; e.g. 9×3 +7=34, etc.]
24. [SHABANA]
25. S C O L D
    C Y C L E
    O C T A L
    L L A M A
    D E L A Y

❑

TEST-6

1. [b; sequence is: + 6 + 5 + 3.]
2. [3]
3. [a; letters skipping two letters in forward and reverse directions.]
4. [2]
5. [N; First letter of each natural numbers.]
6. [d; others are divisible by 11.]
7. [55; $N = n^2 + (n-1)^2 + (n-2)^2 + (n-3)^2 + \ldots$ where N is total number of squares and n is the number of small squares in a row.]
8. [4; arrow in same direction.]
9. [d. 715154; A = 1, B = 2, C = 3, etc.]
10. [b; in others two letters are being skipped.]
11. [4; horizontal diameter; the two small lines move 90º in anti-clockwise direction]
12. [6 digits in a PIN Code.]
13. [AGARKAR]
14. [TRA: TRAUMA]
15. [4; number of strokes decreasing and the small circle is moving one unit of length inside the triangle clockwise.]
16. [120º; if any two vertices inside the hexagon are joined to make a triangle, the biggest angle is 120º]
17. [B]
18. [c; twice the sum of all the four digits on the left.]
19. [b]
20. [C]
21. [79; other numbers are divisible by 3.]
22. [REINS; RINSE; SIREN]
23. [2; '+' and '–' signs alternate their positions and so do the '×' and '÷' signs.]
24. [4]
25. [ASSEMBLE]

❑

TEST-7

1. [b; multiple of 11 plus subsequent prime numbers starting with 2.]
2. [d; group of letters skipping two letters in forward and reverse directions.]
3. [1]
4. [a; in others three letters are skipped.]
5. [(a) Barely; (b) Barely; (c) Bleary]
6. [135º; angles at the centre = 366º/8 = 45º; 180º – 45º = 135º]
7. [LIT]
8. [1; in others, the number of sides of the inside figure is one less than that of the outside figures.]
9. [LOAF]
10. [LEG + END = LEGEND]
11. [2; the black dot will come up and other figures get oriented.]
12. [b; A=1, B=2, etc. then subtract the sum of first two letters from the third letter.]
13. [d; Ankita is 9th from the back but ahead of Chanda who is 8th from the left, since Bindiya is in between, therefore,
 - - - - - - - C B A - - - - - - - - -]
14. [C]
15. [4; number of sides of the innermost figure is increasing by one and the circle should enclose the other figure.]
16. [18; (43 – 37) × (41 – 38) = 6 × 3]
17. [MAN]
18. [BOTSWANA; Other countries contain seven letters]
19. [a; sequence is: αβββγ, αβββγ, αβββγ]
20. [1]
21. [COMMON]
22. [ASHADHA]
23. [c; Rahim < Ahmed ; Rahim > Daler > Etmad; Etmad > Fahim; therefore height in descending order is: Ahmed > Rahim > Daler > Etmad > Fahim]
24. [4; black and white dots change their positions alternately. The small 'cut' rolls clockwise.]

25. [The missing number is 6; the number in the middle of each triplet is the same as the digits of either end's number when added together. 3+7=10=8+2 and so on.]

❑

TEST-8

1. [c; $n^3 - n^2$]
2. [BEES SAAL BAAD]
3. [91; formula is the same as that used in squares, i.e. $N = n^2 + (n-1)^2 + (n-2)^2 + (n-3)^2 + \ldots$ where N is total number of squares and n is the number of small squares in a row. Here $n = 6$, therefore the total is 91.]
4. [3]
5. [b; if the numbers are assigned the values A=1, B=2, Z=26, then in each case sum of the letters is divisible by 10 except (b).]
6. [d; dingo is 'Natasha'; mingo is 'is'; lingo is 'beautiful'; ringo is 'becomes'; jingo is 'actress'; and bingo is 'star'.]
7. [HANUMAN]
8. [STONE]
9. [3]
10. [SHEIKH]
11. [2; multiply each pair of the two numbers facing diagonals and get the difference, e.g. (5×4) ~ (6×3) = 2.]
12. [RAT]
13. [EARING, GAINER, REGAIN, REGINA]
14. [4; in others, the intersecting lines are parallel.]
15. [BUTTON]
16. [c; the sequence is: $\frac{1}{4}\frac{1}{3}\frac{1}{2}\frac{1}{3}\frac{1}{2}\frac{1}{4}\frac{1}{3}\frac{1}{2}$]
17. [b; $AD = (AE + DE)^{\frac{1}{2}} = 10\sqrt{2}m$]

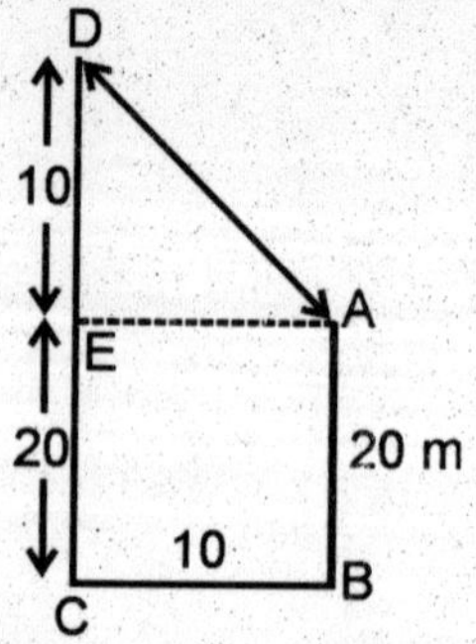

18. [TEN]
19. [3; the dot will come to the right side and the lower portion of the square is shaded.]
20. [Coach]
21. [B; D; G; P; T]
22. [3]
23. [FOREGO]
24. [888+88+8+8+8=1000]
25. [4; black and white dots move alternately so do the figure inside and the black 'cut'.]

❑

TEST-9

1. [108º; angle at the centre = 360º/5 = 72º; required angle = 180º – 72º = 108º]
2. [2]
3. [140; $N = n^2 + (n-1)^2 + (n-2)^2 + (n-3)^2 + \ldots$ where N is total number of squares and n is the number of small rectangle in a row.]
4. [a; in others the 'sum' of letters is 40.]
5. [a; obviously Abha and Uddhava are Phizo's parents.]
6. [d; A=1, B=2, etc. the code is: 1918945229]
7. [1]
8. [d; Greek notation]
9. [WETHER]
10. [TAR]
11. [3]
12. [DYNAMO; other contains just one vowel.]
13. [VIETNAM]
14. [0; the numbers are in alphabetical order: (eight, five, four, nine, one, seven, six, ten, three, two, zero.)
15. [b; 731<u>34</u>943287<u>93</u>2731863240<u>136</u>2321398632<u>736</u>]
16. [10,000; numbers in bigger parts of circles are fourth power of the numbers inside the smaller parts of circles.]
17. [Firm]
18. [Finch]
19. [TEHRAN]
20. [3; the slanting lines on squares are on opposite sides.]
21. [42; sum of numbers inside the figure minus sum of numbers outside the figure]
22. [PISTOL]
23. [2; number of segment decreasing.]
24. [EAR]
25. [4; mirror images.]

❑

TEST-10

1. [a; in others four letters are being skipped.]
2. [5; e.g. (8×9) – 12 = 60; 60/15 = 4; similarly, (5×12) – 10 = 50; 50–/10 = 5]
3. [d; $2n^2 + 1$, where $n = 0, 1, 2, 3,\ldots$]
4. [1]
5. [c; series is: ψψψωωχ ψψψωωχ ψψψωωχ]
6. [Letter C: CUSEC](A measure of the rate of flow of fluid)
7. [c]
8. [2; others do not suffer lateral inversion.]
9. [RUM]
10. [c; in others 2nd letter is 13 placed ahead from 1st; 3rd letter is 1 placed ahead of 2nd and 4th letter is 13 placed behind the 3rd.]
11. [2; figures are moving clockwise; arrows are moving 90 degrees anticlockwise.]
12. [114; e.g. (9+27) + (27–9) = 36 + 18 = 54; similarly, (19+57) + (57–19) = 76 + 38 = 114]
13. [20.]
14. [ENVOY]
15. [55; each number is the sum of the 2 preceding numbers. It is known as Fibonacci number.]
16. [HOUR]
17. [CHITAL]
18. [MARSHY]
19. [3; another triangle is on right side with a line.]
20. [Hide]
21. [8; 1st figure: 10 = 2 + 8; 8 – 3 = 5 and 3 – 2 =1]
22. [d; sa=Lata, re=is; ga=singer; ma=sings; pa=songs; dh=are; ni=melodious. Lata sings melodious songs = sa ma ni pa]
23. [LIFE]
24. [C]
25. [3]

❑

TEST-11

1. [c; n^2 + Prime Number, where $n = 1, 2, 3$, etc.]
2. [d; group of two letters with difference of 13]
3. [1/4; see the first figure: ½ -- ¼ + 1/3 = 7/12; second figure: 1/3 – ¼ + ½ = 7/12; similarly, ¼ – ¼ + ¼ = ¼]
4. [2; The figures are halved and dot moves to the left sides.]
5. [a; in each case the second letter is 13 places ahead and the third letter is 10 places behind the second.]
6. [b; series is: xy xxyy xxxyyy]
7. [c]
8. [d; the sequence is: 2nd letter = 1st letter + 2; 3rd letter = 2nd letter + 11; 4th letter = 3rd letter + 2.]
9. [13]
10. [4; in others, the line divides the figure into two equal halves.]
11. [AAMIR KHAN]
12. [GOLD]
13. [KAYAK]
14. [1]
15. [OUR]
16. [3]
17. [IGNORE]
18. [SATURN]
19. [PACKAGE]
20. [1; a line of figure gradually vanishing.]
21. [4]
22. [Cardinal
23. [RIDICULE; in others all the letters are different.]
24. [c; number at the third column of each row = (cube of first number – number in the middle).]
25. [C]

❑

TEST-12

1. [d; in other figures there are four parts inside.]
2. [1]
3. [c; in each column, fraction in the 3rd row = product of fractions in the 1st and 2nd row.]
4. [b; Two series: 1st: Difference of 8; 2nd: Difference of 12.]
5. [a; in others the 3rd letter is '1/3rd' of the 'product' of remaining two if A = 1, B = 1, etc.]
6. [d; in the first figure: 24 + 35 = 59; 59 – 14 = 45; in the second figure: 28 +38 = 66; 66 – 21 = 45; similarly in the third figure: 20 + ? – 5 = 45 therefore, ? = 30.]
7. [2; one-third part of the figure is cut.]
8. [BRANCH; others contain the word "RUN".]
9. [STY]
10. [b; let "t" be the time in years. Therefore, (32 + t) = 3 (8 + t); or, t=4.]
11. [ALLAHABAD]
12. [b]

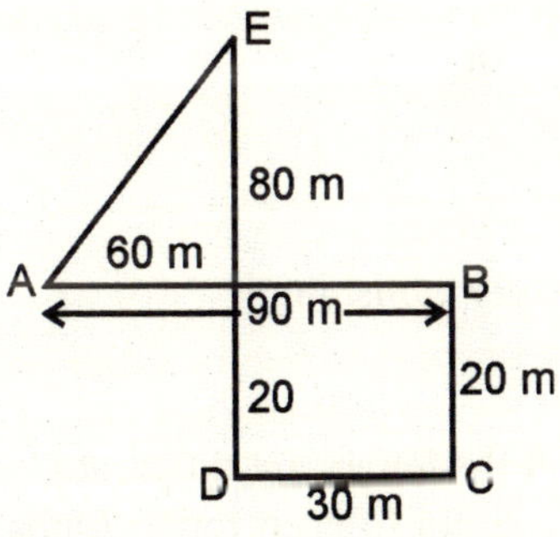

$$AE = \sqrt{3600\,m + 6400\,m}$$

$$= 10\sqrt{100}$$

$$= 100$$

13. [3; in others, the arithmetical operators are in an order, i.e. (?), (+), (×), (÷).]
14. [FINE]

15. [GOBLET]
16. [38; in each square unit there are eight triangles; two more triangles are added for additional square unit.]
17. [1]
18. [BREAK; BAKER; BRAKE]
19. [4; arrow is changing its direction with dot inside the small circle.]
20. [BRAZIL]
21. [a; take the square roots of the two numbers on the left and add them.]
22. [ALLA RAKHA]
23. [4; e.g. $(2^2+5^2) - (3^2+ 4^2)=4$]
24. [c; if A=1, B=2, etc. multiply all the four letters as per their numerical values.]
25. [D]

❑

TEST-13

1. [d; in others, the 3rd letter is 'half' of the 'sum' of remaining two if A = 1, B = 2, C = 3, etc.]
2. [d; the sequence is: ▲▲▼▼, ▲▲▼▼, ▲▲▼▼]
3. [b; other letters are formed using more than one line.]
4. [6; e.g. $(7^2+4^2) \sim (6^2+5^2)$, etc.]
5. [2; in such case when two faces bear the same numbers, the remaining number will be opposite to the one in question.]
6. [b]
7. [3]
8. [194; the differences are multiple of 17, e.g. 17, 34, 51, … etc.]
9. [REVOLUTION]
10. [8; in each quadrant, the inner number is twice the difference of the outer numbers, e.g. 14 is 2 (34 – 27)]
11. [VENUE]
12. [1; in others, the lines are intersecting from all the edges.]
13. [RIB]
14. [b; successive difference of 4, 6, 8, 10,…]
15. [1]
16. [30]
17. [CITADEL; DELTAIC; DIALECT]
18. [STALE; STEAL; SLATE]
19. [1; two lines between R and its image.]
20. [Harper]
21. [3]
22. [Flat]
23. [PET]
24. [d; other figures contain six parts.]
25. [R]

❑

TEST-14

1. [c; n^3-1 where n = 1, 2, 3, etc.]
2. [2]
3.

K	I	L	O
I	C	O	N
L	O	U	T
O	N	T	O

4. [3872; rotating the numerals.]
5. [d]
6. [d; in others 2nd letter - 1st letter = 15; 2nd letter – 3rd letter = 13; and 4th letter – 3rd letter = 11.]
7. [VIRUS; others have letters in reverse alphabetic order.]
8. [T]
9. [4; middle line(s) is/are removed.]
10. [ANDY ROBERTS]
11. [OUTRAGE]
12. [SUMMER]
13. [VAST; in others the third letter is a Roman numeral.]
14. [1]
15. [a]
16. [T; other letters have curved lines along with straight lines.]
17. [1; in others, the two figures intersect.]
18. [AGE]
19. [DINAR; NADIR; DRAIN]
20. [2]
21. [9/4]
22. [CORSET, COSTER, ESCORT, SECTOR]
23. [11; in each row the sum of alternate number is equal.]
24. [RUN]
25. [b]

TEST-15

1. [17; in each quarter, the number at the centre is obtained by the difference of the squares of the remaining two numbers.]
2. [3]
3. [c; the series is: αααββγ, αααββγ, αααββγ]
4. [a; letters at odd numbered-placed advance one place and letters at even numbered-placed move back one place.]
5. [HOT]
6. [2]
7. [3; in others, the number of sides of inside figure is one less than that outside.]
8. [56]
9. [CLI: CLIMAX]
10. [CHROME; other words have a two-letter word in the middle.]
11. [4]
12. [APT]
13. [ACCUSE; others are in alphabetic order.]
14. [4]
15. [MENTAL]
16. [165; in each circle, if number starts from 1 in the first circle (4 in 2nd circle, 6 in the 3rd circle), the 3rd number is the sum of the previous two numbers (Fibonacci series).]
17. [HAWKER]
18. [3; dotted square.]
19. [MANIAC]
20. [2; vertex of the figure is changing in opposite directions.]
21. [DEBATE]
22. [PLASTER; PSALTER; STAPLER]
23. [HEAPS; PHASE; SHAPE]
24. [400; the numbers are squares of successive numbers 17, 18, 19, and 20.]
25. [3; the figure inside is exactly the same as outside.]

❑

TEST-16

1. [b; $(2n) - 1$, where n = 1, 4, 9, 16, … square numbers.]
2. [100HI5050I; substituting letters for Roman numerals, it is CHILLI which is a vegetable; others are animals: LLAMA, BULL, LAMB.]
3. [3]
4. [20]
5. [512; the numbers above the lines are the squares of the numbers below the lines.]
6. [d; similar figure inside.]
7. [NOTES; STONE; ONSET]
8. [BOW]
9. [BHAGAT SINGH]
10. [BEGILD; in others, letters are in alphabetical order.]
11. [4; in others, arrows are perpendicular to the tangents.]
12. [d; correct sequence is: – 1 – 2 + 1.]
13. [31; e.g. (4–2) = 2 and (7–3) = 4, etc.]
14. [SILENT; anagrams of each other.]
15. [OUT]
16. [2]
17. [HOT]
18. [Even]
19. [ULTIMATE]
20. [1]
21. [80; if you reverse the digits of each number and add them, you will arrive at this result.]
22. [PEN]
23. [CUR: CURFEW]
24. [D]
25. [3]

❑

TEST-17

1. [b; $n^3 - n^2$]
2. [d; the letter series is qppqr qppqr qppqr]
3. [C]
4. [SCIENCE]
5. [T; alphabet are expressed as the initial letters of first twelve numerals.]
6. [4; dots with lines are alternating their positions.]
7. [Jordan]
8. [3rd upper line of the keyboard of a type writer.]
9. [4]
10. [b; proper sequence is: – 1 + 4 + 1]
11. [TALC]
12. [6; in such figures, number of triangle (N) is given by N= (n+1) where n is the number of lines inside the triangle.]
13. [3; in others, the number of lines joining the ends is seven.]
14. [BHUBANESWAR]
15. [RIM]
16. [529; all the numbers are square of the successive prime numbers.]
17. [RECKON]
18. [4; curved triangle.]
19. [PAL + ACE = PALACE]
20. [B, M, N, P, T, W]
21. [4]
22. [SHOOT]
23. [DECRIAL; others are anagrams of each other.]
24. [2]
25. [NER]

❑

TEST-18

1. [ROCKET]
2. [Flower]
3. [Notice]
4. [ALERT; ALTER; LATER]
5. [8; e.g. (8×12) ~ (4×16) = 32; (28×30) ~ (26×32) = 8]
6. [3]
7. [4; the number of sides of inside figure is one less than outside.]
8. [3; in others the number of sides of inside figures are one more than the outside figures.]
9. [13; in such figures, number of triangle (*N*) is given by *N*= (*n*+1) where *n* is the number of lines inside the triangle.]
10. [WALRUS]
11. [T]
12. [RAN or LAN]
13. [5; in such case when two faces bear the same numbers, the remaining number will be opposite to the one in question.]
14. [24; in the first figure all the four outer numbers are multiples of 17, the number at the centre is obtained by adding the number of times 17 is multiplied. Same is the outcome with 18 and 19.]
15. [VASCO DA GAMA]
16. [2]
17. [3; these are the first ten digits of π (pi) 3.141592653.]
18. [VIRGO]
19. [3]
20. [LINE]
21. [b; gap of 12 letters.]
22. [8; 12345679 × 9 = 111111111; 12345679 × 18 = 222222222, and so on.]
23. [c; in others the result is 0.1.]
24. [b; the series is: ♠♣♥♦, ♠♣♥♦, ♠♣♥♦,]
25. [4; two curves are separated by a line with opposite face.]

❑

TEST-19

1. [a; denominator is even.]
2. [36; opposite numbers in each case are squares.]
3. [3; in others, the shaded portions form triangles.]
4. [DOOR]
5. [1999; these years constitute the prime numbers.]
6. [d; sequence is: – 2 –3 +1.]
7. [(a) RETARD (b) TRADER; (c) DARTER.]
8. [56; e.g. $(3^2 - 2^2) + (7^2 - 5^2) = 29$ OR 84; e.g. $(7 \times 5) - (3 \times 2) = 29$, etc.]
9. [a; the dots and diagonals are alternating their positions.]
10. [Wind]
11. [ENDEAR]
12. [REGIMENT]
13. [c]
14. [2]
15. [Party]
16. [BEHEAD; others contain the letters A, B and C.]
17. [2]
18. [ANT]
19. [7416; in others, middle two digits are obtained by multiplying the other two digits.]
20. [LIT]
21. [2]
22. [LONG]
23. [3; in such case if in two different positions of a dice, the position of a common face be the same then the opposite faces of the remaining faces are in the same position.]
24. [d]
25. [2; the circle is moving anticlockwise.]

❑

TEST-20

1. [d; the first is placed as far from A as the remaining letters from Z.]
2. [41; the number inside the middle circle is the average of the four numbers outside the middle circle.]
3. [TIRANA]
4. [3]
5. [3; in others, the shaded portions are moving a unit length.]
6. [A FAMILIAR BIRD!]
7. [42]
8. [BEAUTY]
9. [UTTARAKHAND]
10. [ADR: ADRIFT]
11. [4]
12. [RAP]
13. [(a) PRIEST; (b) SPRITE; (c) STRIPE]
14. [1; the half-shaded circle turns up and two parallel lines come inside.]
15. [TIP + TOP = TIPTOP]
16. [R]
17. [4]
18. [38; the number at the centre is the sum of numbers surrounding it.]
19. [c; in others, denominators are squared numbers.]
20. [Fast]
21. [2]
22. [TAILS; others are anagrams of each other.]
23. [LOG]
24. [2; arrow is moving clockwise alternating between two dots and two circles.]
25. [WISER
INTRO
STEAD
ERASE
RODEO]

❑

TEST-21

1. [17; 21. Three series (i) Square numbers 1, 4, 9, 16 (ii) Skipping prime numbers: 2, 5, 11, 17 (iii) Numbers increasing by 4, 6, 8, etc: 3, 7, 13, 21.]
2. [c; difference of three letters forward and two letters backward.]
3. [d; other words contain three vowels.]
4. [c; the digits of first three numbers are reversed in last three numbers.]
5. [2; the arrows are moving towards the curved ends.]
6. [W; others are made using three lines only.]
7. [c; In each row, the third number is obtained by doubling the middle number and adding to it half of the first number.]
8. [c; sequence is: –7 –2 + 5.]
9. [END]
10. [1; the shape changes and parallel lines come inside with white dot.]
11. [SERVANT]
12. [96; e.g. 42/6 = 7 and 54/6 = 9, then 7×9 = 63, etc.]
13. [4]
14. [CANDID]
15. [FOR]
16. [11 and 10; looking across each rows the sum of alternate numbers is 15 in each row. There can be more solutions]
17. [UDAY SHANKAR]
18. [b; other sentences read the same: forward or backward.]
19. [3]
20. [2]
21. [DEVIL]
22. [DRAWER, REDRAW, REWARD, WARDER]
23. [RUN]
24. [4; sum of the upper numbers is half the sum of lower numbers.]
25. [3]

❑

TEST-22

1. [24; the number 37 has a unique property; when it is multiplied by the multiple of 3 it yields interesting results.]
2. [RAT]
3. [1; in others, the black dot lies on the right side of the figure "T".]
4. [QUA: QUARTZ]
5. [a; In each row (1st number = (2nd number) ^2 + 2×3rd number).]
6. [b; other words contain two "SS"s]
7. [ENE: ENERGY]
8. [3]
9. [OUT]
10. [Niger]
11. [d; others have successive consonants.]
12. [2; the inside circles cover the outside figure with two crosses in opposite direction.]
13. [ALLURE]
14. [NAP + KIN = NAPKIN]
15. [Egret]
16. [c]
17. [307; multiply the first number by 3 and deduct 1; multiply the second number by 3 and deduct 2; multiply the third number by 3 and deduct 3, and so on.]
18. [1; unshaded, shaded and solid figures are changing in clockwise direction.]
19. [BILLET]
20. [1]
21. [7]
22. [c; the series is zyxxyz zyxxyz zyxxyz]
23. [LOG]
24. [18; in such cases, $N = 3n$, where N is the total number of triangles and n is the number of lines inside the triangle.]
25. [2]

❑

TEST-23

1. [103; here A=26, B=25, ... Y=2, and Z=1, then add: BARACK = 25+26+9+26+24+16 = 126, therefore OBAMA = 12+25+26+14+26 = 103.]
2. [c; in others one letter is being skipped.]
3. [317; multiply the first number by 2 and add 3; multiply the second number by 2 and add 3, and so on; 157 x 2 = 314, then add 3, it equals 317.]
4. [2; in others, there is only one line with a black dot??.]
5. [1; the small square inside is at the corner of the figure.]
6. [1]
7. [74; digits of the diagonally opposite numbers are reversed.]
8. [4]
9. [FUL]
10. [3; e.g. (16+14)/(12–7) = 6, etc.]
11. [ROTTER; others can be spelled backward to form words.]
12. [d; other words contain same vowels through out.]
13. [RUDIMENT]
14. [58; sum of previous three numbers starting from the 4th number.]
15. [Letter E: ElitE]
16. [d; in others, last digit is the square of 1st digit.]
17. [4; inside figures are either moving clockwise or anticlockwise.]
18. [SUSHMITA SEN]
19. [BEAVER]
20. [3]
21. [15; in each row, the middle number is obtain by the sum of digits of the first number, and the third number is obtain by the sum of the digits of the remaining two numbers.]
22. [d; (2nd number = (1st number)^2 - 3rd number).]
23. [b]
24. [2]
25. [1; the small circles moves just across.]

❑

TEST-24

1. [51; $2n^2 + 1$; $n = 0, 1, 2, \ldots$]
2. [91; $6^2+5^2+4^2+3^2+2^2+1^2$]
3. [COURT]
4. [4; the horizontal arrow moves in opposite direction, the other moves 135º.]
5. [7; 18+9–10/7×14=27–10×1/7×14=7]
6. [FRAUD]
7. [164; in each row the third number is obtained by the sum of the first two numbers.]
8. [241; others are multiple of 19.]
9. [26; A=1, B–2,...Z=26]
10. [11 + 29 – 1 = 39]
11. [3; the square figure is within the right-angles.]
12. [b; A=1, B=2,...Z=26; the given coded letters advances 13 places.]
13. [WAR]
14. [d; subsequent letters advances +2, +11, +2 respectively.]
15. [1]
16. [c; series becomes a b a a b b a a a b b b.]
17. [TALES; STEAL; LEAST]
18. [2; two similar items inside are in each figure and two different items in each cell.]
19. [2; faces having 1, 3, 5, and 6 black dots are already appeared.]
20. [Letter "T"; TaughT]
21. [b; Lion]
22. [3]
23. [ANT]
24. [18; each number on the left side is successively multiplied by 0, 1, 2, 3, etc.]
25. [4]

❑

TEST-25

1. [5; add the squares of three numbers of each figure, then whatever result comes add the digits to obtain the number in the middle.]
2. [MARKET]
3. [LARGE is anagram of GLARE; therefore LARGE is 23415.]
4. [3]
5. [b; in other group of letters the 3rd letter is obtained by adding the 1st number and twice the middle number. Here A = 1, Z = 26]
6. [PET]
7. [3; number of arrows is increasing by half and the dots are changing positions.]
8. [63; n^3-1]
9. [PART]
10. [81, square numbers are revealed on reversing the digits in others.]
11. [d; the figure turns 90º clockwise with a reduction of one side.]
12. [RUIN]
13. [OVER]
14. [B in GO i.e. Bingo]
15. [2; the number of sides increases by 2, the lens-like figure turns through 90º.]
16. [d; Shehnai]
17. [FRAGMENT]
18. [54; in such case, number of sides whose one face is painted $= 6\ (x-2)^2$ where x is the length of one of the sides which is 5.]
19. [20%; number of students who got distinction in at least two subjects = 10+5+15+10=40; hence required percentage is 40/200=1/5=20%.]
20. [4; in others the inside figure is oval in shape.]
21. [EMIL ZATOPEK]
22. [D]
23. [SEESAW]
24. [(a) CHASER; (b) SEARCH; (c) ESCHAR]
25. [2]

❑

TEST-26

1. [21; alternate series with a difference of 6.]
2. [SPROUT]
3. [d; Painting]
4. [MANJREKAR]
5. [4; in others, the three figures on the faces of a dice are different.]
6. [SUB: SUBURB]
7. [712; e.g. in the first figure $(12 \times 2) + (12 \times 5) = 24 + 60 = 84$]
8. [KUALA LUMPER]
9. [1, 2, and 3; $1 \times 2 \times 3 = 6$ and $1 + 2 + 3 = 6$]
10. [3]
11. [HAS]
12. [2]
13. [ARABIAN]
14. [c; Code is: A= 26, B=25….Y=2, Z=1]
15. [NAP + KIN = NAPKIN]
16. [10; sum of the numbers in upper semi-circle equals sum of the numbers in lower semi circle!]
17. [SPLIT]
18. [2]
19. [3]
20. [ART]
21. [2; the arrows turn in opposite directions; shaded portion turns into blank one.]
22. [AGE]
23. [d; others are in the ratio 1: 4.]
24. [4; all the three figures are different.]
25. [2; the number of sides of both inside and outside figures is the same.]

❑

TEST-27

1. [1/24; e.g. ½ × 1/3 = 1/6, then 1/6 + 1/6 = 1/3, finally inverse of 1/3 is 3.]
2. [100; these are Roman numerals.]
3. [2; one rectangle covers the other one having horizontal and vertical lines crossing each other. The slanting lines are also in the same direction.]
4. [a; the series is 233112 233112 233112.]
5. [RED]
6. [a; 0/0 is an indeterminate quantity, others are infinity.]
7. [33; in such cases, $N = 3n + 31$, where N is the total number of triangles and n is the number of lines inside the triangle.]
8. [64; each number is thc sum of previous numbers both across and down.]
9. [b; correct sequence –2 +3 –2.]
10. [Project]
11. [Indore]
12. [d; its sum is 24, others' have 26.]
13. [2]
14. [2]
15. [d]
16. [(a) LISTEN; (b) SILENT; (c) TINSEL]
17. [d; by elimination]
18. [ANDRE AGASSI]
19. [NOW]
20. [3; in others, the number of sides increases in a definite order.]
21. [PER: PERIOD]
22. [PARTY]
23. [$2^6 - 63 = 1$; here 2^6 is 2×2×2×2×2×2 = 64!)
24. [2]
25. [3]

❑

TEST-28

1. [c; Pluto is no more a planet but a minor planet.]
2. [2]
3. [15; in each circle, halve the left number and double the number on right, then add the two numbers; e.g. 10/2=5, 4×2=8, 5–8=13.]
4. [23; LHS: square root of left and right digits = RHS; e.g. 4 = 2 and 9 = 3, number on the right is 23.]
5. [HALF]
6. [c; it is anagram of PERCOLATION]
7. [180; $n^3–n^2$]
8. [(11.5)(2.5)10; Here A=0.5, B=1, C=1.5, D=2…Y=12.5, Z=13]
9. [b; the series is kllmn, kllmn, kllmn.]
10. [18 Chapters of *Mahabharata*.]
11. [OUT]
12. [3; in others square figure is at the centre.]
13. [RETURN]
14. [35; e.g. square roots of upper numbers in each figure are multiplied together (3×5) and cube roots of lower numbers are multiplied together (4×5); then the results are added (15 + 20) = 35.]
15. [kaRATe]
16. [2; first arrow moves anti-clockwise through 90º, other arrows move clockwise through 135º.]
17. [d; in others each subsequent letter is not advanced by four places.]
18. [Mean]
19. [d]
20. [DENOTE; others contain numbers]
21. [one-fourth; Area of a circle = πr^2]
22. [2; the circles change position one step.]
23. [BOY]
24. [CALORIMETER]
25. [b]

❑

TEST-29

1. [c; each letter is advanced by one letter.]
2. [500; $n^4 – n^3$]
3. [B; the darker portion moves 45º anti-clockwise and the shaded portion moves 45º clockwise.]
4. [It remains the same; Area of a triangle = ½ (Base × Height.]
5. [30; numbers with last digits as 4 is 5; numbers divisible by 4 = 25; total numbers = 30.]
6. [DON]
7. [c; China]
8. [1/2; divide the product of the upper set of numbers by the product of the lower set of numbers and halve the outcome.]
9. [TUTOR]
10. [3; the figure turns 90º clockwise and all the small circles come inside.]
11. [CALABASH; other words contain four "A"s.]
12. [TARIFF]
13. [P = 8; Q = 5]
14. [ATE]
15. [4]
16. [PARDON]
17. [Twice of the original volume.]
18. [6; $2x – x/2 = 9, x = 6$]
19. [POWDER]
20. [AMOL PALEKAR]
21. [3]
22. [IMPS
MALT
PLEA
STAY]
23. [1224; Here A=2, B=4, C=6, etc.]
24. [b]
25. [3]

❑

TEST-30

1. [32; n^2 – prime number, where $n = 1, 2, 3, 4$, etc.]
2. [142857]
3. [3]
4. [Coins]
5. [a; in others, the sequence of letters is –2 + 1 + 2]
6. [43]
7. [1; e.g. (1/2 × 1/6)/(1/3 × 1/4) = 1, etc.]
8. [ARSHAD; in others the names contain three vowels.]
9. [REVOLUTION]
10. [1; others are symmetrical.]
11. [IRAQ; letters of other countries form anagrams: IRAN → RAIN; PERU → PURE; LAOS → ALSO.]
12. [AUT: AUTHOR]
13. [B; unequal parts are rising up.]
14. [8; in each quadrant the number in the bigger circle is obtained by multiplying the two numbers and dividing **by 18.]**
15. [ONE]
16. [1]
17. [VENDER]
18. [c]
19. [ADDLED]
20. [a]
21. [9; in each row, go on adding digits of preceding numbers.]
22. [Net]
23. [RICHARD ALLEN]
24. [3; arrows move anti-clockwise through 90° and the line moves anti-clockwise through 90°; the '+' sign moves clockwise through 90°.]
25. [128(5/7)°; central angle = $\frac{360^\circ}{7}$ where 7 is the number of sides. Required angle = $180^\circ - \frac{360^\circ}{7} = \left[128\left(\frac{5}{7}\right)\right]^\circ$

❑

TEST-31

1. [a; in others three letters are being skipped.]
2. [100 sons of Dhritarashtra]
3. [AKALIDAL]
4. [24 and 12; in each row the second number is obtained by multiplying the digits of the first number, and the third number is obtain by multiplying the digits of the second number.]
5. [1]
6. [9; 923076 = 4 × 230769]
7. [REC: RECOUP]
8. [AABCIR; others form countries when letters are reshuffled.]
9. [O; all are four-letter words: QUAY, ZINC; SWIM, and VET(O)]
10. [50]
11. [9; difference between square numbers 1, 4, 9, 16, etc.]
12. [3; in others, the figures are divided into four equal parts.]
13. [ROW]
14. [b; every letter is advanced to fourth place, i.e. A=E, B=F, C=G, etc.]
15. [3, 2, 8]
16. [DERANGE; GRANDEE; GRENADE]
17. [d]
18. [b; A=½, B=1,..F=3, G= 7/2....O=7½, etc.]
19. [4; triangle turns upside down like mirror image.]
20. [44; In each hexagon the number at the centre is the difference of sum of upper three numbers and sum of lower three numbers, e.g. (3+7+11= 21; (13+17+19=49); 49 21=28, etc.]
21. [BITTEN]
22. [b]
23. [Accra]
24. [1]
25. [4; half arrow moves through 180º; the small line at the end moves anti-clockwise through 90º; black dot is on the same side as half arrow.]

❑

TEST-32

1. [GALLANT]
2. [2 and 3!]
3. [SACK]
4. [c]
5. [e; others have four lines.]
6. [63; squares of even numbers – 1]
7. [DEPRIVE; Other words form anagrams: CUPRITE=PICTURE; DEVISER=DIVERS; REFOUND=FOUNDER]
8. [(b) others are having curved lines also.]
9. [RUIN]
10. [AIL]
11. [1; figure turns 90º clockwise and two arrows are added.]
12. [₹ 475; total cost price = 300 + 50 = 350; Profit = ₹ 125; Now selling price = ₹ 350 + 125 = 475.]
13. [d; others follow the rule: $n^3 – n^2$; n=1, 2, 3,..]
14. [1; in others, arrows move in anti-clockwise directions.]
15. 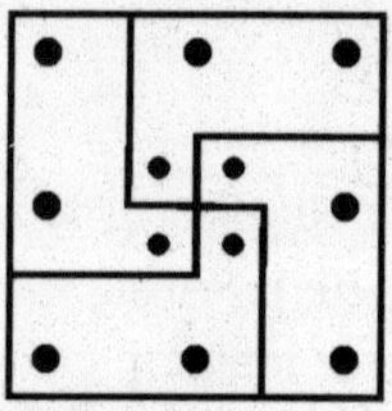
16. [123; which is two more than 121 (=11x11) and two less than 125 [5×5×5]
17. [a; in others four letters are being skipped.]
18. [2]
19. [Y]
20. [3; the number of arrows are increasing an the same directions alternately and dots alternate on left and right sides.]
21. [d; Calligraphy and Graphically are anagrams, so are Incorporate and Procreation.]
22. [AKSHAY KUMAR]

❑

23. [C]
24. [ACT]
25. [2; in each figure there are two pairs of each item, each pair has similar items but are placed opposite.]

❑

TEST-33

1. [d; in others sum of digits is 8.]
2. [2; number of sides increases by one.]
3. [AGE]
4. [CUT]
5. [b]
6. [TRIANGLE]
7. [FACETIOUS; though all these words contain all the vowels—AEIOU—but this particular word contains the vowels in the correct sequence.]
8. [c; in others the black dot is at the end of arrow.]
9. [EMBALM; others are anagrams of each other.]
10. [a; correct sequence is: natural occurrence of alphabets.]
11. [Bill]
12. [c; the series is $\frac{7}{8} \cdot \frac{5}{8} \cdot \frac{5}{8} \cdot \frac{7}{8} \cdot \frac{3}{8} \cdot \frac{7}{8} \cdot \frac{5}{8} \cdot \frac{5}{8} \cdot \frac{7}{8} \cdot \frac{3}{8}$]
13. [27; number of small cubes = volume of bigger cube/volume of smaller cube.]
14. [49; difference between numbers is successive multiple of 3.]
15. [MELODIC]
16. [HASTEN]
17. [1; Add the upper digits. Now divide the sum of the lower digits by the sum of upper digits. The result is the number at the centre.]
18. [THRONE]
19. [d]
20. [EAR]
21. [N; TINE -N = TIE; BID + N = BIND]
22. [1; the sum of number of parallel lines on the left is twice the sume of parallel lines on the right.]
23. [LANGUR]
24. [63 e.g. A = 1, B = 2, C = 3, etc. add the numbers.]
25. [1; arrow is moving anti-clockwise throw 45º; parallel lines are alternately placed up/down and left/right.]

❑

TEST-34

1. [44; each number indicates its position in the grid, e.g. 21 means 'second row and first column'; 32 means 'third row and second column', etc.]
2. [LEAVE]
3. [1 and 7]
4. [HAVOC]
5. [85 (1st letter × 2nd letter) + 3rd letter; if A = 1, B = 2, Z = 26]
6. [11; difference between numbers is 7, 19, 37, 61, etc. i.e. Prime number skipping 3rd, 4th, 5th, …primes in between respectively, i.e. (11, 13, 17), (23, 29, 31), (41, 43, 47), (53, 59, 61).]
7. [D; in other figures the black spot is near the arrow.]
8. [abc = 141]
9. [d; the sequence is abba abba abba…]
10. [MOTHER-IN-LAW]
11. [3; number of circles are doubled with dots inside.]
12. [GURU]
13. [FLAMBEAUX]
14. [15; these are all non-prime numbers.]
15. [ILL]
16. [4; the horizontal arrow moves left and right and the vertical arrow moves up and down; small circle moves up and down.]
17. [(a) PHRASE, (b) SHERPA; (c) SHAPER]
18. [a]
19. [LOTION]
20. [O; others are formed by straight lines.]
21. [b; each subsequent number is two more than a squared number starting with 1, i.e. $n^2 + 2$]
22. [25]
23. [C]
24. [1]
25. [a; carving.]

❑

TEST-35

1. [c; 1st series: a, b, c, etc., 2nd series: q, p, o, *n*.]
2. [Dear]
3. [64, 69]
4. [1]
5. [CHA: CHASTE]
6. [1 and 5; e.g. 1st two columns: 9 × 4 = 36 (numbers in 2nd row); 3 × 6 = 18, numbers in 3rd row), etc.]
7. [b; proper sequence is: –1 + 3 + 1.]
8. [3; other figures do not have dots at two ends.]
9. [O; The top row of letters in the middle on a key board of a typewriter!)
10. [CIVIL, as its all the letters are in Roman numbers.]
11. LAM: LAMBDA]
12. [b; next number is half of the previous number.]
13. [4; the centre portion disappears.]
14. [AGO]
15. [2.65; the numbers are the successive square roots of 1, 2, 3, 4, 5, 6 up to two decimal places.]
16. [c]
17. [27; the second number on the left side is halved.]
18. [d; Each subsequent number is three less than a cubic number in reverse order, i.e. $n^3 - 3$]
19. [NOEL (the other name of Christmas), there is L missing, or the alphabet contains "No eL"!]
20. [4; number of dots are two less than number of sides of the figures.]
21. [SUGAR]
22. [MAL]
23. [3; half arrow moves up and down of the diagonal in opposite direction; '+' and '–' signs are placed up and down alternately.]
24. [FREEZE; other contains three consecutive alphabet.]
25. [3]

❑

TEST-36

1. [256, 16: two alternate series: N^4 and N^2]
2. [c; others follow the rule: $2n^2 - 1$; n=0, 1, 2, 3.]
3. [One thousand years in a millennium.]
4. [40; A=1, B=2, C=3, etc., C×A×T=3×1×20; therefore B×A×T=2×1×20=40.]
5. [c; in others one letter is being skipped.]
6. [FEEDBACK]
7. [1144; these are the successive square numbers of 1, 2, 3, 4, 5, 6, 7, 8, 9, 10, 11, and 12 split into groups of four.]
8. [1; in others, central line divides the figure.]
9. [ENG: ENGYME]
10. [c; the first two letters of each of her daughters are the notes of the musical scale: Do Re Me Fa Sol La.]
11. [WIN]
12. [2]
13. [Vinita; the sitting arrangement is like this: Vinita Nalini Malini Pratima Ankita.]
14. Y; these are units of time: Second, Minute, Hour, Day, Week, Month, and Year!]
15. [A and C]
16. [MUSK DEER]
17. [29; in each figure the number at the top is obtained by adding the bottom numbers in such a way that the left number is halved and the right number is doubled.]
18. [MAN + AGE = MANAGE]
19. [B; one – fourth of the figure.]
20. [Couple]
21. [d; number of lines increases by 2.]
22. [D]
23. [READER; others start and end with the same two letters.]
24. [MAN]
25. [2; arrows are alternately changing their positions.]

❑

TEST-37

1. [c; others follow the rule: $2n^2 + 1$; n=2, 3, 4, 5.]
2. [EGN]
3. [4; the parallel lines go up and join the shaded portion.]
4. [420; $(n^2 - m)$ where n and m are multiple of 3.]
5. [IN, SIN, SING, STING, STRING, STARING, STARTING, and STARTLING.]
6. [NURSED]
7. [d; sequence is: +3 + 2 + 2.]
8. [4; in others, a rectangle is inside the figure.]
9. [10, 13; two series: even numbers, successive prime numbers.]
10. [TRITON; others have just one vowel.]
11. [MENTAL]
12. [AMIABLE]
13. [Sixty four Squares on a Chess Board.]
14. [Line]
15. [d]
16. [c; the sum of digits successively increases by 1.]
17. [4]
18. [Lark]
19. [R]
20. [PROPER]
21. [BADE GHULAM ALI]
22. [a, combination of English and Greek alphabets.]
23. [B and E]
24. [SUPREME]
25. [3; all the lines are alternately changing their positions.]

❑

TEST-38

1. [5, 7, 22; three series: 1st series: natural numbers; 2nd series: natural numbers; 3rd series: successive difference of 4.]
2. [PRESENT]
3. [B and D]
4. [ANT]
5. [MILD, as its letters suggest Roman numerals.]
6. [0.111; fractions start from ½ = 0.500, 1/3= 0.333, etc…1/9 = 0.111.]
7. [50; A = 1, B = 2, Y = 25, Z= 26 then DO = 4 × 15 = 60 ∴ BY = 2 × 25 = 50]
8. [1; in others, the number or side increases by one.]
9. [32, 27; 1st series: difference between numbers is doubled; 2nd series: successive decreasing one third of the previous number.]
10. [T—they all rhyme.]
11. [a; in each case the second letter is 13 places ahead and the third letter is 10 places behind the second.]
12. [4; the small rectangle turns 180º and crosses the circle.]
13. [VIVEKANANDA]
14. [SIXTH]
15. [DANGER]
16. [3]
17. [b; three series: Natural numbers; constant difference of 2; n^2.]
18. [180; e.g. in 1st figure, $2^3 + 3^2 = 17$; $4^3 + 5^2 = 89$; now 17 + 89 = 106, etc.]
19. [PARTS; STRAP; TRAPS]
20. [IMPEND]
21. [a; proper sequence is: + 6 + 5 + 5.]
22. [B; number of lines increasing.]
23. [Grant]
24. [2; all the arithmetical signs are occupying the sides of triangles one after the another.]
25. [ANT]

❑

TEST-39

1. [41, 51; 1st series: successive difference is 8; 2nd series: successive difference is 12.]
2. [3; the number of black dots is the same as the number of sides and dots are situated at the corners of each figure.]
3. [PLANTAINS]
4. [d; the series becomes: mallalalla, mallalalla.]
5. [144; e.g. $9^2 = 81$, $9^3 = 729$, $9^4 = 6561$]
6. [85; A = 1, B = 2, C = 3, etc. H is = $(H \times I) + S = (8 \times 9) + 19 = 91$; $\therefore$ HIM = 72 + 13 = 85.]
7. [MAHARAJAH]
8. [3]
9. [61; Successive prime numbers.]
10. [L; other letters are formed using three lines.]
11. [GAL: GALAXY]
12. [3; in this case the triangle is turned wrongly.]
13. [HORSE]
14. [AND]
15. [Twelve Signs of the Zodiac.]
16. [GOD]
17. [a; LUSTER; (b) RESULT; (c) RUSTLE]
18. [46; add the number around the central number which gives the sum.]
19. [4; the lower portion remains intact and upper one turns.]
20. [MIDGET]
21. [29; average of the five numbers at the vertices of the pentagon is equal to the number at the centre.]
22. [C]
23. [UNCOMPLIMENTARY; the only word to have all the five vowels in reverse order!]
24. [2; the main figure is moving clockwise 135º and small circle is moving clockwise two units of length.]
25. [LET]

❑

TEST-40

1. [c]
2. [c; others are powers of 6.]
3. [49; numbers are the sum of first six prime numbers and squares of first six natural numbers.]
4. [d]
5. [d]
6. [WAY]
7. [c; average of number values if A=1, B=2, Z=26.]
8. [a; in others, the figures are increasing in size.]
9. [MAN]
10. [a; (15 + 21) – 1 = 35]
11. [b; couple means two persons; number of sons =5; 5 daughters-in-law, number of grand sons = 20; number of family members: 2 + 5 + 5 + 20 = 32.]
12. [BEZOAR; others have alternate consonants/vowels.]
13. [c; three series: Difference of 3; difference of 4; multiple of 3.]
14. [2; the next figure is horizontal with two arrows.]
15. [366 Days in a Leap Year.]
16. [c]
17. [Reservation]
18. [C and E]
19. [STARTLE]
20. [b; number of sides of outer figure is decreasing by one and number of sides of inner figure is increasing by one.]
21. [ORNAMENT]
22. [c; the first two letters of all of her daughters suggest the scale of Indian music, i.e. sargam!)
23. [D]
24. [2; as per English alphabet, the numbers as in found placement in the dictionary are: Six, Ten, Thirteen, Three, Twelve, Two.]
25. [A]

❑❑❑